Second Edition

ILLUSION AND DISILLUSION: THE SELF IN LOVE AND MARRIAGE

John F. Crosby
University of Kentucky

Wadsworth Publishing Company, Inc.
Belmont, California

Sociology Editor: Stephen D. Rutter
Designer: Dare Porter
Production Editor: Larry Olsen

ISBN 0-534-00450-4
L.C. Cat. Card No. 75-36884
Printed in the United States of America
4 5 6 7 8 9 10—81

Acknowledgments

American Psychological Association—for excerpts from Abraham H. Maslow, "A Theory of Human Motivation," *Psychological Review*, Vol. 50, 1943, pp. 370–396. Reprinted by permission of the American Psychological Association; Appleton-Century-Crofts—for excerpts from *The Family in Search of a Future: Alternate Models for Moderns*, Herbert A. Otto, Editor. Copyright © 1970 by Meredith Corporation. Reprinted by permission of Appleton-Century-Crofts, Educational Division, Meredith Corporation; Columbia University Press—for excerpts from Andreas Capellanus, *The Art of Courtly Love*, abr. and ed., Frederick W. Locke. Copyright 1941 by Columbia University Press. Reprinted by permission of Columbia University Press; Dorrance and Company—for a poem by Tom McFee, from *Love and Other Painful Joys*, Dorrance and Company, 1970. Used by permission; Harper & Row, Publishers,

About the Author

John Crosby received the B.A. degree in philosophy from Denison University and the B.D. degree in theology from Princeton Theological Seminary. He served as a pastor in Congregational and Presbyterian Churches from 1956 until 1967, when he began work on his Ph.D. at Syracuse University. In 1970 he completed doctoral studies and also earned clinical certification as a marriage and family counselor in the American Association of Marriage and Family Counselors. From 1970 until 1976 he taught in the area of marriage and family relations at Indiana University. In 1976 he became chairman of the Department of Human Development and Family Relations in the College of Home Economics at the University of Kentucky. Dr. Crosby is married to the former Marjorie Eastwick and they have three teen-age sons. Marjorie Crosby received her Master's degree in nurse-midwifery at the University of Kentucky in 1976.

Preface

Those who love the truth
Must seek love in marriage,
Love without illusions.

Albert Camus, *A Writers Notebook*

This second edition of *Illusion and Disillusion* represents an attempt to weave my continuing experience as a marriage counselor and my former experience as a clergyman into a framework which helps explain the disillusionment couples often experience in marriage. I hope that what I have said speaks equally to the married and the unmarried in more than an academic or intellectual way.

As Rollo May has said, a writer usually writes because he is struggling with his own thoughts and ideas. Certainly I am. Readers may disagree with many of my ideas; to this I can only reply that if the disagreement is based on sound insight and widely observed phenomena rather than on the strength of custom, tradition, and romanticized folklore, I welcome it. I wish to challenge the reader to think of marriage as an opportunity for the enrichment of life, as a relationship between two self-aware people open to change and growth and thus not bound to traditional societal role definitions and expectations.

If these pages serve to raise the reader's anxiety level and make him or her feel uncomfortable, then I am glad, because I fail to see how real change will take place in our marital system until people begin to seriously question the premises and assumptions underlying it. When serious challenges are made upon our traditional belief system there is bound to be some degree of internal agony and pain, restlessness and uncertainty, doubt and insecurity.

A book of this nature must, of necessity, draw upon a host of disciplines, including psychology, sociology, philosophy, anthropology, and sexology. The popularly heralded claim that marriage is either passé or in a state of decline and the parallel claim that the family is in a state of breakdown is worthy of reply. Charges so easily made are not so easily refuted, if only because refutation requires theoretical, clinical, and empirical evidence from the various disciplines mentioned above. The major methodological foundation for *Illusion and Disillusion* is theoretical and clinical.

In addition to the five new chapters, those who have read the first edition will note several changes of emphasis in this second edition. These changes reflect (1) my attempt to give increased emphasis to the details of learning how to interact with a partner, and a more thorough treatment of the characteristics of the Growth Model of marriage; (2) my intention to rely less on the supportive statements of my thought mentors (Rollo May, Erich Fromm, Viktor Frankl, Paul Tillich, and Karen Horney); and (3) my own growth and change as a person, a husband, a father, a teacher, and a counselor. I hope the reorganization of the material in three main sections will make it easier for the reader to make sense of the progression of material and its emphasis.

There are many friends who have had either "seen" or "unseen" hands in this book. I wish to thank them all. To Steve Rutter, an editor become friend, a special thanks. Most of all, thanks to Marj, with whom I have shared the experience of life, love, and parenting. We have experienced enough of what I have written about to confirm the authenticity of these pages—the ups, the downs—the joy, the pain—the ebb, the flow—the renewal, the growth.

I would like to thank Boyd Gibson (Susquehanna University), Jackie Webb (Texas A & I University), and Morgan Shelley (Grossmont College) for their suggestions and comments on the manuscript.

I wish to acknowledge a very real debt to those who have contributed personal statements in the form of case studies, and also to all those whose struggles for marital meaning contributed to several of the "fabricated" case studies. Also, a warm note of thanks to my students at Indiana University. Naturally, I take full responsibility for the content of the book and for the interpretations I have placed upon the thought of others.

John F. Crosby

Contents

For the Five of Us—

Rick

Andy

Scott

Marj

John

Second Edition

ILLUSION AND DISILLUSION: THE SELF IN LOVE AND MARRIAGE

FOCUS ON THE PAST AND PRESENT: WHERE WE ARE

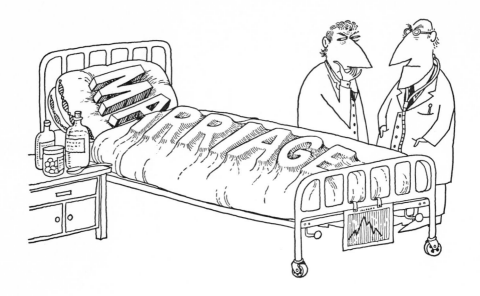

ONE
WHAT'S WRONG? THE ROOTS OF MARITAL DIS-ILLUSIONMENT

Disillusionment

Had It

I've had it! That's all! I've taken all I can take. The whole thing stinks! Marriage—ha! All that talk about love and caring and giving and taking. I'll tell you, I gave and gave and what did he give? You tell me. He wanted to own me—control me—possess me. I was supposed to be grateful—grateful for being his wife and the mother of the kids. Be beautiful —be sexy—be a good mother, a good housekeeper, a good social secretary —entertainer, passionate lover, adoring wife, taxi driver. I tell you . . . it's no use . . . all we do is fight. I should have known better . . . I thought we would be different—that our marriage would be something beautiful—that fighting and bickering, bitching and criticizing—well, that's the way it was for others but it wouldn't be that way for us—that's what I told myself. I'm sick of it—do you hear—sick of it and the whole sorry mess. Marriage is crazy. For me—no way—ever again.

Bitter

I admit I'm bitter. You would be too if you worked your ass off for your family and all you got was a turn-off from your wife. You'd think I was some sort of sex pervert if you listen to her. Look, all I want is some loving—some affection—some tenderness, instead of all this nagging and picking about all the things I'm doing wrong or not doing. She expects me to be some sort of a model husband—dedicated to making her happy—praising her—fussing over her but never—and this is the worst part of it—never having any needs of my own. She should have married a guy who was handsome, athletic, handy with tools, good with kids—yet completely sexless. When I'm out of this thing you can bet I'm not going to tie myself down again—ever! Marriage is for the birds.

Disillusionment is the state we reach when our hopes and dreams are destroyed. The two statements quoted above were made by a wife and a husband who were bitter and angry. Each had been hurt and had suffered pain at the hands of the other. In despair, both of them gave vent to deep-seated feelings of anger, resentment, and futility. The marriage ended soon after these statements were made. Counseling was too little and much too late. Both partners had entered the marriage with high hopes and lofty dreams. Their mutual expectations were fantastic—but, sadly, those expectations never really were talked about. Each wanted the personality and behavior of the other to conform to images they brought to the marriage. Each wanted the individuality of the partner to be obliterated. Neither was willing to allow the other to be a separate person.

Both partners protested the rotten deals they had received. Both swore they would not marry again. Both will probably remarry. Both will carry new or renewed bundles of fantastic expectations into their new relationships, and both will make some of the same mistakes again. And it is safe to assume that they will not talk about their expectations or deal with them in creative or productive ways. Our culture still believes (with some exceptions, of course) that love, romance, sex, and marriage are instinctual, the result of "doing what comes naturally." After all, what is there to learn about marriage? What is there to learn about sex and conflict, fighting and hurt, relationships and communication, expectations and assumptions?

Educational and governmental institutions in the United States spend billions of dollars annually on almost every conceivable type of education except education that deals with the self and with primary relationships. Millions are spent on research, yet very little research has been concerned with discovering answers to the basic question: What are the ingredients of a truly vital and dynamic marriage? Few clinical researchers have studied problem marriages to discover the factors that contribute to marital health. Few experimental researchers have explored the factors that keep couples together and satisfied. In the pages that follow we shall examine attitudes toward love, sex, and marriage in the hope that we can discover some of the factors that contribute to vitality and joy in intimate relationships.

Illusion

Dictionary definitions of *illusion* include references to misperception of reality, distortion of reality, the state or condition of being deceived, and deception caused by false impressions. I use *illusion* to refer to beliefs that are rooted in the folklore and folkways of the culture but that are either inaccurate or only partially accurate. Thus, illusions lead to assumptions based on unexamined expectations. Marriage, the family, interpersonal relationships, sex, intimacy, and conflict—these are all substantive areas of deep personal importance and all are obscured by illusions of many types. Countless illusions surround the "romance—sex—love—marriage—family" theme.

Illusion indicates a personal investment in a belief. Each person creates illusions according to his personal **ego-investment** in the particular idea or concept. Illusion is a form of self-deception that enables us to perceive what we wish to perceive and prevents us from perceiving the reality of a situation. Freud claimed that an illusion is not the same thing as an error. Illusions, according to Freud, are derived from human wishes. "Thus we call a belief an illusion when a wish-fulfillment is a prominent factor in its motivation, and in doing so we disregard its relations to reality."[1] For example, if one believes that "the expression of anger is bad," then one operates under the illusion that "a good marriage has no anger in it." The illusion is based on the belief and on the wish to have the belief be true. The stage is set for disillusionment: "My marriage is bad because I feel anger toward George."

Disillusion

Disillusion is the process of dealing with our illusions in such a way that the illusions no longer have power over us, either to control us or to influence us unduly. We deal with **myths** by de-mythologizing; we deal with illusion by dis-illusioning ourselves—by examining and dealing with the assumptions that are the bases of our illusions. By investing energy in the process of dis-illusioning ourselves, we hope to avoid the despair and bitterness that result from feelings of being let down, hurt, or betrayed.

ego-investment an investment of the self in something, such as investing time in a relationship or making a commitment to a course of study.
myth a belief given uncritical acceptance by the members of a group, especially in support of existing or traditional practices and institutions.

To rid ourselves of illusions, we must have both an intellectual commitment and an emotional commitment. The intellectual process requires an
open-mindedness as we investigate the various beliefs, myths, customs,
and traditions that surround marriage, romance, sex, and love. Although
these customs and traditions have become a part of our common culture
and have been transmitted from generation to generation, they are not
necessarily meaningful or appropriate to us. The questioning of traditional attitudes and belief systems may cause some anxiety and emotional
discomfort, but these are inevitable if we are to eradicate the illusions
that have become deeply ingrained in our emotional beings.

Scapegoating and Moralizing

Critics of marriage and family life sometimes blame particular ideas and
practices for all the difficulties associated with marriage and the family.
Such doubters offer the following explanations for the breakdown of
marriage:

Young people today have no morals.

*No one under thirty understands the meaning of
duty, commitment, and responsibility.*

People divorce because they are selfish.

*Marriages among the younger generation do not
have strong religious foundations.*

*Marriage is a dying institution, because people
today do not believe in its indissolubility.*

Are these really the causes of marital breakdowns? They may be factors,
but I do not believe they are basic causes. These reasons are used as
scapegoats. By definition, a scapegoat is a falsely accused offender. The
explanations listed above focus attention on factors outside of the marriage.

In any discussion about marriage and the family, the entire list of scapegoats is eventually brought into the conversation, either directly or by

implication. In discussions of marriage, there are at least two types of scapegoating. The first would blame the institution of marriage, and the second would single out moralistic (not necessarily moral) reasons. The former is likely to be expressed by those who are disillusioned, embittered, or feeling somewhat trapped. They probably consider freedom the central issue in marriage. The second is likely to be expressed by those who emphasize the importance of responsibility, rather than freedom, in interpersonal relationships.

Those who blame the institution cite divorce statistics as proof that the institutions of marriage and the family are decaying. Their solution is, of course, to retreat to the past, to glory in nostalgia. They would have us believe that the American family—from the arrival of the Mayflower until the end of World War II—was a happy, functional unit composed of several generations who lived harmoniously under one roof, had few divorces, little serious maladjustment, and even less sexual activity.

Other critics of marriage in contemporary society point to the divorce rate as an indication of the need for change. But instead of suggesting a return to the past, they prescribe a daring future that includes new life styles and new structures for mating, raising children, and intimacy.

In short, the radicals and the conservatives agree that the institutions of marriage and the family are in deep trouble. The only significant difference is that those on the left seek to restructure these institutions while those on the right seek to refortify them. A peculiar characteristic of our society is our tendency to polarize alternatives into either-or propositions. Unfortunately, when attitudes toward marriage and family are polarized, the mass media seize the sensational shocker and the eye-catching headline, which is bound to disturb or delight readers and viewers.

Although scapegoating is neither honest nor valid, it is a common practice. Scapegoating is a game with this prime rule: always shift the blame away from yourself onto someone or something else; never accept responsibility for yourself or your own situation. Scapegoaters must do this or be forced to look to themselves. If a person is serious in his attempt to get at the truth, he avoids scapegoating.

Before making value judgments, we should attempt to differentiate among **value structures** without prejudicing the several positions in either a positive or negative direction. That is, we must work as scientists —investigating and gathering data—before we arrive at value judgments.

If we are to rid the subject matter of both moralistic and antimoralistic implications, we should consider the following questions:

1. By what criteria is marriage failure determined?

2. By what criteria is family breakdown determined?

3. Is the institution of marriage at fault, or is family structure? (Does the coming of children negatively affect the marital relationship?)

4. Do the differences between expectation and reality produce disillusionment?

5. Does an idealized, romanticized, and sexualized image of marital bliss create a double bind in which we are entrapped no matter which alternative we choose? Does society create images, standards, and illusions that frustrate the conjugal pair who attempt to live up to these stereotypes?

6. Does pursuit of the illusive and ill-defined concept of happiness create resentment in innocent and naive marriage partners?

7. Does the **legal-ecclesiastical** stance of the American judicial system make marriage a lifelong contract with no escape clause? Does this system make it impossible to update or revise the contract without a plaintiff-defendant encounter in court?

8. Does our education-oriented society consider education for marriage, family life, and human sexuality to be unnecessary and an invasion of domestic privacy?

---

value structure the hierarchy of values an individual believes in; when a higher (more important) value is in conflict with a lower (less important) value, usually the more important value wins out over the less important value.
legal-ecclesiastical referring to the repository of laws, customs, and traditions that have evolved from the Judeo-Christian tradition and have been officially codified in the Anglo-Saxon and American bodies of law and court systems.

9. To what extent are marriage problems created by partners who bring to the marital union a set of stereotypes, roles, needs, models, idealized images, personality hang-ups, defense and escape mechanisms?

10. Is it possible that the culprit is not marriage, but rather the socialization process that is part of child rearing?

11. Is it possible that the root cause of the dilemma is an internal emptiness, an **existential** vacuum within which there is little meaning or purpose to life itself? Does our existential anxiety attach itself to the domestic situation?

12. To what extent does sex determine the quality of the marital relationship? Is sexual technology the key to marital happiness? If a sensuous woman marries a sensuous man, does their sensuality increase the prospects for marital happiness (a) drastically, (b) somewhat, (c) a little, (d) not at all?

13. Is it possible that today's preoccupation with sex belies a fear of emptiness, despair, meaninglessness, and death?

14. To what extent are marriage and family problems related to issues of women's liberation? What implications does **equalitarianism** between the sexes have for the marital and familial relationships? Is it possible for the female to be liberated without the male also becoming liberated from traditional role expectations and performance?

A study of marriage and family must examine carefully each of the ideas implicitly or explicitly stated in the preceding questions. Simplistic answers would be of no value. Thus, we should distinguish here between a *moralistic* position and a *moral* position. Moralistic positions are based on traditions and customs that are authoritarian in origin. One does the "true and right" thing because tradition says it is true and right. Conversely, a moral position shuns easy answers and depends on a rational approach to the **ethical dynamics** of a situation. The two positions are

---

existential concerning the nature and meaning of human existence.
equalitarianism a belief in absolute equality among human beings; refers here to equality between the sexes without reservation, condescension, or mental equivocation.
ethical dynamics the forces that determine or govern one's moral values and choices.

poles apart. By now the reader is aware of my bias in favor of the latter approach. The process of ridding ourselves of our illusions is not well served unless we avoid the pitfalls of scapegoating and moralizing.

The First Root of
Disillusionment: Marriage as an Institution

An *institution* is "an organization or establishment devoted to the promotion of a particular object, especially one of a public, educational, or charitable character . . . a well-established and structured pattern of behavior or of relationships that is accepted as a fundamental part of a culture, as marriage."[2]

Marriage is an institution. It has legal definition in the United States, it is protected by the courts, and procurement of a license is a necessary step toward legalization. As an institution, marriage encompasses the full range of ecclesiastical tradition that guided the lives of many of the English colonists in prerevolutionary days. The roots of this tradition are Judeo-Christian. The tradition has been transmitted to us by St. Paul, St. Augustine, the Protestant Reformation, the Council of Trent (the Roman Catholic reply to the Protestant Reformation), the Puritans, Victorianism, and the Great Awakening of the American frontier.

Many scholars believe that Christianity is antisexual, largely as a result of the antisexual bias of St. Paul and St. Augustine. But it would be more accurate to say that the Christian *tradition* has become rigidly antisexual, even though Jesus gave little indication of being antisexual. St. Paul counseled chastity because of his commitment to the belief that people should be totally freed of earthly ties if they are to be ready for the coming end of the world (1 Cor. 7:1–9). Marriage, of course, would weaken this commitment. He was also antipermissive about sexual relations outside the marital state; his acceptance of sex within marriage seems to come out most clearly in his advice that it was better to marry than to be aflame with passion.

According to our historical traditions, the Puritans were committed to sexual purity. Actually, the Puritans were a very sensuous people, and they relied on their many laws and regulations to keep the population in line. The Victorian era was characterized by prudishness toward anything vaguely related to sex or to natural body functions. **Victorianism** had the effect of removing the genitals from the self in a pretense that our sexual natures were inferior to our spiritual natures and embarrassing to our more noble selves. Victorianism has had a significant effect on marital standards and expectations in the late nineteenth and twentieth centuries in the United States.

The focal point in our analysis of the ecclesiastical tradition, however, is the belief in the indissolubility of the marital union. This belief is not a matter of tradition alone (as are attitudes toward sexuality). Jesus and Paul were advocates of indissoluble unions except on grounds of adultery. The Old Testament is not clear about this matter, despite the commandment regarding adultery. Before Moses, there was an acceptance of divorce, and after Moses, **concubinage** and sexual relations with non-Hebrew females continued. The ancient Jews believed adultery was wrong because it involved taking what rightfully belonged to another person. Thus the sin of adultery was offensive, not because of the sexual conduct involved, but because of the violation of the property rights of other Hebrews.

The Judeo-Christian tradition influenced the course of marriage and family relationships in Western societies more than any other single tradition or doctrine. The legal tradition in both Anglo-Saxon and American cultures has reflected the Judeo-Christian belief in the indissolubility of marriage.

Most sociologists, anthropologists, and historians agree that any society has a vested interest in the mate-selection process and in the establishment of a societal definition of legality in the marital union. This interest is rarely based on concern for the happiness of the married partners, but rather on concern about the socialization of the forthcoming generation.

Victorianism a style of living popularized during the reign of Queen Victoria of England (1837–1901); manners and morals which are stuffy, hypocritical, or prudish.
concubinage the practice of keeping a concubine, a woman who shares sexual intimacies with a man, or, in some societies, a secondary wife who enjoys protection and support but who lacks the status of a primary wife.

A legal definition of marriage and a societal dependence on some form of family structure have been indispensable in all known societies. In America, all of the states have traditionally upheld the indissolubility of marriage. As has been pointed out, this is not a cross-cultural phenomenon, but rather a result of our cultural tradition.

The legal system in the United States has reflected this tradition in its full judicial process for divorce. This process includes a plaintiff, a defendant, a judge, and legal counselors representing the plaintiff and the defendant. Underlying this practice is the assumption that there is a guilty party and an innocent party in the marital dyad; one has been wronged or harmed by the other. Within this system collusion is illegal. And, under the present system, if a couple agrees to waive the issue of guilt and present the court with a mutual agreement to dissolve their relationship, that is considered collusion.

Other contracts have clauses stating the conditions under which the contract may be dissolved or revised. The marriage contract is indissoluble in most states unless there is a court order following a hearing attended by attorneys, plaintiff, defendant, and judge.

There is much antipathy toward this system. Nevertheless, the American Bar Association has not been able to arrive at any consensus about how to change it, and until the bar changes its position it is unlikely that divorce procedures will change drastically. Meanwhile, treatment of such issues as alimony, child support, division of property, and visitation rights for the spouse not retaining custody of the children continues to make the entire system a farce. Lying and perjury are encouraged by the system. Legal grounds for divorce such as adultery and mental cruelty become catchalls and hence meaningless.

The postdivorce testimony of many is that they intended to part amicably but ended up embittered, vengeful, and hating. Why? Could it be because their attorneys transformed the proceedings into a contest for money, privilege, and property? Several states have made progress in changing the adversary nature of the divorce proceedings. Florida's no-fault divorce law is one attempt to remedy this unhappy situation.

To Make Divorce Less Painful

Florida's new "no-fault" divorce law is an intelligent effort to take the conflict and bitterness out of divorce proceedings, and make the painful dissolution of a marriage a little more civilized. In fact, that is how the new law refers to the process—not as divorce but as a dissolution of marriage. And it permits the dissolution without the hurtful and often fraudulent accusations of adultery, cruelty, or wrongdoing that most states still demand.

Adultery, cruelty, or any of the other legal grounds for a divorce are, after all, merely surface indications of the inability of two people to live together harmoniously. And that is what the law is designed to do—let two people dissolve their marriage when it no longer has any productive meaning. No witnesses will be required to testify to the breakdown, or the evil of either partner. Alimony, available to both man and wife, will be allotted not as a punishment but as a means of allowing the disadvantaged partner to gain a new start. Custody of children will be awarded strictly on the basis of the children's welfare, with both partners regarded as equal claimants.

These provisions make sense. Our divorce laws were intended to protect the sanctity of the home and the welfare of the children by making divorce difficult. As divorce rates show, they have not worked. Instead, they have only made the procedure hurtful and costly, thus impairing the ability of the divorced people to regain a normal life, and taking from them money needed to support the children in a critical period.

There was a time when a woman, in order to protect herself against the stigma of divorce, needed to prove herself guiltless of wrong, and to show that her husband was at fault. But the stigma is not what it was, and there is no longer any justification for forcing two already anguished people to further embitter, debase, or perjure themselves in order to dissolve an already broken and meaningless relationship.[3]

It is easy to understand why thousands upon thousands of divorced people attack, criticize, and in other ways try to discredit the institution of marriage. Our feelings are not so much the result of our intellects as of our experiences. Is it any wonder that women and men who have gone through the devastation of marital dissolution henceforth place most of the blame for their troubles on the institution of marriage? Nevertheless, as pointed out in the section on scapegoating, we should not be content to single out one major cause and ignore all other factors. If we are to conduct a truly critical evaluation of marriage, we must acknowledge that the legal-ecclesiastical definition of marriage and its effect on subsequent enforcement of the marital contract is *one* factor—but only one—to be examined.

The Second Root of Disillusionment: Societal Influences

In what ways does society contribute to marital disillusionment? The answer to this question is complex. But certainly it is safe to say that society encourages marital disillusionment by fostering unrealistic and romantic expectations.

A reading of Andreas Capellanus' *The Art of Courtly Love*, a thirteenth-century statement on the nature of love, provides a glimpse of the forerunner of the movement known as romanticism.

Now let us see in what ways love may be decreased. Too many opportunities for exchanging solaces, too many opportunities of seeing the loved one, too much chance to talk to each other all decrease love, and so does an uncultured appearance or manner of walking on the part of the lover or the sudden loss of his property. Love decreases, too, if the woman finds that her lover is foolish and indiscreet, or if he seems to go beyond reasonable bounds in his demands for love, or if she sees that he has no regard for her modesty and will not forgive her bashfulness. Love decreases, too, if the woman considers that her lover is cowardly in battle, or sees that he is unrestrained in his speech or spoiled by the vice of arrogance.[4]

In the light of such a statement, it is not difficult to understand why Albert Ellis says:

[T]he general marital philosophy of our society is quite opposed to such acts as lovers limiting the period of their love, becoming varietists, engaging in plural affairs, consciously renouncing their loves, or arranging a suicide pact with their beloveds. Instead we espouse what might be called the most illogical climax to romantic courtship and love: consummation. For sexual and marital consummation indubitably, in the vast majority of instances, maims, bloodies, and finally kills romanticism until it is deader than—well, yesterday's romance.[5]

Our society has inherited the courtly-romantic tradition as well as the Victorian-puritan tradition. Both traditions are essentially antisexual and both emphasize purity of motive and spiritual oneness between lovers. If we look to the opera, literature, drama, movies, television, magazines, newspapers, and advertising of our past and present, we see how deeply the concept of romance has influenced our cultural heritage. This heritage is transmitted by our courts, our religious institutions, our educational institutions, and our familial institutions.

Societal expectations concerning marriage, especially among the middle classes, include the following: People should marry for love; sex should be an expression of love; lovers should become a fused unity; individual identities should merge into couple identity; love will flourish once the right love object comes along; falling in love is the appropriate response to the opposite sex; love conquers all obstacles; love that is genuine need not include **eros;** love and hate are opposites, and one cannot love if one hates nor hate if one loves; conflict is always destructive and to be avoided; unity implies uniformity; males should be more dominant, females more submissive; good women are for marriage—bad women are for sex; men enjoy sex—women tolerate it; men enjoy orgasm—women should not really need it or want it; children strengthen a marriage— marriage without children is abnormal; individual happiness is the supreme goal of marriage; one's partner in marriage should fulfill all needs for love, affection, romance, sex, companionship, and friendship; marriage should satisfy all domestic, economic, and status needs.

eros traditionally, the physical love between man and woman; specifically, that type of love characterized by passion, tenderness, and intimacy, involving a desire to give as well as receive, to procreate, to create, and to enhance the partner's humanity.

These expectations are not all the result of romanticism nor are they all the result of Victorianism. They are the product of a fusing of traditions within American society. When a people embraces a Judeo-Christian cultural heritage, a courtly-romantic view of love, a Victorian-puritan view of sex, rugged individualism, a belief in self-determinism, a semideistic veneration of the founding fathers, and idolatry of the flag, God, and motherhood, then inevitably societal expectations of marriage become contradictory and naively idealistic.

The Third Root
of Disillusionment:
The Socialization Process

Socialization cannot be separated from societal expectations. These expectations determine the customs, mores, beliefs, attitudes, and life style into which the child is indoctrinated. It is useful to examine the process of socialization as carried out by the institutions of family, education, and religion.

The family is the most powerful socializing agent in society. Each partner brings to marriage his or her life orientation, life style, value structure, religious-**metaphysical**-existential viewpoints, and personality structure. The marriage is consummated, and children are born. These children are socialized by the combined orientations of their parents.

The family is the first transmitter of moral values and the various components of the common culture. Children begin to learn sexual and marital roles shortly after birth. This learning is not a formal process but an internalizing process in which children copy, imitate, and mimic their parental models. Sex-role typing takes place long before school age. Little girls wear dresses, play with dolls, and learn how to keep house, "just like mommy." Little boys wear pants, play with toy guns and cars, and compete in sports, "just like daddy." Little girls are taught to be pretty, passive, and domestic. Little boys are taught to be assertive and competitive.

metaphysical a philosophical term referring to the study of principles and problems connected with understanding the ultimate source of life and the universe.

Recently the Women's Liberation Movement has begun to advocate that men and women should restructure much of their sex-role stereotyping. In this view, women should work outside as well as inside the home, and men should assume greater responsibility for child care and household chores. Parents who agree with these views are attempting to break down rigid stereotyping of sex roles in the socialization of their children. Hopefully, this new approach will allow children to develop their individual potential and assume a variety of roles in adult life. Whatever the outcome of this new approach, it remains true that children learn to be adults by imitation of significant models. It is unrealistic to expect children to assume adult roles for which they have no model.

Children likewise develop their attitudes toward sexuality by imitating the attitudes of their parents and other significant adults. These attitudes are learned early on an emotional level, and they become a deeply believed and accepted part of the self. If a boy scratches his penis and his mother or father scolds him or tells him he is being "dirty," "naughty," "not nice," then an aura of mystery begins to surround this organ of his body. Erik Erikson has shown us that shame and doubt develop quite early in a child's life, as do guilt and feelings of inferiority.[6] (Erikson's system is referred to as a **psychosocial** system, as contrasted with Freud's **psychosexual** system. Here again we see the emphasis on the importance of society and the common cultural tradition.)

Since children learn attitudes toward sex and marriage early in childhood, we must ask whether parents are successful in providing realistic models for their children to emulate. Two questions seem especially crucial for the socialization of the child: Why do many parents resist sharing intimacies with each other when children are present? Why do some parents consider it a virtue not to fight in front of their children? By refusing to share the realities of love and conflict, could parents be denying their children meaningful models? Sometimes in adult life the people who avoid conflict are those who lacked models who faced conflict directly, fairly, and creatively. How many times in the course of a month do marriage counselors and psychotherapists hear their clients say, "My

psychosexual and **psychosocial** abbreviations for the terms psychological-sexual and psychological-social, which are used to refer to a system of thought relating psychology to human sexuality and social dynamics, respectively.

parents never fought and never argued." Such a remark would indicate one of several possible situations: (1) one of the partners usually gave in on all issues; (2) both partners repressed and suppressed their feelings, attitudes, and beliefs; (3) they let it all out when no one was around or behind closed doors. Where did our parents, our grandparents, and our great-grandparents get the idea that conflict was evil and destructive? Where did they learn that honesty is wrong? Certainly it is dishonest and hypocritical to withhold one's thoughts, attitudes, and feelings. **Intrapsychic** and **interpsychic** honesty require—even demand—the facing of conflict.

A society that emphasizes the importance of the family in the socializing of its young contradicts its own popular expectations when it makes little provision for educating its young in human development, human sexuality, marital preparation, and family development. As a society, we have socialized our children into sexual anxiety in the most effective negative way possible: we have taught rigid sex roles and ignored sexual dynamics. What passes for mental health education, sex education, and family life education is all too often a sham. Educational institutions disclaim responsibility in this area, pointing instead to church and family. Increasingly, some religious denominations, usually in the more liberal traditions, are seeking to do an adequate job. However, conservative and authoritarian groups continue to contribute to the problem by indoctrinating their young in the tradition (aesthetic and romantic unions, an antisexual stance, and an ethic that places duty above self-fulfillment and **self-actualization**) that places our entire society in its double bind.

This denial of responsibility by both educational and ecclesiastical institutions increases the pressure on the family. If marriage is a dehumanized arrangement, it seems logical to assume that the family also has become dehumanized. What do I mean by "dehumanized"? Dehumanization is the process of depriving us of our essential dignity as individuals. We become things—objects for manipulation and exploitation. In playing roles, we become unreal, false, or inauthentic.

intrapsychic psychic or mental forces within the self (intra = within, psychic = self).
interpsychic psychic or mental forces between two or more people (inter = between).
self-actualization similar in meaning to self-fulfillment or self-realization; the process of developing one's human potential.

The dehumanization of marriage and family is the result of the same double bind. Marriage is said to be the relationship that offers the greatest happiness, but marriage is also held to be the keystone of human misery. There is a conspiracy of dishonesty wherein the brave pretend to be happy and in so doing destroy their greatest opportunity for human growth. If marriage and family life are to become humanized, hypocrisy, illusion, pretense, and dishonesty must be replaced by relationships based on real feelings and conflict resolution rather than on authoritarian traditions.

While parents have ignored education in sexuality, they have socialized their children to adjust, succeed, produce, and accomplish. Underlying this process is the idea of the "marketing orientation" described by Erich Fromm.[7] Fromm points out that in our society the value and worth of a human being is contingent on the price his personality and abilities can command in the marketplace. Many parents feel guilty about not having "made it" and expect their children to fulfill their own lack of fulfillment. (Be what I never was able to be—make my life worthwhile by making up for my own lack of fulfillment—complete my incompleteness—fill my cup for me because I did not fill it myself.) No human being should ever or can ever fulfill another's lack of fulfillment, but many young people are socialized to make just such an attempt. The parents who socialize and the children who are socialized in this manner are usually unaware that such programming results in loss of autonomy, selfhood, and identity. Thus, such programming sows seeds that produce self-doubt and shame, forerunners of guilt.

The socialization process undermines the growth of self-confidence by emphasizing external controls—such as rules, norms, and ethical codes—rather than encouraging self-discovery. Thus, adult overconcern about drugs, sex, and morals tells us more about the anxiety level of the adult than about the inclinations of the young. Consider the inherent contradictions in the following parent–son interaction:

Poor Bill Thompson

The scene is the living room of the Thompson residence. Bill Thompson, age sixteen, has just asked his father if he can use the car for the evening.

Mr. Thompson responds: "Frankly, I don't see why I should let you take the car. After all, you don't help me keep it clean, wash it, or wax it. When's the last time you even volunteered to put gas in it? Every time you take the car, something goes wrong with it."

"But, Dad, would you please listen to—"

"Wait a minute—you listen to me. Your mother and I trust your judgment, you understand, but we just don't think you are ready for the responsibility of taking the car out alone at night."

"In other words, you don't trust me."

"Now, Bill, of course we trust you. It's just that you're a little young to handle certain situations."

"Like what?"

"Well, son, if I have to spell it out for you. You're at the age when girls and sex and cars and drugs all seem to go together. It's not that I don't trust you—it's the others I'm leery about. You know how disappointed your mother was when she discovered that pornographic stuff in your dresser drawer. You should be ashamed of yourself, hurting her like that. Seems to me you could show a little gratitude occasionally—we try to give you every advantage . . ."

"I suppose you were never curious about what a naked girl looks like . . ."

"That's enough of that kind of talk out of you . . ."

This father and son are talking, but they are not communicating. Why does the father react the way he does? He professes trust, but in fact trust is withheld. Love is extolled, yet love is used as a shaming technique. Honesty is ritualized, yet honesty is replaced with hypocrisy. People fear what honesty might reveal to the children—namely, that mother and father are two human beings, each strong and weak, loving and hostile, selfless and selfish, reliable and fallible, autonomous and dependent, self-loving and self-devaluating.

The socialization process within the family is cyclical—the transmission of myths, folklore, and expectations is self-perpetuating. Unless the cycle is broken, parents impose these patterns on their children, who in turn transmit the myths, folklore, and expectations to their children. Talcott Parsons has suggested that the **superego** is formed not merely from the internalization of parental standards, but also from the various beliefs, norms, tenets, folklore, taboos, and standards of the common culture:

If the approach taken here is correct, the place of the superego as part of the structure of the personality must be understood in terms of the relation between personality and the total common culture, by virtue of which a stable system of social interaction on the human level becomes possible. Freud's insight was profoundly correct when he focused on the element of moral standards. This is, indeed, central and crucial, but it does seem that Freud's view was too narrow. The inescapable conclusion is that not only moral standards, but all the components of the common culture *are internalized as part of the personality structure.*[8]

A large part of the socialization process is the teaching and learning of roles. Roles are usually learned in pairs and clusters rather than singly. As a child learns what it means to be a little boy, he also learns what it means to be a little girl. Fathering roles depend on mothering roles, and husbanding roles depend on wifing roles. The learning of roles and role expectations is stressed, as Parsons points out, by all the components of the common culture. The primary group (the family) is the most instrumental during the very early years. But it is important to recognize the powerful influence of other cultural components—such as educational institutions, organizations like Boy Scouts and Girl Scouts, men's lodges and service clubs, women's auxiliaries, religious institutions, and civic and political institutions.

This discussion of socialization and its effect on marital disillusionment should clarify the hierarchy of expectations we work with: marital disillusionment is partly due to unrealistic expectations; such expectations are due to one's socialization; socialization in turn is the product of the society and its traditions.

superego as used here, refers to the symbolic depository within the self of all the rules the individual has learned about how to think, feel, and act.

The Fourth Root of
Disillusionment: Personality
and Character Orientation

The fourth source of marital disillusionment is intrapsychic in nature. Not only do we need to look at role analysis and the sex-role typing that is culturally transmitted, but we also need to look at what psychic needs people expect the marital situation and the spouse to meet for them.

Erich Fromm has described four basic character orientations that seem to predominate. These character orientations are important in marriage, because they determine the needs a person brings to the marriage and his expectations of the partner. Each orientation has a common payoff—a sense of intrapsychic security, security within oneself. The goal is to allay anxiety and depression, meaninglessness and emptiness, dread and guilt. But at what price? Usually at the price of satisfactory marital relationships.

The primary trait of the individual with a *receptive* orientation is dependence. He looks to others to take care of him and meet his needs. Freud's **oral phase** of development is marked by traits similar to those of the receptive character orientation. The receptive person needs to please others, never wants to offend, needs constant reassurance, and represses feelings of anger, resentment, and hostility. He gains security by submission to authority. His feelings of self-worth depend on other people's view of him. Because he does not have much genuine self-esteem, he depends on others to dote on him, to give him succor, praise, and accolades. He is afraid of risk because he lacks confidence in himself. Consequently, he is more likely to be a follower than a leader. At heart he does not trust in his own powers nor does he accept himself thoroughly.[9] Karen Horney describes this personality as one who moves "toward" others.[10]

A person with a fairly strong receptive orientation will place many unrealistic demands on the marital partner. Implicit in these demands will

oral phase the first phase of personality development postulated by Freud, during which the mouth is the primary erogenous zone through which the child gratifies himself and experiences pleasure; as personality develops, oral characteristics may manifest themselves in the form of mouth-centered pleasure.

be the same request posed many different ways: "Take care of me; I'm so helpless. I need you in order for me to be me. Reassure me. Don't fight with me, I can't stand conflict. I trust you implicitly to be right . . . and (sensed but never spoken) I'm afraid to disagree with you because you won't love me anymore." A receptive person is not at all without power— his is the power of manipulation through helplessness. The predictable result of the normal–receptive marriage is that the normal will tire of his mate's dependency and gradually feel resentment and a falling out of love.

Fromm's second type of character orientation is *exploitative*. Exploitative traits are akin to the characteristics of the **anal phase** described by Freud. The exploitative person gains security by being "one-up" or "over" others. He cannot tolerate equality because he needs to retain the feeling of power and control so that he himself will not be controlled or manipulated. He is manipulative and sometimes ruthless in his attempts to maintain control. Karen Horney describes this type of person as moving "against" others.[11]

People who reveal marked tendencies to dominate threaten the happiness of any relationship, and certainly a marriage relationship. The implicit and explicit message is always a variation of the theme, "Be what I want you to be; do what I want you to do. Live, think, act, breathe the way I tell you. I am right. I am leader. You are less—not quite a person. If you forget who you are and what your position is, you will threaten me for I cannot tolerate insubordination. I demand your love." The outcome of the exploitative–normal match is identical to the receptive–normal—chaos, disillusionment, falling out of love, resentment, and dehumanization.

A third type of orientation is characterized by *hoarding*. According to Fromm, "This orientation makes people have little faith in anything new they might get from the outside world; their security is based on hoarding and saving, while spending is thought to be a threat."[12] Because love can be thought of as a possession, the hoarding personality is generally incapable of granting freedom and independence to the beloved. The saving characteristic also manifests itself in a tendency to hold on to memories

anal phase Freud's second phase of development, which is characterized by the child's concern and attention on the anus and toileting habits; anal personality traits are considered to be cleanliness, obstinacy, orderliness, and a desire to hold onto and possess.

of the past, collecting things, and clinging to orderliness and punctuality. Somewhat parallel to this concept is Karen Horney's concept of moving "away" from people.[13]

A hoarding–normal match can be destructive because of the hoarder's overpossessiveness, jealousy, and sometimes extremely conservative attitude toward money and other possessions. A hoarder needs to be constantly reassured of love, never feels sated, and hence never really learns to trust in himself as lovable, no matter what reassurance he gets from his partner. This type of relationship is likely to have financial problems because the hoarder cannot part with the money that is one symbol of his security.

The fourth type of orientation is the *marketing* orientation. Fromm said of this orientation: "In order to understand its nature one must consider the economic function of the market in modern society as being not only analogous to this character orientation but as the basis and the main condition for its development in modern man."[14] Briefly, the individual possessing a marketing orientation allows his value to be determined by his exchange value in the marketplace. Instead of valuing himself as a unique and worthwhile individual, he allows the market to do the valuating. That is, he bases his identity on his success in the world of business, sales, industry, commerce, and politics. He depends a great deal on the role he fulfills and the status he commands, thus attempting to create a locus of worth essentially outside of himself. Rollo May has given an example of this process:

For example, there is the curious remark made regularly nowadays at the end of radio programs, "Thanks for listening." This remark is quite amazing when you come to think of it. Why should a person who is doing the entertaining, who is giving something ostensibly of value, thank the receiver for taking it? To acknowledge applause is one thing, but thanking the recipient for deigning to listen and be amused is a quite different thing. It betokens that the action is given its value, or lack of value, by the whim of the consumer, the receiver—in the case of our illustration, the consumers being their majesties, the public.[15]

This loss of a sense of self runs through the marketing orientation. In our society it is little wonder that retirement for men and the empty nest for women are such threatening and often disillusioning experiences. Because their identity as persons has been co-opted from their station, role, status, and salary, they are at a loss to create new centers within themselves.

The marketing–normal match is the most difficult to uncover due to its subtlety and its status as a culturally patterned defect. Nevertheless, the person with this orientation finds his value only in the worth the marketplace ascribes to him. He is more likely to seek his identity in the work world than to place importance on achieving a fulfilling marital relationship. Whenever a marriage partner depends on the value others ascribe to him, rather than on his own sense of self-value, the result is bound to be a weakening and deterioration of the marital relationship whenever the expected valuation from the marketplace is not forthcoming. When we lack inner feelings of self-acceptance and self-fulfillment, marriage is unfulfilling.

Summary

This chapter has included a discussion of the meaning of the terms illusion, disillusion, and disillusionment and has considered several areas that produce marital disillusionment. Although scapegoating—singling out one cause as the culprit in creating marital dissatisfaction—is a common practice, in actuality many intertwining beliefs and practices contribute to marital dissatisfaction.

Four social and individual influences on marriage were discussed: the legal-ecclesiastical definition of the institution of marriage, societal expectations stemming from Western cultural traditions, the socialization process, and the intrapsychic or personality makeup of the individuals who enter marriage.

Marital disillusionment can rarely be attributed to a simple or single factor such as the institution, society, socialization, personal needs, or character orientations. Rather, various factors interact to create a feeling of disillusionment—sometimes mild, sometimes severe, and often repressed. The roots of marital disillusionment are powerful and create inner feelings of guilt, anxiety, disappointment, misery, and depression. A prescription for treatment must be based on an honest evaluation of ourselves and our implicit and explicit expectations in the context of contemporary institutional, societal, and socialization practices.

As we have seen in examining Fromm's postulated character orientations, and as we shall see in the next chapter, the net effect of expecting a mate to meet one's faulty or excessive ego needs is to drive the mate into the unfulfilling position of deficit-filler.

Questions for Study

1. In the two statements at the beginning of the chapter, find the ideas that reflect each of the four sources of marital disillusionment.

2. Criticize the radical and conservative attitudes toward marriage as described in this chapter. In what ways are these stances valid or invalid?

3. List specific ways in which the legal-ecclesiastical establishment has affected marriage. What changes in this establishment reflect or respond to changes in marriage?

4. List the traditional belief systems that are prevalent in our society, and analyze how each contributes conflicting beliefs concerning marriage.

5. What specific factors in *your* early socialization in the school and family affect your present thoughts and beliefs about yourself, sexuality, sex roles, and marriage?

Reading Suggestions

The Fractured Family by Leontine Young. New York: McGraw-Hill, 1973. An analysis of the strengths and weaknesses of the traditional American family structure.

The Death of the Family by David Cooper. New York: Random House, 1970. An exploration of the effects of the family on the individual.

Sanity, Madness and the Family by R. D. Laing and A. Esterson. Middlesex, England: Penguin, 1964. A theory of the relationship between family functioning and schizophrenia.

Readings on the Family and Society edited by William J. Goode. Englewood Cliffs, N.J.: Prentice-Hall, 1964. Readings on the effect of society on the family, illustrated by an examination of various cultures and historical periods.

Husbands and Wives by Robert Blood, Jr. and Donald Wolfe. Glencoe, Ill.: Free Press, 1960. An historical sketch and an empirical analysis of the social dynamics of American marriage.

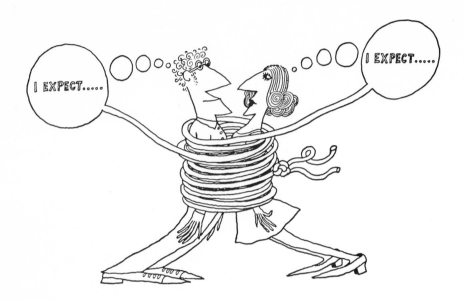

TWO
THE EXPECTATION BIND: NEED FULFILLMENT IN MARRIAGE

34

**The Expectation Bind:
Need Fulfillment in Marriage**

Marital Expectations

Happiness and Pleasure

Legitimate and
Illegitimate Need Fulfillment

The Neurotic Need for Affection

Deficiency Needs and Being Needs

The Origin of Illegitimate Needs

Deficiency Love and Being Love

Dependence—
Independence—Interdependence

Summary

Questions for Study

Reading Suggestions

Marital Expectations

Jean in Premarital Counseling

Jean: *Since you are asking what I expect of Carl and our marriage I want to first say that I don't really think Carl and I have many expectations of each other. We believe that if we love each other deeply enough this is the most important thing. Love always finds a way.*

Counselor: *Yes, Jean, but what exactly does this mean to you? For example, do you expect Carl to ever be angry at you?*

Jean: *Oh, I suppose so, but he'd better have a good reason. I don't think people who love each other need to get angry. You know that line from Love Story, "Love means never having to say I'm sorry." I like that because it means love is strong enough to override all the possible problems.*

Counselor: *What might those problems be?*

Jean: *Oh, I don't think we'll have many problems. When someone loves you they just know what you are feeling and what to do.*

Counselor: *What do you think Carl expects of you?*

Jean: *He expects the same things I do. He expects me to do my share of the deal. He expects me to be a good wife.*

Counselor: *Jean, I'm wondering how you will feel if Carl doesn't pay enough attention to you—or behave the way you expect him to.*

Jean: *Carl has never disappointed me! He has always been set on his career and he'll be earning a good income. We've decided to go ahead now and buy an oversized house so we'll be ready when we have children.*

Counselor: *Children?*

Jean: *Yes, we want at least three children. Carl will make such a fine father. I really want a close-knit family where we depend on each other and really enjoy each other. I think children need to be close to their father—don't you?*

Counselor: *How much time will Carl have for you and the children if he is concentrating on his professional responsibilities?*

Jean: *Oh that's no problem: Carl will always find the time. He'd better! I need him. That's why I'm so happy . . . he meets my needs so well.*

Jean Six Years Later

Carl expects me to keep a clean house, do all the cooking, manage the budget, be a good mother who never yells at the kids, greet him with a cocktail when he gets home from work—all gussied up in something sexy—I'm even supposed to feel sexy. I'm supposed to have dinner ready on time and the kids bathed and in bed on time. What does he do? He enjoys his work. He has lots of friends to rap with and secretaries to make passes at.

Carl Six Years Later

Who says marriage is supposed to meet all of a person's needs? I need lots of people and lots of different experiences in order to be happy. Jean says I'm supposed to meet all of her love needs, all of her sexual needs, all of her friendship needs, all of her social needs, fun needs, recreation needs, financial needs, and companionship needs. Hell, I can't do it! And she can't do it for me either. Look, I'm a person, okay? I have needs all my own—privacy needs, solitude needs, social interaction needs, sexual needs—does marriage mean that each of us is expected to meet all of each other's needs and no one else is supposed to meet any? Look, I've been sexually faithful to Jean, but is there anything wrong with me talking with and being with other attractive women?

Jean and Carl's problems reflect a number of factors: their premarital romanticized concept of love and its staying–holding–healing power; Jean's blindness regarding her expectations of Carl and marriage in general; the sex-role division of labor along traditional lines and Jean's feeling that she is getting the worst of the bargain; implicit demands that each is supposed to be the need-filler for the other—without any other sources of input; and Jean's implicit assumption that individual identity is unimportant—the only important thing is couple identity.

People generally expect marriage to satisfy most of their basic needs. They expect their partners to meet their physical needs, **affect** needs, romance

affect refers to emotion; affect needs are emotional needs.

needs, communication needs, sharing needs, sexual needs, economic needs, and social needs. There are few societies, if any, that expect as much from the marriage relationship as our society does.

Our children are socialized in ways that create marital expectations which are not consistent with a realistic assessment of marriage. Our society places marriage on a pedestal and bemoans divorce; it idolizes sex, yet refuses to educate for human sexuality; it glorifies romance, yet insists that romance is for the young and immature. We learn roles from the time we are infants. We internalize the teachings and examples of our role models, who, during the first years of our lives, are almost exclusively our parents. We build up **ego ideals** of ourselves and of our future spouses. And our role-learning, ego ideals, mate ideals, cultural expectations, and romantic longings lead to a high divorce rate.

The focus of this chapter is the bind in which we put ourselves when we fail to recognize and identify the expectations we have of our partners. Very few people are in touch with all their expectations. But far too many of us are in touch with only a few of our expectations. The result is that we unwittingly put our partners in a bind by expecting them to operate in conjunction with a set of norms that we are not aware of and have not openly discussed. Expectations usually arise out of what we perceive as our inner needs. We all have needs that must be met one way or another —by the self, the mate, others, or by various interests and pursuits.

Before we delve into a more thorough discussion of needs and expectations, let us examine happiness, the desire most people express when asked what they expect from married life.

Happiness and Pleasure

Young people frequently (if not always) maintain that their chief goal in married life is happiness. Happiness is the great god of married life. "We want happiness together more than anything else."

---

ego ideal an idealized image of oneself that is indicative of the way a person would like to be; the ideal self; the fantasied self-image as contrasted with the actual self-image.

Of course! Why not? Everybody wants to be happy. The advertising industry knows this quite well. Happiness is a trip to Hawaii. Happiness is a bottle of this or a taste of that. Happiness may be a new husband, a new wife, a new sex partner, a new car, a new snowmobile, a new garden tractor. There is no doubt that the advertising industry is aware that most Americans are restless most of the time, that they nurse feelings of disappointment and disillusionment, that they are largely unfulfilled and non-self-actualizing.

Aristotle identified happiness as a state of self-fulfillment. W. T. Jones, summarizing Aristotle's thoughts about happiness, writes:

Pleasure is the name we give to immediate satisfaction, which is all that is open to the animal. Happiness is the name for that longer range, more complete satisfaction which reason gives us the possibility of achieving . . . the possibility of more ignominious failure than any animal has experienced is the risk the rational soul must run for the possibility of a much greater fulfillment. . . . Happiness, then, is what we experience when we are virtuous, that is, when we are living at our best and fullest, when we are functioning in accordance with our nature, when our end is realizing itself without impediment, when our form is becoming actual.[1]

Note the phrases "living at our fullest," "functioning according to our nature," "realizing ourself," and "form becoming actual." This same emphasis is being heard today from people in many different disciplines. Abraham Maslow writes: "[F]or writers in these various groups, notably Fromm, Horney, Jung, C. Buhler, Angyal, Rogers, and G. Allport, Schachtel, and Lynd, and recently some Catholic psychologists, *growth, individuation, autonomy, self-actualization, self-development, productiveness, self-realization,* are all crudely synonymous, designating a vaguely perceived area rather than a sharply defined concept."[2]

The concept of self-actualization can be traced from the time of Aristotle to the present. People may quarrel about formal definition, but the essentials of the concept are clear. There is more than a theoretical relationship between happiness and self-actualization. There is a *functional* relationship on the level of feelings, attitudes, values, and behavior, and its focal point is the self-concept. That is, self-actualization constitutes the emotional freedom and autonomy that are as necessary as breathing space for the human psyche. Without space and freedom to evolve, the psyche becomes stymied, constricted, blocked, and shut in on itself, depriving the individual of the basic ingredients of happiness.

There is, however, a conceptual and theoretical difference between happiness and pleasure. Can a happy person experience tragedy and grief, yet remain an essentially happy person? Can an unhappy person experience pleasure and joy, yet remain basically an unhappy person? Yes, in both cases. Why? Because we are talking about two different things. Many essentially happy people go through tragedy and sorrow. Experiencing these feelings does not significantly alter personality makeup.

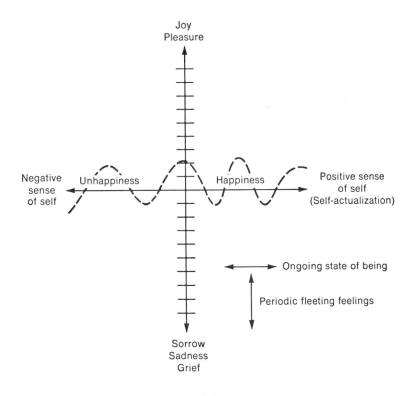

Figure 2–1
The Ongoing State
of Happiness vs. Periodic Fleeting Feelings

Nor is a little pleasure for an unhappy person likely to significantly change his basic personality. Following this line of reasoning, let us ask, "What words can be used to describe the opposites of happiness and pleasure? Figure 2–1 pictures two intersecting continua—one axis polarizes happiness, the other polarizes pleasure. There is room for a wide range of possibilities on each continuum or line.

Both lines represent emotions. Yet there is a difference between the two. The "Happiness-Unhappiness" line reflects a state of being that is more or less constant—an ongoing inner state subject to mild mood fluctuations yet relatively constant. The "Pleasure-Sorrow" line reflects a different quality of feeling based on periodic or fleeting experiences. The very nature of a peak experience or of a joyful feeling is that it waxes and wanes. Sorrow and sadness likewise come and go. They are not normally thought of as permanent, ongoing emotional states.

Happiness is more directly related to personality than to marriage. It is reasonable to expect happiness in marriage, if the marriage partners have happy personalities. If, however, an essentially unhappy person believes that marriage will somehow change his basic personality from an unhappy to a happy one, he is probably deluding himself.

Legitimate and
Illegitimate Need Fulfillment

Aron Krich has said:

[M]arriage will not make an unhappy person happy. Marriage is the relationship that most adults find conducive to attaining satisfaction from life, but marriage in itself does not create happiness. . . . Marriage can add to one's feeling of self-worth if one enters it feeling worth loving in the first place. But the love of a husband or wife cannot make up for the love one failed to get as a child. Countless people approach marriage counseling complaining of the inadequacy of their spouse's love, when actually no amount of love would be enough to make them feel good about themselves.[3]

If a person is essentially happy, he or she will not seek a marital partner to make up for a love deficit. The needs that one partner expects the other partner to fulfill will be reasonable—that is, they will be needs that have a rational basis. Among these needs one could list sharing, communication, friendship, erotic love, and nonerotic love. The expectation that a mate will meet the major portion of each of these needs is legitimate, because these are ongoing *being* needs—needs that arise in the present rather than out of deficits accumulated in the past.

It is reasonable to say that any need is legitimate—even the need to be immature—if the individual honestly feels the need as real. If, for example, a person has never felt the security of being loved, certainly that need for love is a legitimate need. But, if that person expects a mate to make up for the early deficiency, that is an illegitimate expectation, because the need arises out of a past deficit. "Please love me and make me feel loved (even though I have never felt lovable)." People who ask for or demand constant reassurance that they are loved are frequently expressing a love deficit. The need may be legitimate, but the expectation of fulfillment by the mate is illegitimate. Throughout the remainder of the book I refer to a legitimate expectation of need fulfillment as a *legitimate ego need*, and to an illegitimate expectation of need fulfillment as an *illegitimate ego need*.

Erich Fromm has described the difference between love based on expectation of legitimate need fulfillment and love based on expectation of illegitimate need fulfillment. He writes of the person who is mature in his love:

To give has become more satisfactory, more joyous, than to receive; to love, more important even than being loved. By loving, he has left the prison cell of aloneness and isolation which was constituted by the state of **narcissism** *and self-centeredness. He feels a sense of new union, of sharing, of oneness. More than that, he feels the potency of producing love by loving—rather than the dependence of receiving by being loved—and for that reason having to be small, helpless, sick—or "good." In-*

narcissism an exaggerated concern with the self, implying a being in love with oneself; not to be confused with self-love or self-esteem.

fantile love follows the principle: "I love because I am loved." *Mature love follows the principle:* "I am loved because I love." *Immature love says:* "I love you because I need you." *Mature love says:* "I need you because I love you."[4]

Illegitimate ego needs arise primarily from the insecurity of not feeling loved in early childhood, late childhood, and adolescence. The experience of being in love is often an emotional response to someone who is perceived as capable of meeting any unmet or partially met needs that we have brought from our earlier development to adulthood. When this happens, "I love you because I need you" accurately describes the condition of illegitimate need expectation. Let us ask what happens when a person loves because he needs. For a while things may go well, but if the spouse is relatively stable and secure he will eventually tire of being leaned on. One day the individual who "loves because he needs" will perceive that he no longer loves his spouse. He will wonder why. "I am falling out of love." "My love has died." In reality the stable, secure spouse has slowly tired of treating the dependent one as a child, of being leaned on and assuming the role of parent substitute. When the dependent subject begins to feel that his love is dying, he is actually experiencing his spouse's inability to meet his illegitimate need demands.

If both partners enter a relationship with an "I love you because I need you" orientation, then there is a symbiosis. That is, they share a mutual dependence that makes it impossible for either to function alone in a truly self-fulfilling, mature manner. Thus, a *symbiotic* relationship is to be distinguished from a genuinely healthy *interdependent* relationship. A symbiotic relationship is built around a mutual meeting of illegitimate needs, whereas genuine interdependence is based on a mutual meeting of legitimate needs. Paradoxically, symbiotic marriage relationships quite frequently endure. Because both partners experience satisfaction in meeting the illegitimate needs of the other and in turn receive gratification of their own illegitimate needs, they have a basis for an enduring relationship, however immature and neurotic it may be.[5] There is, however, no such thing as a half-symbiosis! If only one partner leans on the other, theirs is not a symbiotic relationship. Chances for survival of the marriage are slim, unless the dependent partner can work through his dependency in counseling or psychotherapy.

Ron and Judy

Ron and Judy have been married for seven years. Judy has had an increasing awareness that she is not happy, and she and Ron have separate appointments with the same counselor.

Judy: *I feel sort of—well, sort of blah most of the time: It's to the point where I only feel happy when we go somewhere special, like to a party. Sometimes I go shopping, just because it makes me feel better. Ron used to make me happy but he seems to be a drag. I love him; but we just don't seem to have any spark left in our marriage. He keeps telling me that I need to get out of myself more—and I'd like to but I don't know how. If only we had more money, then we could do more things together and enjoy life a little. I've thought of getting a job—and I might just as soon as Suzie reaches first grade. Then both children will be in school and I'll have more freedom. Maybe then I'll be happy. Ha! (long pause) I really feel it's Ron's fault. We both agreed when we got married that the most important thing we wanted was happiness. That's a laugh!*

Ron: *I don't know what it is with her, but lately I feel totally frustrated. She seems depressed, low—and always expecting me to pull her up. We've spent money like crazy—buy this, buy that, go here, go there: Yet— nothing seems to make her happy. We have sex about twice a week and I enjoy it—and she seems to—but then, she's still miserable. I suppose I should have been more encouraging when she mentioned she would like to get a job. I'm not against it—although I admit I'm not crazy about the idea. It's starting to get me down. I've thought of divorce and of having relationships with other women. But . . . I guess I'm worn down too— I keep feeling guilty because I can't make her happy. There are times I just have to push all my feelings into the back of my mind. I wonder if I even love her anymore.*

Ron and Judy cannot be analyzed on the basis of such short statements, but for our purpose it is sufficient to point out the probability that Judy's unhappiness (restlessness, depression) is not the result of Ron's attitude and behavior. Judy's problem lies within Judy. She believes she would feel better if Ron would make her happy, but it is not within Ron's power as a human being to fill the unfulfillment of Judy. It is within

Ron's power, however, to become more supportive of Judy's desire to take a job outside the home. Judy may be a very gifted woman who is trying to find her fulfillment through her husband rather than through her own career efforts. If this is the case, Judy's lack of adjustment to the wife–mother pattern may, in fact, be a sign of emotional health. Nevertheless, Judy appears to be an emotionally dependent person who expects her husband to make her happy. This expectation is illegitimate; it can be safely assumed that her present unhappiness stems from emotional deficits she experienced as a child.

The Neurotic Need for Affection

Karen Horney has contributed to our understanding of legitimate and illegitimate ego needs by reviewing the characteristics and attributes of the neurotic need for affection.

Although it is very difficult to say what is love, we can say definitely what is not love, or what elements are alien to it. One may be thoroughly fond of a person, and yet at times be angry with him, deny him certain wishes or want to be left alone. But there is a difference between such circumscribed reactions of wrath or withdrawal and the attitude of a neurotic, who is constantly on guard against others, feels that any interest they take in third persons is a neglect of himself, and interprets any demand as an imposition or any criticism as a humiliation. This is not love. . . . Of course we want something from the person we are fond of—we want gratification, loyalty, help; we may even want a sacrifice, if necessary. And it is in general an indication of mental health to be able to express such wishes or even fight for them. The difference between love and the neurotic need for affection lies in the fact that in love the feeling of affection is primary, whereas in the case of the neurotic the primary feeling is the need for reassurance, and the illusion of loving is only secondary. Of course there are all sorts of intermediate conditions.

If a person needs another's affection for the sake of reassurance against anxiety, the issue will usually be completely blurred in his conscious mind . . . all that he feels is that here is a person whom he likes or trusts, or with whom he feels infatuated. But what he feels as spontaneous love may be nothing but a response of gratitude for some kindness shown him or a response of hope or affection aroused by some person or situation. The person who explicitly or implicitly arouses in him expectations of this kind will automatically be invested with importance, and his feeling will manifest itself in the illusion of love. . . . Such expectations . . . may be aroused by erotic or sexual advances, although these may have nothing to do with love.[6]

It is imperative to underline Horney's remark that there are "all sorts of intermediate conditions."[7] One individual does not have just legitimate ego needs or just illegitimate ego needs. We all have some of each. But some of us have more of one and less of the other—it is a matter of degree.

The extremes are relatively uncommon. Because most of us have a mixture of both legitimate and illegitimate ego needs, we need to examine the balance of the mixture (see Figure 2–2 for representation of various

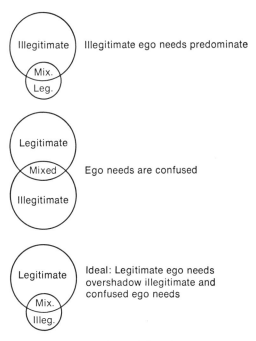

Figure 2–2
The Degree of Mixture
of Legitimate and Illegitimate Ego Needs

mixtures). There is a point at which, even though the illegitimate needs are present and operating, they can be handled without placing too much stress on the marital relationship.

Deficiency Needs and Being Needs

Abraham Maslow offers us a third way of looking at legitimate and illegitimate needs. His concept of "deficiency needs" (D-needs) and "being needs" (B-needs) is similar to the distinction between legitimate and illegitimate ego needs. Maslow outlines four deficiency needs that are *pre-potent* in nature—that is, they are basic needs that must be met before a person seeks fulfillment of less basic needs.[8] The higher or more elementary the need, the stronger its power, force, or influence. According to Maslow, the following make up the hierarchy of D-needs: (1) physical needs, such as food, drink, sleep, warmth; (2) needs for psychological and physical safety from harm; (3) the need to be loved; and (4) the need for esteem, both self-esteem and that bestowed by others. A person may be operating fairly effectively in meeting his esteem needs, but if he were suddenly cast adrift in a lifeboat in the Pacific Ocean his esteem needs would be of no importance because he would revert to his pre-potent physical needs and safety needs.

Each D-need must receive some degree of satisfaction before a person can move up the ladder to the next need. Any level may collapse at any time because of specific circumstances and crises. Maslow's D-needs are needs that have to be satisfied in some manner, regardless of why they are still unsatisfied. These D-needs are illegitimate because they arise from a developmental deficit of the individual who thrusts the responsibility for their fulfillment onto another person. Unfortunately, the person who most often inherits this responsibility is the spouse.

William Glasser has pointed out that whenever we look to others to do what we ought to be doing for ourselves we are, in effect, shifting responsibility for ourselves onto the other person.[9] The individual who accepts his own deficiency needs and becomes aware of his own ploys, methods, and strategies to get others to fulfill his lack of fulfillment is in a position to begin to deal with his deficiency needs. Then he need no longer play the game of shifting responsibility to others, which Eric Berne and Thomas Harris have described as "Look what you made me do" or "Look what you did to me."[10] It could also be described as "Be what I need you to be."

The Origin of Illegitimate Needs

Illegitimate ego needs arise from feelings of self-doubt, shame, guilt, and worthlessness. If a person feels unworthy, helpless, and weak, he is likely to need to cling to and possess his mate. If he lacks self-trust, self-belief, and self-faith, he will look toward the other to provide strength, succor, and feelings of esteem. A lack of self-confidence can lead him to attempt to maneuver his mate into constantly bolstering his self-image. Needless to say, such a demand is insatiable and eventually leads to feelings of disgust and resentment in the mate. Self-esteem implies self-acceptance.[11] Erich Fromm has persuasively contended that self-love is not to be confused with selfishness or with narcissistic **egocentricity.**[12] Most counselors and therapists contend that the person who lacks self-love will be a nonaccepting, selfish manipulator of others.[13]

Basically, however, illegitimate ego needs are the result of an actual love-security deficit or a perceived love-security deficit. Such a deficit usually results from socialization by authority figures who are bent on molding the child or teen-ager into a particular behavior **syndrome.** The authority figures love the child but fall into the trap of withdrawing love, of failing to reassuringly demonstrate their esteem for the child as a person. Constant shaming and demeaning may not seem very harmful or detrimental, but such negative messages make a major contribution to the child's negative self-image. The child quickly learns patterns and methods of handling his emotions that form the groundwork for later neurotic tendencies. Any maladjustment or neurotic behavior in the parents contributes to the negative self-image of the developing child, who in later life brings that negative self-image to his adulthood and thus to his marriage and his children.

egocentricity the state of being self-centered.
syndrome characteristics or patterns that form a consistent set.

Illegitimate ego needs usually do not become apparent in nonintimate relationships. Some people exhibit an amazing capacity to avoid deep interpersonal relationships, even though they have no awareness of their avoidance tactics or their need to protect themselves from being known by others. The great majority of people do not avoid intimacy. But most fail to achieve genuine intimacy because of the intrusive negative effects of illegitimate ego needs learned in childhood. The greater the degree of closeness and intimacy, the more likely that illegitimate needs will take command of the personality, causing the individual to make impossible, unreasonable, and illogical demands and requests of the partner.

Deficiency Love and Being Love

Under the circumstances just described, love can become confused with the partner's capacity to meet both legitimate and illegitimate ego needs. When an individual is able to unlearn illegitimate ego needs (an admittedly slow and painful process), he is freer to express genuine love, which in its ideal state we call B-love or "being love." However, illegitimate ego-need fulfillment can give a person such a strong illusion of security (however temporary it may be) that he mistakenly perceives fulfillment of his needs as the essence of love. When this happens, the person is experiencing D-love or "deficiency love," which is really a type of gratitude: "I am feeling love for you; I am grateful that you fill my needs."

D-love contributes to disillusionment in marriage because it is born of illegitimate expectations. The D-lover lacks a strong sense of emotional security, and so his identity is excessively dependent on his partner's ability to provide constant support and love-reassurance.

Dependence—
Independence—Interdependence

Marriages and other intimate relationships based on D-love usually involve dependency or symbiosis. This is referred to as an A-frame relationship (Figure 2–3). Each partner has a weakened self-identity; the relationship has a strong couple identity. Removal of either partner (by divorce, death, or prolonged absence) deprives the other partner of support.

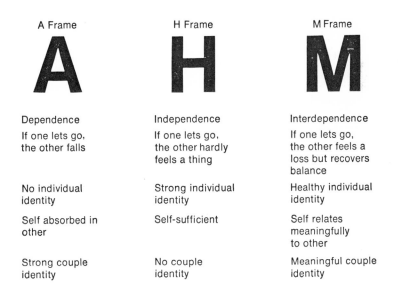

A Frame	H Frame	M Frame
Dependence	Independence	Interdependence
If one lets go, the other falls	If one lets go, the other hardly feels a thing	If one lets go, the other feels a loss but recovers balance
No individual identity	Strong individual identity	Healthy individual identity
Self absorbed in other	Self-sufficient	Self relates meaningfully to other
Strong couple identity	No couple identity	Meaningful couple identity

Figure 2–3
Dependence—Independence—Interdependence

Many young people today express a strong desire for H-frame relationships (Figure 2–3). Each partner has a strong self-identity and each partner disclaims any deep need for the other. They want mutuality but no dependence. They want total individual autonomy but no couple identity. In an H-frame marriage there is total independence. If either partner is removed, the other is hardly affected.

A third type of relationship (discussed in depth in Chapter 12) is a modification of the A-frame and the H-frame. I call it the M-frame (modified) marriage (Figure 2–3). The emphasis is on a strong individual identity for each of the partners, and on a strong commitment by each to the other. It is crucial to the future happiness, fulfillment, and satisfaction of the relationship that each partner have a clear individual identity. Similarly, a meaningful intimate relationship requires a commitment to the other in addition to the self. The M version combines the best qualities of both the A-frame and the H-frame into a relationship that is characterized by individual identity and a meaningful measure of couple identity but that does not foster so much couple dependence that one partner would collapse if the other were removed. In this arrangement the partners are committed to trying to meet the legitimate (being) needs but not the illegitimate (deficiency) needs of their mates.

"But," you may ask, "Isn't it right to expect the mate to meet the needs of the spouse?" Of course! Rational needs that result from mutual interdependence should claim the help of the mate. If the couple is joined by the kind of love expressed as "I need you because I love you," then certainly we can expect mutual need-satisfaction. Legitimate ego needs arise from a commitment born of trust, honesty, freedom, and caring. Illegitimate ego needs are born of dependence and an unconscious desire to make another person responsible for "who I am."

Love based on legitimate needs implies an "active concern for the life and the growth of that which we love."[14] Love based on illegitimate needs does not encourage the growth, freedom, fulfillment, and actualization of the spouse. Legitimate love implies responsibility for the beloved; illegitimate love implies a deterioration of responsibility into manipulative domination and possessiveness. Legitimate love implies respect for the beloved as he or she is; illegitimate love implies oneness with the other in the exploitative sense of needing "him to be as an object for my use."[15] Legitimate love implies a knowledge of the other that transcends the concern for oneself—that is, knowledge that is used to enhance one's ability to give to the other; illegitimate love implies a knowledge of the other gained by self-preoccupation—that is, knowledge of the other that is used to facilitate one's power over and ability to manipulate the other.

Phil and Sandy

Phil and Sandy have been married two years and they have a one-year-old daughter. Phil sought out a psychotherapist and explained his situation.

I came here because I'm afraid I am doing some things that are hurting my relationship with my wife. I might be mistaken . . . (pause) . . . but—I mean to say, it might be a mutual marital problem—but I really don't think so. I keep on finding fault with Sandy—over little things. At times I am beastly to her . . . almost like it's her fault I am me. I get angry and I feel resentment. It's always over little things. She doesn't do the things I think she ought to do. She irritates the hell out of me sometimes. Like the other day—I really wanted her to fuss over me a little and when she didn't I felt hurt—then I got angry. Later I felt depressed and I kept thinking it was all her fault. It's often that way. I seem to be picking at her about little things and afterwards I resent her all the more . . . (long pause) . . . and yet deep down I feel that I'm being unfair because she can never win! It's like something inside of me keeps coming out on her. . . . Do you follow what I'm saying? It's almost like she's responsible for the way I feel . . . it's her fault and I take it out on her.

Many dynamics may explain this episode, including role definition, role expectation, displacement of anger, internal conflict, and anxiety-hostility. Basically, Phil has correctly sensed a contradiction in himself, and he is correct (on the basis of the evidence presented here) in concluding that this is more his problem than his and Sandy's problem. Phil resembles the passive-aggressive personality that characteristically expresses aggression in mildly safe, passive ways. The real target of Phil's anger may or may not be Sandy, but he holds her responsible for whatever it is that bothers him. Phil is shifting responsibility for himself to Sandy, making her the target of his hostility-anxiety. In the passive-aggressive framework there is no way for Sandy to win. The problem is Phil's and he would benefit himself and the marriage if he could discover the source of his anxiety-hostility. Discovery alone is usually not sufficient to change behavior. But until a person gains some insight into his maladaptive behavior patterns he is usually unable to identify the concrete changes that need to be made.

Phil's illegitimate demands on Sandy result from anxiety-hostility. When he feels and expresses anger and resentment toward Sandy, he is condemning her for not being what he wants her to be and for not doing what he wants her to do. Thus, Phil dehumanizes Sandy by focusing on feelings based only on his illegitimate ego needs and bypassing feelings based on an understanding and acceptance of her as she really is. Phil's reaction is bound to become increasingly resentful and, if he had not sensed it in himself, would probably have led to three things: (1) Sandy would eventually tire of Phil's unreasonable and illegitimate demands because she would come to realize that no human being can supply the insatiable demands resulting from Phil's developmental deficits; (2) Sandy would "fall out of love" with Phil because his behavior would eventually destroy her positive regard for him; (3) Phil would be likely to conclude that he no longer loved Sandy because she was unable or unwilling to meet his (illegitimate) needs. To the extent that Phil loved Sandy because he needed her, he would experience love turned to resentment.

Summary

This chapter began with a discussion of marital expectations and then considered legitimate and illegitimate ego needs, the nature of happiness, B-love and D-love, and dependence, independence, and interdependence. Our expectations arise from several sources. Among these are our needs, our emotional-security level, our happiness level, societal norms (including sex-role stereotyping and the sex-role division of labor), and the entire socialization process.

As we go through the process of ridding ourselves of illusions, we realize that the ego state of a person is the key factor. A person who can accept his own legitimate needs and who is aware of and can identify his illegitimate needs has probably achieved a fairly reasonable degree of identity and autonomy. The next step is to begin to fill one's own illegitimate ego needs. This is the ongoing process of filling one's own cup, rather than going through life expecting others to fill it.

If a person is essentially unhappy and seeks happiness by marrying someone who promises to make him happy, the prognosis is one of disillusionment, disappointment, and despair. He is, in effect, saying to his intended, "You must make me happy. You will be to me what no one has ever been to me. You will make up for all my previous unhappiness. You will make up for my own lack of fulfillment." No human being can rightfully expect another to bear such a burden for him. If a person is essentially happy—if he has positive feelings of self-worth, self-acceptance, self-trust, and self-esteem—he can legitimately say, "I need you because I love you. I anticipate a happy relationship as we grow together in caring, trusting, and being ourselves."

Erich Fromm wrote:

[L]ove is an activity, not a passive affect; it is a "standing in," not a "falling for." In the most general way, the active character of love can be described by stating that love is primarily giving, not receiving. . . . Giving is the highest expression of potency. In the very act of giving, I experience my strength, my wealth, my power. This experience of heightened vitality and potency fills me with joy. I experience myself as overflowing, spending, alive, hence, as joyous. Giving is more joyous than receiving, not because it is a deprivation, but because in the act of giving lies the expression of my aliveness.[16]

The fulfillment of legitimate ego needs takes place in B-love, which creates love by giving, and experiences happiness as the state of inward fulfillment that comes from the active loving of another person. Illegitimate ego needs find expression in D-love, which takes love from another in an attempt to achieve happiness. It is not wrong to desire happiness in the marital relationship, but marital happiness lies *primarily* within oneself and *secondarily* in the other.

Questions for Study

1. Is it possible for all human needs to be met in a marriage? Is it desirable?

2. Discuss the difference between Fromm's two statements: "I love you because I need you" and "I need you because I love you." Relate these statements to the concept of legitimate and illegitimate ego needs.

3. Do you agree that the person who lacks self-love will be a nonaccepting manipulator of others? Why do you think this is true or not true?

4. Describe a marriage that you would classify as an A-frame, and one that you would classify as an H-frame. Specifically what types of interaction characterize each?

5. Is the modified M-frame marriage workable? Would it work for you? Why or why not?

Reading Suggestions

Toward a Psychology of Being by Abraham Maslow. Princeton, N.J.: Van Nostrand Company, 1962. A theory of personal growth and creativity; includes a discussion of B-needs and D-needs.

The Art of Loving by Erich Fromm. New York: Harper and Row, 1956. A theory of love and its practice in Western society.

The Neurotic Personality of Our Time by Karen Horney. New York: W. W. Norton, 1937. An analysis and description of prevalent neuroses, including the neurotic need for affection.

The Ability to Love by Allan Fromm. North Hollywood, Calif.: Wilshire, 1966. A comprehensive review of the dimensions of love and the various experiences of love; emphasis on the importance of self-love.

THREE
ROMANCE, SEX, AND MARRIAGE: AN UNLIKELY TRIAD

58

**Romance, Sex, and Marriage:
An Unlikely Triad**

Love Theme—Vintage 1174

Love Theme—Vintage 1869

Love Theme—Vintage 1886

Courtly Love

Romanticism

American Romanticism

Sex, Eros, Philos, Agape

Love as a Configuration

Summary

Questions for Study

Reading Suggestions

Love Theme—Vintage 1174

A Judgment in the House
of the Countess of Champagne

We declare and affirm, by the tenor of these presents, that love cannot extend its rights over two married persons. For indeed lovers grant one another all things, mutually and freely, without being impelled by any motive of necessity, whereas husband and wife are held by their duty to submit their wills to each other and to refuse each other nothing. May this judgment, which we have delivered with extreme caution, and after consulting with a great number of other ladies, be for you a constant and unassailable truth.

Delivered in this year 1174, on the third day before
the Kalends of May, Proclamation VII.[1]

Love Theme—Vintage 1869

Marriage is the great civilizer of man; the organizer of society; the peace-giver and joy-giver of the world. Its condition among a people is the true measure of their spirituality. If all men and women were married and their marriages were perfect, wars would cease; diseases would disappear; supreme order would prevail; love universal would reign; heaven would descend to earth . . . verily sex, love and marriage are eternal . . . the sexuality of man and woman consists really in the sexual differences between their souls, which are thence anatomically represented in their bodies . . . Sex is therefore spiritual. If spiritual it is eternal. Love is the attraction, the very life of the sexes; marriage is their union, their eternal life, their heaven.

William H. Halcombe[2]

Love Theme—Vintage 1886

At the outset of this important subject, we stop to correct a gross, but widely received popular error. Every woman, every physician, nearly every married man will support us in what we are going to say, and will thank us for saying it.

It is in reference to passion in woman. *A vulgar opinion prevails that they are creatures of like passions with ourselves; that they experience desires as ardent, and often as ungovernable, as those which lead to so much evil in our sex. Vicious writers, brutal and ignorant men, and some shameless women combine to favor and extend this opinion.*

Nothing is more utterly untrue. Only in very rare instances do women experience one tithe of the sexual feeling which is familiar to most men. Many of them are entirely frigid, and even in marriage do they ever perceive any real desire . . . The above considerations, which all married men will do well to ponder, should lead them to a very temperate enforcement of their conjugal rights. They should be always considerate, and not so yield themselves to their passions as to sacrifice their love to the woman they have married.

George H. Napheys, M.D.[3]

Courtly Love

Hugo Beigel has delineated three periods of history in which the ideals of courtly love have surfaced in different ways. The ideals originated in the twelfth century, were expressed in changing ways in the eighteenth and nineteenth centuries, and are now present in modern American love which he sees as "a derivative, modified in concord with the conditions of our age and based more on ego demands than on ideal demands."[4] Thus, romanticism has changed as it has been adapted to the needs of a particular age. Beigel characterizes courtly love as

l'amour de lohh (*distant love*), *or* minne, *and many documents, poems, and epics depict its form and the feelings involved. . . . Courtly love was the conventionalization of a new ideal that arose in the feudal class and institutionalized certain aspects of the male–female relationship* outside marriage. *In conformity with the Christian concept of and contempt for sex, the presupposition for* minne *was chastity. Being the spiritualiza-*

tion and sublimation of carnal desire, such love was deemed to be impossible between husband and wife. By application of the religious concept of abstract love to the "mistress," the married woman of the ruling class who had lost her economic function, was endowed with higher and more general values: gentleness and refinement. Unselfish service to the noble lady became a duty of the knight, explicitly sworn to the oath the young nobleman had to take at the dubbing ceremony.[5]

Denis De Rougemont claimed that courtly love was an arrangement contrived outside of legal marriage and was incompatible with marriage. Courtly love was also opposed to the satisfaction of love.

Romanticism

In its formative stage, romanticism was antisexual; chastity was the norm. This, of course, contributed immensely to feelings of unrequited love and intensity of emotion. The beloved was sexually unattainable and so the innocence of purity and chastity was ensured.

The romantic movement of modern times is an outgrowth of the courtly tradition of the twelfth century. Historic romanticism is characterized by the predominant recurrence of several basic themes:

1. Love and marriage are incompatible.

2. The beloved is idealized.

3. There is a sense of distance between the lovers.

4. Love cannot be satisfied in an ongoing relationship.

5. Feelings of the present should remain unchanged and time should stand still.

6. Love is to be celebrated exclusively as a feeling.

Not until the second phase, known as the romantic movement, did sexual expression become explicitly acceptable:

*Under the increasing discomfort in a changing civilization, the aristo-
cratic class had found a way to alleviate the defeats of a family-
prescribed monogamous marriage by dividing duty and satisfaction; the
woman reserved her loyalty for her husband and her love for her gallant.
Continuing on the tracks laid by the concept of courtly love, the nobles
of the seventeenth and eighteenth centuries in Austria, Spain, France, and
the Netherlands, etc., still adhered to the tenet that love and marriage
were irreconcilable.*[6]

However, sex and love were well integrated, if only outside marriage.

During the modern period, love and marriage have become integrated.
"No longer was there to be a cleavage between the spirituality of love
and the marital sex relation; but the latter was sanctified by the former."[7]
This type of love became a hallmark of the literary and operatic works
in the romantic tradition. Hence, in these three stages we see: (1) *the
courtly period:* love outside marriage but normatively without sex; (2)
the romantic period: love outside marriage with sexual permissiveness;
and (3) *the modern period:* romanticized love and sex united within
marriage.

Such generalizations are, of course, oversimplified, and exceptions to the
ideal in each period were legion. Nevertheless, note the trend of drawing
sex and love into an adulterous union and then into a legal union. Note
also that the chief symbol of romanticism seems to be an idealized
woman who is an object of veneration and adoration with or without
sexual relations.

American Romanticism

Today romanticism takes the form of a societal emphasis on certain
aspects of the historical reality. The American version of romanticism is
unique in that it attempts to combine romanticized feelings with sexual
expression within the institution of marriage. Our society transmits
this message: Love is the ultimate justification for marriage; marriage
alone justifies sex; sex and love are therefore the two basic hallmarks of

the marital union and neither sex nor love are culturally acceptable outside of marriage.

Love in America is celebrated exclusively as a feeling, with little honest recognition that the basis of the feeling may be unrealistic and superficial. Consequently, when a marriage is contracted with the expectation that the intense feeling (the chemistry, the electrifying, magnetic attraction) will continue unabated and unchanged, disappointment and disillusionment are inevitable. Other western cultures have attempted to combine romanticized love and sex within marriage, but it is unlikely that any culture has ever expected as much of the conjugal union as we do in the United States. We are unique, if not in combining romance and sex within marriage then certainly in the naive and intense expectation that romance and sex are and will continue to be the most important ingredients in marriage. The judgment of the house of the Countess of Champagne recognized the incompatibility of romantic love with marriage. Yet we still cling to a grand illusion.

This belief regarding romanticized love and sexuality has given birth to a whole series of phenomena. A survey of television shows and commercials, movie and confession magazines, advertising and popular songs reveals that romantic love and sex are useful in marketing many commodities.[8] Deodorants, hair sprays, cosmetics, shaving lotions, and perfumes are multibillion-dollar sellers. Advertising, which is aimed not only at the unmarried but increasingly at the married as well, uses a blend of romance and sex to lure the consumer. Sex is packaged as the ticket to romance; the romantic illusion is, in fact, the acceptable cultural cover for using sex to sell merchandise. One suspects that this implication—romance justifies sex—makes it possible for the general populace to accept sexual connotations. Without the romantic motif, we would be face to face with sex for its own sake. Perhaps this would be more honest but, as advertisers know quite well, it would not sell. The citizens of this country are not ready to view sex objectively.

X-rated movies that portray adults engaged in various sexual acts suggest the frank embracing of physical sexual pleasure without any reference to love, commitment, value, or meaning. The success of some of these movies is an indication that increasing numbers within our population can accept sexual activity devoid of any romantic or other rationalizations; to this extent, this attitude may be considered honest. I would guess that this type of sexual stimuli will always be accessible but that after the stimuli have endured one or two generations they will lose their impact. Slowly but surely the American citizen will learn to live with sexual frankness and interpersonal sexual honesty. However, what has been culturally repressed for several centuries is not likely to be released without an intermediate overreaction.

Rollo May has said that puritanism is based on love without sex but that today's "neopuritanism" wants sex without love.

In our new puritanism, bad health is equated with sin. Sin used to mean giving in to one's sexual desires; it now means not having full sexual expression. Our contemporary puritan holds that it is immoral not to express your libido. . . . This all means, of course, that people not only have to learn to perform sexually but have to make sure, at the same time, that they can do so without letting themselves go in passion or unseemly commitment—the latter of which may be interpreted as exerting an unhealthy demand upon the partner. The Victorian person sought to have love without falling into sex; the modern person seeks to have sex without falling into love.[9]

Beigel assesses the romantic movement as a necessary antidote to social breakdown and feelings of helplessness. Albert Ellis does not see redeeming features in romanticism. To Ellis, romanticism is an "idealized, perfectionist emotion" that "thrives on intermittent rather than steady association between two lovers."[10] Contrary to popular assumptions, romantic love does not necessarily thrive on increased sexual expression or on offspring, nor is it guaranteed to survive the lover's aging process:

Consequently, the utter, terrible disillusionment of many or most romantic lovers becomes eventually assured . . . the romantic lover exaggerates, overestimates, sees his beloved as she really is not . . . when their expectations are ultra-romantic, and hence unrealistic, failure to achieve their level of aspiration must inevitably ensue: with consequent unhappiness and a tendency toward emotional disturbance.[11]

Ellis sees romanticism as essentially antisexual, for sex is employed only as a means of attracting and holding the male:

The pattern of courtship in America and in practically all of Western civilized society is that of the Sex Tease. In following this pattern, the modern woman, whether she consciously knows it or not, is forcibly striving to do two major things: First, to make herself appear infinitely sexually desirable—but finally approachable only in legal marriage. Second, to use sex as a bait and therefore to set it up as something special. If she gives in too easily to sex pleasure, she loses her favorite man-conquering weapon. Hence she must retain sexuality on a special plane, and dole it out only under unusual conditions. . . . Where romance is the rule, sex is virtually never enjoyed for itself. It is invariably hemmed in by idealistic, nonpractical love restrictions. Romanticism, hand in hand with the sex tease game of American courtship, often plays up the verbal and plays down the active expression of human sexuality.[12]

Ellis faults romanticism chiefly on these two counts: creating unrealistic expectations and using sex as a lure, as a means to an end rather than as an end in itself. Beigel, writing from a sociohistorical point of view, holds to the alternate thesis that courtly love and romantic love are expressions of a process of reconciliation between human needs and frustrating sociocultural conditions. Beigel feels that romanticism has been unfairly blamed as being the villain in present-day marital disillusionment. Ellis thinks that romanticism is one of the chief villains.

While there may be truth in both of these positions, it is imperative that we recognize that the romantic tradition has had a powerful impact on American mating patterns, marital expectations, and sexual customs. The female has been idolized and idealized; young people are taught that love is the sole basis for marriage; love and marriage are described in terms that cannot possibly be realized. We are a people who have been socialized to fall in love with love, and sex has been enshrined as being acceptable *only* when justified by feelings of love. Romantic feelings and sexual ardor are to be consummated only within a legalized union. After the honeymoon stage is over, the folklore says that we should mourn the declining intensity of the relationship as well as the loss of passionate excitement celebrated by the lovers before their legalized union.

The problem still remains: Sex and love are reconciled in Victorian-puritanism which denies sex while affirming love; and in neo-Victorian-puritanism which denies love while affirming sex. The sexual reductionists want sex for its own sake, devoid of all extraneous feelings, values, meanings, and sentiments. The romanticists use romance as the rubric under which sex is legitimate, whether within or without marriage. In neither tradition does one find any reference to a single permissive standard, such as "permissiveness with affection."[13]

The problem, however, is not simply to arrive at a consensus on a single sexual standard to replace abstinence or the double standard. The challenge is to combine a "sexual" standard with an "affect" standard in order to make possible an integrated, viable union of two people over time. This, then, is our central question: can sex, love, and marriage be combined into an enduring relationship that will not compromise authenticity? Is there an alternative to the modern derivative of romantic love, one that will not do violence to sex, love, or marriage? One could wish for an easy answer, but the history of marital customs, love relationships, and sexual expression precludes any possibility of an easy solution.[14]

I believe that romanticism is one of the culprits that creates unrealistic marital expectations. These, in turn, breed disillusionment, despair, and resentment. If we are to rid ourselves of illusion, we must come to terms with romantic marital expectations.

Perhaps the kindest thing our society could do with its romanticism is to give it the dignity of a decent burial. In order for something to be born, often something must first die. Romanticism has bequeathed to us much that is good, as Ellis points out, but it has, in the process, been directly and indirectly responsible for unrealistic expectations about emotional satisfaction in marriage, sexual satisfaction, and the raising of children. The role of conflict between spouses, the facing of anger, resentment, disappointment, sadness, tragedy, and crises of all kinds, and the possibilities for self-fulfillment and self-actualization are precluded by a romantic frame of reference. The following hypothetical question–response dialogue may be helpful in understanding the need for some new frame of reference regarding romantic love.

Question: *Is there no place left for romance?*
Response: *No, if by romance we mean romanticism as a tradition; however, there is another kind of romance that places value on affection, commitment, trust, and tenderness. If this kind of romance is combined with other approaches—open confrontation of one's feelings, honest handling of conflict, mutual exploration of sexual needs, desires, and preferences, forthright acceptance of responsibility for oneself, acceptance of the challenge to change and grow, self-fulfillment, self-actualizing experiences, freedom to be oneself and to avoid manipulative techniques in relating to the other—then there is a basis for keeping romance in marriage.*
Question: *Then why use the word "romance" at all? Aren't you talking about love?*
Response: *Yes, of course, but it's not necessarily the same as traditional romantic love, or the way the romanticist approaches love.*
Question: *How is it different? What's wrong with being romantic?*
Response: *There's nothing wrong with being romantic, but you can be romantic without being a romanticist. The kind of love I am referring to is not for romanticists. The romanticist idealizes the love object. The romanticist does not allow for the creative facing of conflict; he avoids conflict. The romanticist thrives in an atmosphere of emotionality. The kind of love I'm talking about accepts the realities of human relationships and thus makes possible a deeper, more fulfilling intimacy than that made possible by romanticism.*

The common expression "the honeymoon is over" is an interesting commentary on our dependence on the concept of traditional romantic love. Lovers who are courting have a distance between them that colors and heightens their interaction when they come together. The honeymoon places them together for a continuous period of time during which they can simply enjoy each other. The experience may prove to be disillusioning, however. Once they have the freedom to enjoy their relationship they discover that there is now less emotionality, because they know that separation is not imminent. When conflict of any kind enters the relationship, there is a threatening, foreboding awareness that the union lacks perfection and that the man and woman are fallible human beings after all. The discovery, often disillusioning and disappointing, that the feverish, romantic, idealistic oneness and enchantment cannot be sustained on a day in, day out basis gives birth to such resigned, antiromantic expressions as "the honeymoon is over."

Hal and Jayne

Hal and Jayne have been married five months. Jayne has felt increasing degrees of loneliness, unhappiness, and depression.

Jayne: *I guess we aren't compatible. I just feel . . . well, like it's all over between us. Before we were married everything was great. We had FUN together! Now . . . well . . . now we just seem to abide each other. Honestly, I don't see how a person could change so quickly. Hal used to be fun! I mean really groovy. But now it's work, work, work! Weekends are even a bore. At least we have a few friends. It's like we—would you believe it—like we don't have anything to say to each other any more. I thought I could make Hal happy. He's happier than I am—that's for sure. He seems content to work all day and then sit and read the paper when he gets home. He's a golf nut. . . . I thought marriage was going to be exciting and fun—Wow! He used to tease me and do things to turn me on— now I feel like all he really wants is sex. We had sex before marriage and it was great. I felt loved and . . . like I was really a part of him. We were one. Now we just seem to go through the motions.*
Hal: *I guess you could say that things have changed. I love Jayne, but (pause . . . and another pause) it's just that I can't seem to do anything to make her happy or perk her up! Of course things aren't dashing and exciting anymore. Look—I enjoy doing the same things now that I did before we were married only now instead of picking her up and going out we begin and end at the same place! How could that change everything? . . . But it does! I work all day and when I get home it's almost like I'm supposed to become a different person and court her all evening long. Sex is different too—but to me it's just as much fun as ever—it's only that now I don't spend two or three hours wining and dining her every time we*

have intercourse. Look—I can't! We don't have that much dough and I've got a lot of other things that demand my time—my boss isn't the most patient guy in the world, you know. . . . What gets me is I never thought Jayne would be like this after we were married. She used to be—well, everything I did was OK with her. Now we're married. Big deal.

Of course the honeymoon is over. The assumption that a relationship will remain the same when its terms are changed so drastically can only be an assumption born of unrealistic expectations. Jayne and Hal probably have a great deal going for them, but they might prematurely separate never having given themselves the opportunity to work through their differences, especially Jayne's disillusionment.

It would be useful to explore Hal and Jayne's role expectations as husband and wife. If we knew more about their individual histories and their methods of handling conflict during their engagement period, we would have a deeper understanding of how their problems developed. At a minimum, however, we can see a carry-over of romantic expectations which now cause the pain of disappointment. The mystique created by distance and time is now erased by a common living arrangement. The honeymoon *is* over, and married life is de-idolized. The crisis that Jayne and Hal face will probably be the making or breaking point in their marriage. Crises of this kind can lead to insight, understanding, and growth provided the partners are able to work through some of their fantastic and unrealistic premarital expectations. Further, they need to redefine their love together so as to create vitality and variety in sex, love, and daily interaction.

Question: *Then what kind of love can survive marriage?*
Response: *Certainly not the romanticized type of love that we've been discussing. Some call nonromantic married love* conjugal love *or* familial love. *Others describe the relationship as* companionate marriage, colleague marriage, *or* partner marriage.

These terms may be helpful in describing a marriage between equals who define their own goals and values. Nevertheless, such a marriage is not sustained by romanticism but by a mixture of sexual, erotic, philial, and agape love.

Sex, Eros, Philos, Agape

The English language is truly impoverished when it comes to the usage and meaning of the word *love*. Love refers to anything from soup to nuts, including football, movies, foods, cars, fashions, experiences, and feelings. We have all heard people say:

I love football.

I love mini-skirts.

I love romantic movies.

I love to ski.

I love martinis and roast beef.

Marital love, conjugal love, companionate love, infatuation, puppy love, sexual love, parent love, friendship love, patriotic devotion, and religious devotion are all covered by the single word *love*.

The ancient Greeks used three words for love. *Philos* referred to friendship, to love between equals. Philos comes down to us as brotherly love (hence the word *Philadelphia*, the city of brotherly love). A second Greek word, *eros*, describes the physical love between a man and a woman. Eros is the drive to create, to procreate, to communicate to another person in the most intimate way possible. *Agape* is the prototype of the unconditional, pure kind of love which, in its theological form, represents love of a deity for man. Agape is unearned, unmerited, unconditional, and undeserved. Agape says, "I love you in spite of" rather than "because of." This is the kind of love parents have for their children, although in a less ideal state. "We love you in spite of the trouble you have gotten into," rather than "We love you because you are such a good boy." In the marital relationship, agape love implies an acceptance of the mate as a fallible human being without implicit conditions or demands to change or to conform to the other's image.

Rollo May points out that in the West we have used sex (lust or libido) to replace eros, which combines physical and psychic intimacy. He suggests that we have detached sexual love from erotic love and left little passion or creativity in sex.

My thesis . . . is that what underlies our emasculation of sex is the separation of sex from eros. *Indeed, we have set sex over* against *eros, used sex precisely to avoid the anxiety-creating involvements of eros. . . We are in a flight from eros—and we use sex as the vehicle for the flight. Sex is the handiest drug to blot out our awareness of the anxiety-creating aspects of eros. To accomplish this, we have had to define sex even more narrowly: the more we became preoccupied with sex, the more truncated and shrunken became the human experience to which it referred. We fly to* the sensation of sex in order to avoid the passion of eros.[15]

Our culture has lost the true life-giving sense of eros. In fact, eros has become a dirty word, indicating lust, deviancy, and carnal degradation. This is, to say the least, unfortunate. Pointing out how our society has separated sex from love, Rollo May distinguishes sex and eros:

Sex can be defined fairly adequately in physiological terms as consisting of the building up of bodily tensions and their release. Eros, in contrast, is the experiencing of the personal intentions and meaning of the act. Whereas sex is a rhythm of stimulus and response, eros is a state of being . . . eros seeks union with the other person in delight and passion, and the procreating of new dimensions of experience which broaden and deepen the being of both persons.[16]

Obviously, eros is what is missing in neo-Victorianism, in sex manuals, and in sexual technology that places such great weight on technique in sexual relations. The erotic element is repressed—the passion, the desire for union in aesthetic as well as physiological terms, the desire for creativity, expression, commitment, and spontaneity. Sex without the feelings, values, and emotions of eros may be caricatured by two machines in bed programming orgasm. As May says, it is not physical nakedness which gives us pause, but spiritual-mental-emotional nakedness. The "machines" may indeed be naked; yet there is a "chastity belt" drawn tight around the inner self of the person who avoids the passion of eros. The chastity belt hides the heart, not the genitalia.

Eros is a release of **id** and affect, sharing and communication. Eros is the deep inner urge to know the other, much as the ancient Hebrew word for know means sexual knowledge. Yet to know only sexually is not to know fully. Eros is the physical abandon of lovers who are enabled to abandon because they care, feel, and trust.

Paul

Paul is twenty years old, unmarried, and considers himself to be liberated from the binds of conventional middle-class morality.

*"I made this appointment because I'm having trouble with a problem,"
remarked Paul to the counselor. "I've had all kinds of girls . . . whores,
pickups, townees, and some real nice bitches here on the campus. As far
as I'm concerned the townees put out the best. They really know how to
make a guy go out of his mind. Well, everything seemed to be going along
fine until the other day. For some time now I've been dating this girl who
I really like—kinda—and, well, she's a little bit different. I've had sex with
her but when I did I had trouble getting an erection—Imagine that! Say,
you aren't going to write this down or report me, are you? Like I was saying, this girl did something to me I can't seem to get out of my mind. I
even started to feel jealous when she told me she had had sex with some
other guy. The thing that really gets me though is that now I'm having
trouble making it with townees. I don't seem to get very excited . . . and
after it's over I get this empty feeling like all it amounted to was a lot of
nothing."*

*On a subsequent visit to the counselor, Paul stated: "I never would have
believed it but I think I've discovered there is more to sex than just
orgasm. Late last week I couldn't make it with a townee. Hell! I just
couldn't get it on! Was I ever disgusted with myself. What would people
think? The guys! Wow! So of course I told a pack of lies to the guys but
inside I was miserable. Then the weekend—and that chick I told you
about, the one who I got jealous about when I found out she had sex with
another guy, well, we had the most fantastic weekend. We did everything*

---

id sexual energy and sexual drive (shortened form of libido).

—we ate together, went swimming, to the movies, studied together, went horseback riding, we really . . . (pause) we really opened up to each other . . . like it was great . . . I really emptied my guts to her and she to me. I never felt so close to another human being in my whole life. We had sex a couple times and it was the greatest I ever had. For the first time in my life I felt I really loved *a girl. We were so close."*

Why is Paul so intent on sexual experiences? What does the variety of sex partners imply about his view of sex? What kind of self-concept does Paul have? What does sexual conquest do for Paul's sense of self and his feelings of masculinity? What is the payoff for Paul when he boasts of his sexual prowess to his male friends? What relationship might there be between Paul's feelings and his occasional impotency?

The case study serves our purposes by showing that Paul had been experiencing many facets of libidinous love. His thoughts about his weekend experience gives testimony to the development of an erotic type of love. We can begin to sense the blending of libido, eros, philos, and agape. Paul experienced a psychic intimacy with a female. That intimacy carried over into the passion-filled eros and included elements of philos and agape. Paul experienced a spiritual nakedness for the first time in his life.

Love as a Configuration

If we are rejecting the romanticized definitions and explanations of love in favor of libido, eros, philos, and agape, then it is essential that we understand the love experience as a **configuration**. Libido, eros, philos, and agape describe the various experiences most frequently associated with intimate relationships. Libido will be dealt with in greater detail in the next chapter. Eros is of central concern here because it most accurately fulfills the passion and the dynamic impetus that most people seem to associate with romantic love. Eros is a much deeper, fresher, and richer experience than the illusory and unrealistic concept of romanticism.

configuration an arrangement of parts to create a blending without conflict. In psychology, a configuration is often called a *gestalt*.

Romance, sex, and marriage are indeed an unlikely triad. But a marriage based on a blending of libido, eros, philos, and agape is a marriage founded on a configuration of values capable of producing meaning and purpose (see Figure 3–1).

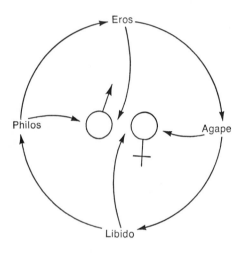

Figure 3-1
A Configuration in Which
the Four Kinds of Love Are Congruent

The fusion of sex, romance, and marriage can be accomplished if, instead of relying on a sexual concept of love or a romantic concept of love, the two partners experience sex, eros, philos, and agape in a relationship that is a configuration—an intimate, growing relationship. If one of the four kinds of love is missing, then the configuration is broken. Furthermore, if either eros or libido love is lacking with one's mate (even if this lack is not being met in extramarital relations), there is still no love-configuration—the four-faceted configuration is broken.

The love configuration is a central premise to which I shall refer often. The love configuration may not create feelings as exciting as being "on top of the world" or as ecstatic as "angel and lover, heaven and earth am I with you." But it does have the capability of producing a rich and satisfying marriage—something that romanticism has never been able to do.

Summary

The focus of this chapter has been on the American attempt to combine romanticized love with sexual expression within the marital union. A brief outline of the courtly and romantic traditions emphasized the American version of romanticism. The chief hypothesis of the chapter was that romanticism as a philosophy of sex and love is destructive of marital satisfaction, because romanticism has a dehumanizing influence on interpersonal relations. Romanticism idealizes and idolizes the beloved and so deprives the relationship of equality and realistic interpersonal expectations.

I have not denied the growth-producing function of romance, but instead have suggested that all of the values of romance can be included in the concept of eros. When a dynamic eros is combined with the other dimensions of love—libido, philos, and agape—a broad foundation is established for the inclusion of sex and romance within marriage.

Many will protest the substitution of eros for romance. It is important to realize that the configuration of libido, eros, philos, and agape need not preclude moonlight, candlelight, roses, wine, and other romantic trappings. Eros involves tenderness and commitment, affection and mystique as well as sexual desire. Indeed, the couple that seeks to actualize the marital relationship will use variety, spontaneity, and imagination to this end. I am suggesting, however, that these qualities imply the death of a movement known as romanticism. Romanticism is a philosophy of relationships between the sexes based on false hopes, unrealistic and idealistic expectations. Consequently, it has created disillusionment, disenchantment, disappointment, resentment, and despair.

Questions for Study

1. Name some fairy tales, popular novels, and movies that reflect the American heritage of romanticism.

2. Discuss May's statement that today's neo-Victorian wants sex without love. What are examples of this neo-Victorianism? How widespread is it?

3. Do you believe, as the author suggests, that romantic love is basically incompatible with marriage? Why or why not?

4. What has happened in a marriage when one or both partners believe "the honeymoon is over"?

5. Do you think people would give up the ecstatic-electric-chemical excitement of romanticism for the love configuration of philos, eros, agape, and libido? Elaborate on your answer.

Reading Suggestions

Love in the Western World by Denis De Rougemont. New York: Harcourt Brace, 1940. This book traces the attitudes toward romantic love in traditional Western literature, religion, and myth.

American Sexual Tragedy by Albert Ellis. New York: Lyle Stuart, 1962. A thorough analysis of American attitudes toward love and marriage as reflected in the popular media.

Love and Will by Rollo May. New York: W. W. Norton, 1969. A comprehensive study of love and its relationship to the mental and emotional functions of intentionality.

The Art of Loving by Erich Fromm. New York: Harper and Row, 1956. A theory of love and its practice in Western society.

"The Styles of Loving" by John Alan Lee. *Psychology Today*, October 1974. An article dealing with the several types and patterns of heterosexual love.

FOUR
SEXUALITY AND VALUE: AN EXISTENTIAL APPROACH

**Sexuality and Value:
An Existential Approach**

The Existential Quest for Meaning

Sex and Psychic Restlessness

Sexuality: The Search
for Value and Meaning

Congruency and Configuration

Summary

Questions for Study

Reading Suggestions

The Existential Quest for Meaning

Russell's Lament

To the amazement of my friends, I am honestly able to pick up the phone at any time and get a bed partner. I can even vary the bed partners as I have more than one. This sounds so smug on my part, yet I say it in amazement. I have sought sex as an avenue to status and find it empty. Do not misunderstand me; sex, even without passion, has its rewards. Yet those rewards are no longer enough. Sex has proved to be a momentary, passionless thing. It has become rewarding only in the short run. At times, I find myself using it as a sleeping aid! . . . Here I am. I am dissatisfied with passionless sex and dissatisfied with a relationship devoid of sex. I seem unable to find both in a single person. I am looking for the total communication that will make someone unique to me and me unique to that person. I seek to have a great value placed on my existence, and to place an equally great value on that person's existence. I hope to raise a family. I want to experience what must be the unique joy of realizing that this communication of two people has created a third individual; different from both, yet the product of both.

A popular brand of cigarettes advertises: "Are you smoking more and enjoying it less?" Let us change the subject of this ad: Are you having more sex and enjoying it less? Are people getting bored with sex? Has sex been oversold? Is it likely that the free-sex ethic can deliver on its promises?

This chapter is based on the premise that what we value in life produces meaning. Therefore, if we value sex, sex is one source of meaning in our lives. Yet many who claim to value a **hedonistic** sexual ethic are experiencing boredom and meaninglessness. Why is this so? Does this mean they do not really believe in the values they claim to embrace? The position taken in this chapter is that sexual attitudes and behavior cannot be separated from the basic and ultimate questions of life. Indeed, in this

---

hedonistic referring to hedonism, a philosophy of pleasure for its own sake; in psychology, the pursuit of pleasure as a motivational force in human behavior.

age of anxiety, the search for meaning and the need for affection, re-assurance, security, and succor often masquerade as the sexual drive. Thus, the existential view of the search for meaning is useful to us if we are to understand the role of sexuality in our lives.

Existentialism focuses on man's responsibility to define the meaning of his existence and to take responsibility for his life. The existential point of view, stated quite simply, is that our existence as human beings precedes our essence—our meaning and our purpose. Existence contains within it essences (meanings) to be discovered. An opposite and more traditional viewpoint states that the meaning of one's life is automatically "given" prior to one's birth—thus, essence precedes existence. One can believe in a God who creates and gives life and also believe that each individual is ultimately responsible for giving meaning and purpose to his life. Phrases that are frequently used in the human potential movement—such as "self-fulfillment," "self-realization," and "self-actualization" (see Chapter 1)—imply that the meaning or essence of life is something each of us must arrive at for ourselves and each in our own ways. I cannot do it for you and you cannot do it for me. We can do it within a religious or a nonreligious framework. It must be done or we experience an inner emptiness that produces despair, dread, ennui, and malaise.

Victor Frankl claims that when an individual fails to experience meaning in life he is caught in an "existential vacuum"—an inner void. Frankl claims that each of us must confront this void and discover meaning and purpose for ourselves.[1] Frankl was opposed to Freud's pleasure principle and to Adler's power principle (the ideas that pleasure alone motivates human behavior or that power alone motivates human behavior). Frankl claims that we are motivated primarily by a deep-seated desire to make sense out of existence by finding meaning in our daily lives. Frankl makes the distinction between his position and that of Freud in his theory of Logotherapy (*logos* is a Greek word that signifies *meaning*):

Logotherapy . . . focuses on the meaning of human existence as well as on man's search for such a meaning. According to logotherapy, the striving to find a meaning in one's life is the primary motivational force in man. . . . Logotherapy deviates from psychoanalysis insofar as it con-

siders man as a being whose main concern consists in fulfilling a mean-
ing and in actualizing values, rather than in the mere gratification and
satisfaction of drives and instincts, the mere reconciliation of the con-
flicting claims of id, ego, and superego, or mere adaptation and adjust-
ment to the society and environment.[2]

Sex and Psychic Restlessness

It is nearly impossible to determine how much of the current preoccupation with sex is an attempt to overcome feelings of impotence in the face
of the existential void. However, it is apparent to many psychologists,
psychiatrists, and other counselors that many people seem to seek out
sexual activity that gives them little pleasure or joy. In line with this observation, it has been suggested that sex becomes a cover for various kinds
of psychic distress and unrest. Karen Horney, for example, has suggested
that "all is not sexuality that looks like it," indeed that sex is very often
"an expression of the desire for reassurance" and that it is often "regarded as more a sedative than as genuine sexual enjoyment or happiness."[3]

Erich Fromm makes a similar point: "An insecure person who has an
intense need to prove his worth to himself, to show others how irresistible
he is, or to dominate others by 'making' them sexually, will easily feel
intense sexual desires, and a painful tension if the desires are not satisfied."[4] However, as Fromm points out, these desires, while interpreted by
the person as genuine physical needs, are merely stand-ins for less obvious psychic needs. A healthy sexuality is not based on such needs but
rather is "rooted in abundance and freedom and is the expression of
sensual and emotional productiveness."[5]

Free-floating anxiety will readily attach itself to the sex drive in such a
way that the subject is totally unaware of the inauthenticity of his sexual
desire. His sexual preoccupation may be acting-out behavior stemming
from repression and suppression of his real ego needs. Frankl has remarked that "there are various masks and guises under which the existential vacuum appears. Sometimes the frustrated will to meaning is

vicariously compensated for by a will to power, including the most primitive form of the will to power, the will to money. In other cases, the place of frustrated will to meaning is taken by the will to pleasure. That is why existential frustration often eventuates in sexual compensation. We can observe, in such cases, that the **sexual libido** becomes rampant in the existential vacuum."[6] The following case study illustrates such unrestrained sexual desire.

Gary

Gary is in his early thirties, married, the father of one child, age eight. Gary was married once before; the marriage was of short duration and he has described it as a union of two incompatible, immature people.

Gary: *I am here because I'm worried about myself. I feel tense and up-tight most of the time; especially when I'm under any kind of pressure at work. My wife doesn't seem to understand and I sometimes feel resentful toward her. Several years ago I began to have sexual relations with a girl I had met at work. She was a lot of fun although I never really had any feelings for her . . . You'd have to understand that except for one or two occasional flings, I was pretty much on the up and up with my wife. I don't believe in extramarital sex but here I am—now I almost thrive on it. I go crazy for women. It's so easy—they are just asking for it . . . so why not? I don't think my wife knows it, although I'm sure she suspects things.*

The trouble is I'm scared! I'm really worried that I'm abnormal. I feel like my sex drive is . . . well, you know . . . like I'm oversexed. I meet a girl and before you know it I'm in bed with her—sometimes I don't even know her name or what she looks like. All I know is that I gotta have her—my whole body vibrates with excitement and I act like I'm pro-grammed to move right in! Then . . . well . . . then I feel better! Usually anyway . . . (pause). I've learned to ignore my conscience—hell, if I let my screwing bother me I'd die of guilt. Sometimes I do get depressed and down on myself . . . and then I make noble vows to myself . . . but

---

sexual libido Frankl here uses the term to refer to the life-energy system within us that is peculiarly sexual in nature; sexual libido is usually referred to as "id."

*. . . well, you know how long I stick to those. First chance I get—right
back at it . . . I guess you could say I love it—but then I hate myself for
loving it.*

Gary is saying several things. He is bothered by his sexual appetite; he
sometimes feels guilt, which bothers him, and at other times he successfully suppresses his guilt feelings; he wishes to be free of his compulsive
behavior. Yet Gary may be saying something on a deeper level. He may be
saying that he has an all-pervading disgust for himself, and he may be
camouflaging his request for help in a request to help him curb his sexual appetite. As in all our case studies, the dynamics go far beyond the
material presented. However, it is safe to say that Gary's behavior is only
an indicator of an inner anxiety. Gary appears to be compulsively driven,
and one can predict that he is highly indiscriminate in his choice of sexual
partners. The case study reveals not only that "not all is sexual that looks
sexual" but also a psychic inner conflict replete with anxiety, self-devalua-
tion, and an absence of meaning and purpose. Under such conditions, sex
is being used to fill the sensed existential vacuum. This is different from a
discriminating sexual liaison. A satisfying relationship that includes sex
as one facet is usually not motivated by an inner restlessness or emptiness.

A great deal of sexual relating is an **acting out** of inner frustration. This
in no way implies that a person who is sexually active within marriage or
outside of marriage is merely acting out. It is important to stress, however, that psychic security—a sense of knowing who I am and where I
am—is the single most important ingredient in a healthy sexuality.

The relationship between the existential void and human sexual behavior
is, indeed, valid. Man is never an isolated sexual creature, nor is he an
isolated organism set apart from the milieu in which he lives, breathes,
works, suffers, and enjoys. He is exposed to great issues and nagging
trivia. Foreign policy, national policy, population crises, ecology concerns,
poverty, law and order, revolutionary movements, and questions of per-

---

acting out a Freudian term (widely accepted even by non-Freudians) indicating that unresolved inner feelings, frustrations, and conflicts play through the individual in such a way
that the person's behavior becomes an outlet for the unresolved material.

sonal and social ethics are problems that are thrust upon us. These increase the frustration caused by our human weakness and impotency. Pressures from large-scale corporations, the all-enveloping political bureaucracy, the economic inflation, and the rising national unemployment can dwarf our individual capacities for effecting change and create in us great frustration and feelings of impotence. People start asking themselves "What can one person do? What is the sense in it all? Where are we going?" And gradually they become apathetic.

This dilemma is due in part to a breakdown of traditional systems that in earlier times protected man from his anxiety. Paul Tillich maintains that, because we are living in a period of great change, the traditional means of coping with anxiety no longer work. The traditional symbols no longer convey the meanings that they did to former generations. Ancient formulas and creedal statements are not relevant to modern man, not because they are wrong but because they cannot be understood today in any meaningful way.[7] This leaves the individual in a frustrating and anxiety-producing situation. If the traditional religious and cultural symbols are no longer meaningful, they cannot be of much use in helping people to find security. The challenge is, of course, to define and discover authentic values and meanings for ourselves. Tillich says "man's being includes his relation to meanings. He is human only by understanding and shaping reality, both his world and himself, according to meanings and values."[8]

And so it is not strange that our restlessness and anxiety drive us to search for concrete channels of expression. The libido is well qualified to serve as this channel. In sexual expression people often find a unique kind of security and peace, even if only fleetingly. Thus, sexual behavior may serve as an outlet for psychic restlessness, as a security-producing mechanism, and as acting-out behavior.

Sexuality: The Search
for Value and Meaning

I use the word *sexuality* for the total fusion of sex with personal identity. Human sexuality includes the entire sexual identity and psychic orientation of the individual. It is part of and dependent on one's self-concept.

The terms *masculinity* and *femininity* describe more than just male and female **genders.** These terms are psychological **constructs** that relate gender identity to the personality structure. When we say that someone lacks confidence about his masculinity, we are not simply speaking of male genitalia. Rather, we are talking about identity and the individual's awareness and acceptance of the essential core of his being. Sexuality is bound up with the total sense of self—self-esteem, self-acceptance, self-confidence, and self-trust.

A value creates meaning only to the extent that the value is honestly and authentically held. Rollo May has insisted that "the degree of an individual's inner strength and integrity will depend on how much he himself *believes in* the values he lives by."[9] (Italics mine.) If the so-called value is really only a pseudovalue, it will be incapable of providing meaning for any prolonged length of time.

Our consideration of value systems begins with hedonism, or the will to pleasure. For some, hedonism works. For others, it only functions superficially to assuage repressed restlessness that gnaws away like a termite. Thus, hedonism probably becomes a pseudoescape for many people, resulting only in redoubled attempts to obtain pleasure when the specter of emptiness raises its ugly head. Is this not the state of much hedonistic preoccupation today? Is it not true that we have experienced, in a deep and profound sense, a loss of meaning and value? Failing to make sense of this loss, we have opted for a shallow hedonism or we have repressed our existential doubts in order to remain faithful to the traditional symbols, creeds, and dogmas within the traditions of Western thought. Some have opted for Eastern thought, but they, too, face a dilemma, because the Western mind is socialized in a Western pattern and cannot readily internalize Eastern paradoxes.

Liberation from the narrow antisensual and antisexual bonds of Victorianism and puritanism is of value. Who among us would wish for the return of a rigidly repressed sexual orientation? In vain these traditions have protested that sex is good, only to have the message contradicted by

gender the physiological identification of a person as either male or female.
construct several definitions that fit together to convey a thought-system or the roots of **a** theoretical idea.

warnings, limits, and preachments that gave a metacommunication, a message about the message. Sex is good and to be enjoyed but be careful, because it is also dirty and essentially enjoyable only to the lower instincts. As Rollo May says, "In Victorian times, when the denial of sexual impulses, feelings, and drives was the mode and one would not talk about sex in polite company, an aura of sanctifying repulsiveness surrounded the whole topic. Males and females dealt with each other as though neither possessed sexual organs."[10]

If Victorianism is hypocritical, does it not follow that hedonism is desirable? I suggest that a moment-to-moment pleasure orientation fails to satisfy man's quest for fulfillment. Many, undeniably, go the hedonistic route and sing its praises. Others attempt to go the hedonistic road and finally confess that their inner states are no better than they were.

I reject hedonism as a satisfactory way to fill the existential void or to compensate for not being able to fill it. With equal conviction I reject the nonsexual, antisexual, repressed-sexual stance of Victorianism.

If we reject both the antisexual emphasis of Victorianism and the prosexual emphasis of hedonism, what is left? What would a synthesis entail? How can man fulfill his quest for meaning and value as well as his desire for pleasure, enjoyment, and fun? What would a synthesis reject from these polar approaches to sexuality? A synthesis would probably reject the essential tenets of the two traditions: that sex is only pleasure and that sex is a necessary but only tolerable function.

An effort to synthesize these two traditions would logically start with an examination of the idea that pleasure is or has the potential to be a value —not merely as a means to some other end but as an end in itself. Pleasure is its own reward. Pleasure is its own meaning because it has value. It does not need to be rationalized, nor does it need justification to make it worthwhile. Pleasure has always been valued for its own sake, regardless of philosophical, theological, and moralistic reservations about the dangers of hedonism. Yet we have been conditioned to find pleasure in the violation of rules rather than in the observance of enjoyment. Thus, the price one pays is guilt. If guilt accompanies a desirable activity, we are assured, that activity is pleasurable.

The greater the taboo against pleasure, the greater the possibility of guilt if the taboo is violated. The taboo against masturbation triggers guilt even in those who only daydream or fantasize about it. If the guilt outweighs the pleasure, then one concludes that the pleasure was not worth the price. If the pleasure wins out over the guilt, then the mental pain (guilt) was more than offset by the rewarding pleasure. We do not need to confine ourselves to explicit sex activities in illustrating the value of pleasure. Fear of pleasure has led to prohibitions against cosmetics, dancing, movies, television, eating, and drinking.

According to some moralists, if man is a creature with a higher, godly nature and a lower, demonic nature, then activities that feed the desires of the lower nature need to be discouraged. Yet man has always succeeded in flirting with pleasure despite the threat of punishment or guilt. If we are to resolve this dilemma, we must reject an ethic that claims that pleasure is wrong or evil, and we must then determine the appropriate role for pleasure to play in a revised value system.

If pleasure is intrinsically valuable and sexual relations are pleasurable, does this imply that the value of sexual relations is exclusively in the sexual act? Not at all. A clear distinction should be made between *intrinsic* and *extrinsic* values. An intrinsic value is inherent to the object that is valued. Intrinsic valuation is philosophically considered to be *objective* in that the value resides in the object itself. An extrinsic value is external to the object and lies in the attitude or mind of the person doing the valuing. It is philosophically considered a *subjective* value. (Beauty is in the eye of the beholder; ugliness is in the eye of the beholder.) I would like to contend for the position that *sexual relations are intrinsically meaningful because they are pleasurable in and of themselves*. Nevertheless, when sexual relations are congruent with other values, a configuration of values is formed which is extrinsic to the sexual relationship itself but serves to enrich the sexual relationship so that it can be both intrinsically and extrinsically meaningful.

Figure 4–1 illustrates the extremes of hedonism and **aestheticism.** It is my position that hedonism gives only intrinsic meaning and aestheticism

aestheticism the cult of beauty and good taste; as used here aestheticism refers to the pursuit, cultivation, and enjoyment of sex along lines of perceived beauty wherein sex is cleansed through the purifying effect of love, devotion, and affection.

gives only extrinsic meaning. Hence, a mixture of intrinsic hedonism and extrinsic aestheticism gives us added meaning, because we are embracing both values—the intrinsic value of sex as fun-filled pleasure and the extrinsic value of sex as a means of expressing love and affection.

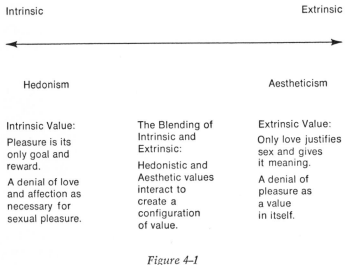

Intrinsic   Extrinsic

Hedonism   Aestheticism

Intrinsic Value:	The Blending of Intrinsic and Extrinsic:	Extrinsic Value:
Pleasure is its only goal and reward.		Only love justifies sex and gives it meaning.
A denial of love and affection as necessary for sexual pleasure.	Hedonistic and Aesthetic values interact to create a configuration of value.	A denial of pleasure as a value in itself.

Figure 4-1
A Hedonistic—Aesthetic Continuum

Congruency and Configuration

Meaning results from what we value. When people have an authentic belief (rather than an adopted or conditioned belief) in the values they embrace, they are likely to experience meaning and purpose in their daily living, devoid of excessive anxiety, depression, or psychic restlessness. They probably experience joy and happiness in reasonable measure. We can say that pleasure is its own value and therefore is its own meaning, but we should also point out that life is not fulfilled when its meaning is confined to one type of experience (here, the pleasurable experience). Fulfillment is a configuration of values, each different, yet each congruent with the others.

Now we need to ask: Can something be of value even if it is not pleasurable? The answer is yes. Suffering is not usually pleasurable, but it can have meaning. Bereavement over the loss of a loved one is not pleasurable, but the experience is meaningful precisely because of a meaningful relationship. Death is a meaningful experience, even though it is painful and nonpleasurable. Indeed, is it not true that as we contemplate our own nonbeing, it gives new meaning and importance to our being? Life as we know it on this planet has a beginning and an end. If we knew that we would never die, would the events in our lives have as much meaning for us?

The existential challenge, by its very nature, is a challenge that each person must meet alone. No one person can ever define or fulfill the meaning of another person's existence. Unfortunately, some try. Unfulfilled parents look to their children for fulfillment. Husbands look to wives and wives to husbands. Children, too, sometimes yearn to remain emotionally dependent on their parents, wanting the parents to help them give their lives meaning and purpose. Parents can give direction, guidance, and a framework for determining values, but they cannot define or fulfill the meaning and intrinsic value of their children's lives.

The establishment of meaning is also thwarted if one adheres to only one value orientation. When meaning is restricted to one kind of value it becomes narrowed, and therefore neurotic. This is the fallacy of hedonism, which focuses solely on the value of pleasure. Similarly, to restrict one's definition of man to his so-called higher nature or lower nature dehumanizes him.

Eastern thought teaches us a great deal about paradoxical logic, whereas Western thought has somewhat rigidly followed the cause and effect of Aristotelian logic. Paradoxical logic teaches us that there would be no cold without heat; there would be no joy without sorrow or pain; there would be no good if there were no bad; there would be no love if there were no hate and anger; there would be no faith if there were no doubt; there would be no passion if there were no stoic dispassion; there could be no security if there were no anxiety; there would be no possibility of "being" if there were no possibility of "nonbeing"; there would be no meaning if there were no possibility of meaninglessness; and there would be no value if there were no possibility of worthlessness.

When values, however paradoxical they may be, form a configuration, and when they are congruent with each other, life takes on its own meaning in the sense that the meaning of human existence is intrinsic to the very process of living. When values are congruent they may be quite different and include a wide range of possibilities, but they are not in conflict. They are compatible, they fit in with each other and form a configuration that consists of many parts. A true configuration of values allows for human diversity, spontaneity, and growth. Thus, the meaning that one chooses to give to his own existence is greater than the sum of the several parts, because these parts interact, complement, and otherwise feed into each other, forming a holistic pattern.

Sex is such a value. It can exist as part of a meaningful configuration. Sex, sexuality, and sensuousness are values, not in isolation, but in relation to each other and to the whole. Similarly, pleasure is a value that must be congruent with other values within the configuration.

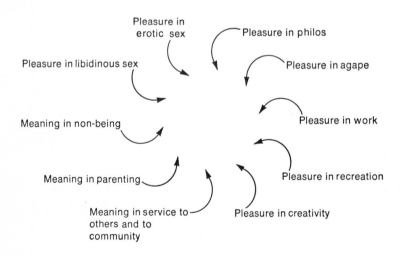

Figure 4–2
A Configuration of Congruent Values

Figure 4–2 illustrates a configuration of values that are congruent. The concept of value congruence is quite similar to the ancient Greek concept of the balanced life. It is a recognition that human beings derive meaning from a wide range of pursuits, interests, and relationships.

Each of the several factors in the configuration delivers an intrinsic value—that is, each factor has an inherent value for the individual, providing he has an authentic belief in the particular value. These several intrinsic values have a very significant cumulative effect when they are congruent. The congruence adds to the total cumulative effect, forming a total configuration of values that contains an extrinsic value of oneness and wholeness. This is what I mean when I say that the whole is greater than the sum of the parts. In Chapter Ten we return to this idea of configuration and look at it in terms of marital and extramarital sex. Here I want to emphasize that when our sexuality is separated from a meaningful framework of values it can quickly become dull and meaningless, lacking in any payoff beyond the orgasm of the moment.

Vivian

Well—this is going to be hard for me—when I was in high school—I was a good girl. I hardly did anything except make out a little. My senior year I met Gene and he kept pressing me. He was patient for awhile but then I started to worry about losing him—and after all, what's so big a deal about having sex? So we did. We went on like that until I went to college. College almost blew my mind. I mean guys just expected it—like it was some sort of payoff for taking me out. . . . Anyhow, I started enjoying it. I guess I had never realized how sensuous I was. For a while I couldn't stay out of bed. If a guy even looked at me—well, you know, a kind of penetrating, inviting look—well there I was—being had. Usually I would see the guy for two or three weeks and then the whole thing would sort of die out. . . . This went on for about two and a half years and it was always the same story. I'd get real interested in a guy and then we'd ball for hours. It was great! I was on the pill and I was always on guard against VD. Then—I guess it was back in February, I was in bed with this dude and after I came I looked at him and all of a sudden I started to feel sick to my stomach. I got real nauseated and I was scared I was sick or something. I got over it okay—but then two or three weeks later I was with this other guy who was just beginning to get it on when I started to cry. . . . He got real scared and asked me if I was a virgin or something and did I want to go home to Mommy. I told him to stick it up his ass.

. . . but that bothered me because I sort of really did want to go home to Mother. Mother and I usually got along pretty well, you know—the usual fights about clothes and boys and stuff—but basically I never had too much flak from her. . . . I just never told her anything important. . . . What I should've done was get someone on campus to talk to but I thought I could handle it. Well, one day I was listening to you in class— talking about that value configuration stuff—and—it really grabbed me. It's like a part of me wants sex but another part of me wants something more than that. I don't like this part of me and I used to keep wishing I didn't enjoy it so much because then there wouldn't be any problem. Then I met Fred. Fred's the greatest! We started the way I always started, but in a short time the sex bit changed into sort of, a, ah, an ego trip you might say. We started really digging each other. We talked by the hour— we played together—we laughed and joked with each other. We even studied together! Well, I'm about to graduate from this place and I'm feeling better about myself than I can ever remember. Fred and I probably will go our separate ways but I know for sure that I'll never settle for straight sex again. I think I must have been trying to prove something to myself—or something like that. Don't get me wrong—I still like sex— it's great fun—but a steady diet of that without all the other aspects of a relationship just isn't worth the bother. Of all the beds I've been in— Fred is the only guy who has ever been a person to me. All the others are dim blurs—nobodies with erections. Well—Ann Landers wouldn't approve —but who cares? I feel really together. I think my body was telling me something. I'm glad I listened.

Vivian certainly won't go down in history as one who is obsessed with sexual purity (a type of "moral athlete"). She will probably invest her sexual activity in places where the rewards are both intrinsic and extrinsic. This is the main theme of an existential approach to sexuality. We are creatures who are a strange mixture of body, mind, and feelings, and it is a form of castration to pretend that the genitals can be separated from the feelings or the feelings from the mind. We are creatures who— perhaps each of us in different ways and in different ethical-moral terms —must make sense out of who we are and what we do. We may poke fun at the values of our parents or our forefathers, of the church or of the synagogue. But unless and until we discover meaning in our own authentic values—sexual and otherwise—we are likely to be living in our own existential voids.

Summary

This chapter has focused on the various ways that sex is used to obscure unresolved feelings and conflicts. The problem is existential because it derives from our inability to define and discover meaning for existence. Meaning is largely the product of what we value. What we do not value will hold little, if any, meaning for us.

Within this framework I suggested that a lot of sexual activity is not meaningful because it has lost its value base. Value in sexuality is derived from both intrinsic and extrinsic sources. Hedonism is an intrinsic value because the pleasure value is in the fun and enjoyment of sexual expression. Many people believe that the value of sex is in the fact that sex is a means of expressing love and affection. Thus its value is extrinsic—the value is not in the pleasure of the act (intrinsic) but in what the act of sex signifies or expresses.

When extreme positions are abandoned, values from two sources form a configuration within which we can experience both intrinsic and extrinsic values—both sexual pleasure for its own sake and sex as an expression of love and affection. When both values are present, the sexual encounter has double meaning. This is not to say that pleasure alone is not a value or that the expression of love and affection is not a value. Both clearly are capable of giving meaning. When value is realized both intrinsically and extrinsically, there is greater likelihood of ongoing satisfaction because there is greater meaning.

Finally, the challenge of defining and discovering meaning is a task each of us must do for ourselves. Our psychic and emotional health depends on the degree to which we believe in our own values, because pseudovalues are inauthentic and incapable of giving meaning. This inauthenticity contributes substantially to feelings of inner emptiness and despair, the hallmarks of the existential void.

Questions for Study

1. Is it possible for people to become bored with sex? Is Russell's statement true for many college students?

2. Does it seem to you that human beings are motivated primarily by the desire for pleasure, by the desire for power, or by the will to find meaning in life?

3. I have indicated that the existential dilemma is caused by breakdown of traditional systems. Is it desirable or possible to restore those systems? Are there other alternatives?

4. Explain how sex can have both intrinsic and extrinsic value and rewards.

5. Referring to Figure 4–2, give specific examples of how each of these values is present in your life. If one or more of the values is absent, would you like to incorporate it in your life?

Reading Suggestions

The Courage to Be by Paul Tillich. New Haven, Conn.: Yale University Press, 1952. A psychological inquiry into the role of anxiety in human existence. This is Tillich's most famous psychological statement regarding human nature.

Man's Search for Meaning by Victor Frankl. New York: Washington Square, 1963. A presentation of the theory of logotherapy, focusing on the human need to find meaning in life.

Man's Search for Himself by Rollo May. New York: W. W. Norton, 1953. This book analyzes the existential dilemma and suggests that there is a need to conquer the insecurities of modern life.

Man for Himself by Erich Fromm. New York: Holt, Rinehart, and Winston, 1947. An exploration of humanistic ethics.

Choosing a Sexual Ethic by Eugene Borowitz. New York: Schocken, 1964. A guide for personal sexual conduct based on the principle of autonomy.

Sexual Latitude, For and Against edited by Harold H. Hart. New York: Hart, 1971. Articles by various writers who argue for and against sexual permissiveness.

FOCUS ON TRANSITION: BARRIERS TO GROWTH

FIVE
RECLAIMING
OUR
SEXUALITY:
OWNING
OURSELVES

102

**Reclaiming Our Sexuality:
Owning Ourselves**

Anxiety about Sex

Owning Our Sexuality

The Process of Self-Acceptance

The Single-Identity Myth

A Conversation:
Sexual Ethics and Behavior

Summary

Questions for Study

Reading Suggestions

Anxiety about Sex

Item: Letter to the Editor,
In Reply to a Proposed Health Class.[1]

You may well believe that most parents would not agree with (their) ideas on the requirements for sex ed. teachers. Being "comfortable with their (the teachers') own sexuality" is hardly proper basis for teaching sex ed. Most "go-go" girls would meet that requirement—yet few parents would be very happy with them as teachers . . . our children are young and innocent for only a short time. They are learning more of life at an earlier age (this is due in part to the school, and in part to television); but they have a right to their innocence and their youth—they should not be forced to face adult issues when they are only children.

Item:
"Sex Educators Are Degenerates"[2]

Sex education is a new scheme designed to demoralize our youth, all part of a giant conspiracy to rape the people, weaken their wills and make them sensuous, atheistic slaves. . . . The sex educators are in league with the sexologists, . . . they represent every shade of gray morality, ministers colored atheistic pink, and camp followers of every persuasion; off-beat psychiatrists to ruthless publishers of pornography. The enemy is formidable at first glance, but becomes awesomely powerful when we discover the interlocking directorates and working relationship of national organizations which provide havens for these degenerates.

When the foregoing items are examined closely we see several themes running through them. The themes are essentially these: Sex is something far too explosive to be dealt with in school, especially in grade school. Sex is so much bound up with morality and values that it should never be taught as we would teach other biological and physiological functions. Preserve the innocence of childhood by protecting and sheltering children from any tinges of debauchery and defilement. Sex education is un-Christian, anti-religious, atheistic, and part of a Communist conspiracy to bring down the U.S.A. As is often the case, such letters reveal more to us about the fears and anxieties of the authors than about the merits of introducing sex education in classes.

The question to which this chapter is addressed is: Do we Americans feel comfortable with our sexuality? Do we incorporate our identity as sexual creatures into our total self-concepts, or do we alienate our true selves from our genitalia? Our culture is a sexually anxious culture. We were born into a transplanted puritanism, we are the inheritors of an antisexual ecclesiastical tradition which claims that sex is good—but only within marriage—and not to be enjoyed for its own sake. These concepts were stressed by the Victorianism of the late eighteen hundreds, a period considered by some to be the age of prudery. Sex as a legitimate topic of conversation has been a cultural taboo for over one hundred and fifty years. How can we expect the American population to be anything but anxiety ridden?

One of the strongest themes running through our cultural heritage is the good girl-bad girl syndrome: Good girls don't enjoy sex—bad girls do. Good girls are for marrying—bad girls are for fun. And then we wonder why some males are impotent with their wives but aren't with pickups, bar girls, prostitutes, mistresses, or even other men's wives. We wonder, too, why some females are so sexy in appearance, yet so nonsexual in their marital sex relations. The answer to these inquiries is, of course, that we have been thoroughly socialized. We behave as we have been taught to behave.

How many among us can close our eyes and imagine our parents having a rip-roaring good time in bed? Is it too much to say that we Americans were brought up as if our fathers and mothers ignored their genitalia except during private bathroom ablutions? We are, after all, a culture that has bundled its babies so that they cannot touch their genitals. We are a culture that passes along old wives' tales about the consequences of masturbation. We are a culture in which everyone knows that the real meaning of sin is s_e_x and that morality refers first of all to sexual morality.

Robert Seidenberg has pinpointed this issue:

Somehow our preoccupation with sexual behavior in general has distorted our moral sense. We have judged the morality and worthiness of people almost solely on their sexual behavior and proclivities. Ergo, a young girl is worthy or valuable because she is a virgin although completely corrupted in values of charity, consideration for others, or ability to love. Similarly, a husband is moral if he has observed fidelity but has enslaved his "loved-one" and kept her mindless. The preoccupation with sex has kept us from exploring and defining more sensible and authentic calipers for worthiness—better things to measure a man or a woman by. . . . One shudders to think of the number of reputations and lives that have been destroyed throughout our history by our largely irrational attitudes toward sex. It is not at all difficult to understand sexual fears and abhorrences. There are optimists among us who feel that mankind can make judgments of a person's worth in factors other than sexual. Perhaps demoralization of sex is a logical contemporary project.[3]

Although I am not advocating a de-moralizing of sex, there is much in Seidenberg's statement that rings true. Each individual needs to create an authentic sex ethic that upholds the dignity and worth of the self, the other, and the relationship without compromising the blending of hedonism and aesthetics. This is a tall order and probably impossible for those with rigid ethical systems. Nevertheless we do have a right and a responsibility to work through our sexuality, including our feelings, desires, and ethical responsibilities.

In doing so, we will be facing the omnipresent anxiety about sex so carefully hidden by so many people. This anxiety is usually signaled by an attitude toward sex that indicates, among other things, that "I would just as soon not discuss it; I think sexual talk or discussion is in bad taste; cultured people need not talk about such matters; the antisexual codes are right, of course; sex is really not compatible with motherhood, God, the flag, apple pie, or baseball." This anxiety is not easily allayed, for it usually protects the self from its deepest feelings and desires. Yet there is simply no way any of us can achieve a strong and healthy total identity without dealing with our sexual identity—indeed, the two cannot be separated.

Owning Our Sexuality

What does it mean to own one's sexuality? Basically, it means to acknowledge and internalize the fact that we are sexual creatures and that sexuality is a vital and dynamic part of our identities. To own it is to acknowledge it and then incorporate it into our identities, to possess it, to accept it as natural, and to enjoy it: It is to affirm, "This, too, is me—really me—and I like it."

A careful definition of terminology is important here. By *sexuality* I mean the feelings, behavior, and experiences associated with maleness or femaleness. I do not mean simply sexual relations, coitus, or orgastic experience. It is a gigantic self-deception to think that we are not instantly aware of the gender of whomever we see, meet, or touch. For example, if I say that I need meaningful friendships with females and males and then deny that there is a difference between these male-male and male-female relationships, I am being naive and self-evading. I am trying to place the male-female friendship on a platonic or sexless level, denying that I am also enjoying the femaleness of my women friends. These are primarily psychic relationships but they are also obviously sexual in that they meet my sexual need to relate to females in a meaningful way.

There does not need to be any genital or orgastic sex for a relationship to be sexual. When males and females deny their gender and relate to each other as if they were both sexless, it is safe to assume that their conscious anxiety level is kept at a minimum by such denial. They dare not admit to themselves any conscious awareness of the other's sexuality, for if they did they would feel uncomfortable and ill at ease. The safest course of action is to live as if they are unaware of their maleness and femaleness.

If we own our sexuality, we are determined to stop running away from our obvious sexual differences. The first step, therefore, toward accepting or owning our sexuality is to be willing to take the risk of discovering that the male human being and the female human being are both highly sexual creatures and that there is no need to be afraid of or anxious about one's sexuality. To do this we must learn a degree of self-awareness. I think it is fair to say that most people who are anxious about their sexuality are afraid of it—and consequently their only security is denial of the importance of sexuality in human relationships.

Self-awareness implies acceptance of one's feelings and fantasies. We have all heard directives aimed at controlling our feelings—"don't allow yourself to have such feelings" and "dirty thoughts make dirty bodies."

Such statements produce feelings of self-doubt and shame, the foundation stones for later sexual guilt. I cannot stress too strongly that feelings are neither right nor wrong. They simply are. That is, a feeling is something we experience. A feeling is neither immoral nor moral. Psychologists have more than adequately established that there is a measurable difference between feeling an emotion and acting on that feeling. Even Jesus' famous statement, that any man who lusts after a woman in his heart has already committed adultery, needs to be taken in context. He was attacking the self-righteousness of the scribes and pharisees who were competing for honors in a game called "see how pure I am" (Matthew 5:28). Jesus simply reminded them that adultery begins in the heart. Yet Jesus notwithstanding, there is a difference, at least among mature adults, between the thought and the act. If feelings were subject to moral censorship, both men and women would be immensely frustrated. As we shall see in Chapter Six, feelings of anger, resentment, distrust, hatred, hurt, and spite are not at all irrational, bad, or sinful. They are the logical result of preceding experiences. How we deal with our feelings is a far more important matter.

The Process of Self-Acceptance

What are the most desirable ways for dealing with feelings? I would suggest three ways, each a useful step toward self-knowledge and self-acceptance. First, we can allow ourselves to feel our emotions—without evasion or denial. Second, we can choose to deal with feelings by tracing down their origins or meanings. Feelings, like dreams, can be clues to our innermost fears, wishes, and desires. Third, if the feelings can be acted on, we need to choose either to act or not to act.

If I feel tired, I can acknowledge the feeling, trace it down, and then decide to take a rest. If I feel angry at you, I can acknowledge the feeling and allow myself to feel the anger; then I can try to figure out the reasons for it; and finally I can choose to express the anger or not to express it. If I feel attracted to a woman, I first acknowledge the feeling and allow it to register throughout my being; then I can try to figure out its origin and any possible meaning it may have (I may have just had a fight with my wife, or I may be feeling very high about myself, my marriage, or my work); and finally, I will decide whether to act on this feeling and how I will express it.

Many people have been socialized to believe that any feeling they acknowledge is an omen that something is wrong. It is widely believed, for example, that a married person should never be attracted to anyone except his mate. And so it is that most of us, when an attraction begins to develop, deny it or **rationalize** it. If we look at this phenomenon closely, we discover that a legal wedding was never a deterrent to sexual attractions. Some people believe that once they say "I do" they will never again be led amiss by a shapely vision or a handsome physique, by warmth or fascinating conversation or a shared interest. Fully grown adults should know better! Mature people do not need to protect themselves with such beliefs. They are able to acknowledge such attractions and deal with them. The popular assumption, especially among those who are most anxious about sex, is that if you acknowledge an attraction, even if only to yourself, it is only a matter of time until you are involved in an affair.

When I was a young boy, a middle-aged man gave me some unsolicited advice: "Beware of beautiful women. The devil lives in them." Fortunately I was long past any danger of believing him, but his words did explain to me why he married such an ugly woman and how he protected himself against attractive temptations. This man did not trust himself to handle such feelings, and so he protected himself from beautiful women by believing that the devil lived in them.

The Single-Identity Myth

A pervasive belief in our time is the notion that each of us has a single **identity** and that the process of psychological development is geared to discovering this identity. I have labeled this the single-identity myth.

rationalize to attribute rational and creditable motives for one's actions, without analysis of true, especially unconscious, motives.
identity one's thoughts and feelings about oneself, especially in terms of ultimate goals and the unity and persistence of personality.

Will the Real Rob Please Stand?

*I am Rob. I see myself as a warm, sensitive,
giving person. I enjoy people. I like to be
friends with everyone.*

*I am Rob. I don't like myself when I get angry
at people. I don't like it when I'm irritable
or short tempered.*

*I am Rob. I love my wife and my children. I am
committed to their well-being.*

*I am Rob. I don't like it when I feel upset with
the kids. What will they think? I really
detest fighting with my wife—people shouldn't
fight or quarrel.*

*I am Rob. I enjoy sex with my wife. We seem to
meet each other's needs very well.*

*I am Rob. I sometimes feel I'm oversexed. At
times I think I'm the world's worst adulterer.*

*I am Rob. I am a person who enjoys solitude,
peace, and quiet evenings at home.*

*I am Rob. I love parties and gatherings, a little
booze, and even flirting.*

The myth is that Rob matches only one of these portraits. If Rob believes
he is exclusively, or even predominantly, one of these **personae,** then he
is bound to be restless and uncomfortable when any of the other Robs
shows up. If he acknowledges only one part of himself he is, inevitably,
ignoring the other parts. We are multifaced creatures, and we each find
our true identity by integrating the various faces, moods, and feelings
into a meaningful whole. There is an identity based on the self-image and

persona the social front, facade, or mask an individual assumes in role-playing; personae
are also individual characters in a play or novel.

the self-concept. But the self is a multiplicity of ego states, and to speak of a single ego state as being the whole is to deny the other ego states.

It is in this context that most people fail to own their sexuality. They dare not admit, even to themselves, that they are sexual creatures who might find great joy and satisfaction in their sexual experiences. To do so would

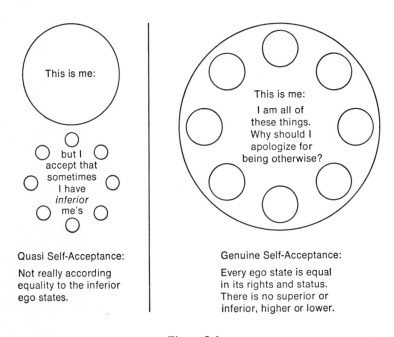

Quasi Self-Acceptance:

Not really according equality to the inferior ego states.

Genuine Self-Acceptance:

Every ego state is equal in its rights and status. There is no superior or inferior, higher or lower.

Figure 5–1
Quasi Self-Acceptance
vs. Genuine Self-Acceptance

be contrary to their natures or to their self-images. When we fail to acknowledge all of our various facets, the excluded facets become alienated from our conscious selves.

Jane—Out of Touch

I enjoy sex as far as that goes, but I think it has its place. I think people make too much of it. If my husband wanted sex every night I wouldn't cooperate. It just wouldn't have any meaning for me. Most of my enjoyment is in trying to please him anyway, but even that gets tiresome. I think there's much more to life than sex. Sure—sex can be fun—but must it be so important? You probably think I'm prudish but compared to my parents I am very liberated. We couldn't even mention the words "sex" or "pregnant." My mother never told me anything much about menstruation except to give me a book to read. "Here—read this—pretty soon something is going to happen to you and you'll wonder what's going on." She didn't teach me anything—that's for sure. I accept sex. I really do. But I can't see getting all excited about it! I could live without it. One of my friends told me she had read that book by "J," The Sensuous Woman *I think it's called. I can't accept that sort of thing. That kind of sex is disgusting. I think sex is meant to be a beautiful thing between a man and a woman, but when it gets into all those perversions it loses its meaning. I can't imagine myself lying in bed fondling my—you know, playing with myself or anything like that. I'd feel like a sex pervert.*

I think it is safe to conclude that while Jane is far from being sexless or frigid or antisexual, she certainly is not a person who feels comfortable with her sexuality. This conclusion is not based on the fact that she finds *The Sensuous Woman*[4] somewhat repulsive. I say that Jane is not comfortable with her sexuality because she seems to take no delight in her femaleness. She could live without sex. Sex to her is sort of a nuisance— necessary for her husband and for others, but not really vital or exciting to her. It is just something that is okay in its proper place. Jane simply has never owned her body. She does not dare to think of herself as a sexual creature, and she does not dare enjoy sexual pleasure. Although she appears to be far more liberated than her mother, in truth she is still very much under her mother's influence. Her ability to discuss sex is a healthy sign—certainly her mother would never do that. Because Jane is able to talk about it she assumes she is far more liberated than her mother. But she is wrong. Jane's deepest feelings are actually similar to her mother's feelings. Jane has accepted sex as a second-class facet of herself—important, but somehow not quite as worthy of status as a full-fledged, first-class facet. Jane is alienated from part of herself. She has not rejected her sexuality, but she accords it only a conditional acceptance. Jane believes that mind and spirit cohabit within her body. Because her sexuality is expressed by her body, she knows she dares not reject sex. But, alas, joyous acceptance and ownership are entirely different from grudging acceptance. Someday Jane may feel inwardly secure enough to incorporate her sexuality, including her sensuousness, into her self-image. But until then we must conclude that Jane does not truly own her sexuality.

When I speak of owning sexuality, I mean far more than a perfunctory nod. I mean accepting and enjoying oneself—one's desires, fantasies, breasts, vagina, legs, penis, arms, face, lips, ears, and eyes. To own is to claim for oneself—not to evade or give a nod to, as if one really should not make too much of those organs, especially those that some have described as the lower part or baser (disgusting) parts of the human body.

We should begin to own our bodies when we are in diapers. There is no reason why any person should grow up being ashamed of his genitals, sex drive, or excretory functions. Early warnings and prohibitions against "touching yourself" create a formidable barrier to the development of a healthy self-image. Fear is learned at a very impressionable age, and it is fear that reinforces messages about what is taboo—fear of masturbation, fear of contamination, fear of punishment, fear of being naughty or dirty, fear of what others might think if they knew our thoughts or feelings, fear of getting caught, fear of feelings, fantasies, and desires, and fear of pregnancy, childbirth, and menstruation. Even venereal diseases need not be feared—only respected as very serious infections that can be avoided or treated if fear and shame do not prevent us from seeking medical care.

It is never too late to begin to truly own and enjoy one's sexuality. None of us can go back in time and make a change here or a switch there. Instead, we must each arrive at an accurate and untainted view of human nature, including human sexuality. Then we must discard the worst taboo of all—the taboo that proclaims that anyone who owns his sexuality cannot possibly be moral or decent. Finally, we can reeducate, reindoctrinate, and resocialize ourselves, laying to rest the inconsistent sexual beliefs we inherited. Much of our ethical heritage may be very sound— that is for each of us to determine. But we must also consider the innuendos, the implications, and the implicit threats that were often used to drive the ethics home. It is these hidden implications that create feelings of shame, disgust, self-doubt, and guilt. The shaming technique remains the greatest single barrier to complete self-acceptance.

A Conversation:
Sexual Ethics and Behavior

The conversation that follows is a condensation of many conversations I have been involved in with college students. Although this particular interchange of ideas is fictitious, it is authentic because the questions and responses are typical of actual discussions. Fran is a college junior; Duane is a sophomore; I am the counselor, John.

Fran: *If people took you seriously, we would all be sexually active. I don't agree with what you're saying. Isn't there any room left for sexual ethics?*
Duane: *He's not saying that everyone should be sexually active. He's only saying that owning your sexuality is not an ethical problem—that you can acknowledge your body and have ethics too.*
Fran: *Oh no he's not. How can anyone learn to own their sexuality if they don't believe in sharing themselves with others? John tells us to get in touch with ourselves—and he also tells us this has nothing to do with ethics.*
John: *If you choose to be sexually nonactive then that's great—as long as it's really your decision and your choice. I respect abstinence; in fact, I think abstinence or maybe a cautious sexual expression has a lot to be said for it. But if you choose abstinence because that's what the culture says—or that's what the church says—or that's what your parents say— well then you haven't made your ethic your own. It's not really a value you believe in. I'm trying to show you that you can be abstinent and still fully own your sensuousness and sexuality.*
Fran: *Oh, come on! How?*
John: *Lots of ways. Mostly—a combination of feeling, thinking, and self-exploration of your own body.*
Fran: *You mean we're supposed to masturbate?*
John: *That's an important part of it—even infants masturbate in the sense of pleasuring themselves by feeling their genitals. Male infants fre-*

quently have erections. This is one reason parents put mittens on babies'
hands and clothing over their bodies—to frustrate this activity. But it
never works, not in the long run.
Duane: *You tell her John. Give it to her!*
John: *You just wait. I've got some questions for you too!*
Fran: *Okay. You're saying that masturbation is not bad.*
John: *I'm saying only one thing about masturbation. It's natural, it's*
normal. It's one part of self-pleasuring. It is not something that one can
put a moral yes or no on because it's as much a part of us as eating or
sleeping.
Fran: *In other words, you believe that we are all just animals—we should*
just do whatever we feel like doing.
John: *I believe we are animals—yes—but we are* homo sapiens. *We have*
minds, we have rational faculties with which to guide our actions and
behavior. Fran, I would like to ask you a personal question. May I?
Fran: *You mean am I a virgin? The answer is no.*
John: *No, I wasn't concerned with that.*
Fran: *That's just my problem with you! Dr. Crosby, you just aren't con-*
cerned with ethics. You—you make me mad.
John: *May I ask you a personal question?*
Fran: *Yes. What is it?*
John: *Do you ever wake up during the night or in the morning with your*
hands over your genitals?
Fran: *Yes—of course. Doesn't everybody?*
John: *That's my point, Fran. In our unconscious or semiconscious state*
we engage in masturbatory activity. Why is it so wrong or so different if
we choose to do this? What is wrong about pleasuring oneself?
Fran: *Because when we are sleeping we aren't responsible for our actions*
or our thoughts. When we're awake we are responsible.
John: *Then you believe it is wrong to engage in any kind of private, pleas-*
urable activity?
Fran: *That depends on what the activity is.*
John: *Taking a bath with bath oils—soaping up in a shower and allowing*
yourself to feel the stroking of lather all over your body—massaging
yourself—any part of your body that you can reach.
Fran: *Oh, everybody does those things!*

John: *Why?*
Fran: *They feel good.*
John: *They are pleasurable?*
Fran: *Yes, they are pleasurable.*
John: *Are they sensuous?*
Fran: *What do you mean by sensuous? Sensuous sounds like sexual to me.*
John: *Yes, sensuous is a word that relates to sexuality. It refers to gratification of the senses. I am using it in the context of acknowledging that your body enjoys pleasuring—that you are receptive to pleasurable stimuli and sensations.*
Fran: *So? What's the big deal about that?*
John: *No big deal—except that I have the feeling that you don't approve of masturbation, although masturbation is a form of self-pleasuring. What makes a soothing bath in oils, or a gentle stroking of one's legs or thighs, so different from stroking the breasts, the vagina, or the penis?*
Fran: *It bothers me that you seem to give the impression that sex before marriage or outside of marriage is okay.*
Duane: *Well, why not? It is good!*
John: *Now hold on a minute, Duane. How can you say categorically that sex before marriage is good?*
Duane: *Well, I agree with Fran that you give the impression that it's good! You goad us into thinking for ourselves. You make digs about adopting wholesale the moral precepts of our parents and society. You challenge us to become autonomous. You encourage us to get in touch, as you put it, with our sexuality.*
John: *Okay. I do goad and dig and, hopefully, challenge. Yet I'm not about to give a carte blanche to unrestrained, unthinking sexual expression.*
Duane: *Why not? What's wrong with it?*
John: *There's a lot wrong with it. You've heard me talk about intrinsic and extrinsic values and about people who are having more sex and enjoying it less. Free sex is no more a responsible alternative than is a total denial of sexuality.*
Duane: *Are you saying that if I meet some chick and she and I want to get it on that that is wrong?*

John: *Perhaps. It depends on whether or not you are using each other—whether or not there is some destructive game-playing—whether or not there is a hidden agenda.*

Duane: *Now you're making* me *angry! Look, I'm not going to go around filling out some sort of a moral checklist before I go to bed.*

John: *What are you afraid of? How is a moral checklist going to hurt you?*

Duane: *I don't think it's necessary. If I want to have sex why shouldn't I? You quoted Seidenberg as saying that our preoccupation with moral values was bad . . . or something like that.*

John: *Yes—I think we become so preoccupied with penises and vaginas that we make them far more important than they really are by deciding all our ethics on the basis of our sexual behavior. But I also think that it's easy to brainwash ourselves by telling ourselves that having sex is the same as seeing a flick or brushing our teeth. It is different! Vastly different! People enshrine sex by placing it on a sacred pedestal and forbidding everybody from calling it by name. But people also insist that there is absolutely no uniqueness or specialness to it at all—as if it were as expected and ordinary as tying your shoes.*

Duane: *Well, if something is good—and you better not deny that you think it's good—if something is good, then why not practice it and do it as much as you can?*

John: *Because that easily becomes nothing more than a habit that necessarily makes the other person into a thing, a penis or a vagina. I still hold to what I said earlier about pleasure being its own meaning. But I believe that indiscriminate sex eventually becomes less and less rewarding—less and less fun. You probably do more harm to yourself than to anybody else, because you fail to attach any meaning except pleasure to sex. Remember the hedonistic fallacy? It isn't that pleasure is lacking in meaning—it's good as far as it goes, but it doesn't go far enough. In the long run pleasure is not capable of meeting some of our most basic human needs.*

Duane: *Like what?*

John: *Like sharing the deeper parts of ourselves, like sharing our ups and downs, sorrows and joys, fears and hopes, the security of being loved in spite of our ugly moods and our orneriness—the love that is eros, philos, and agape.*

Duane: *Yes, I know all that, but I'm looking to straight sex to satisfy my libido—nothing else. I can get those other kinds of love any time. Why are you so against straight body-centered sex?*

John: *Because students and counseling experiences convince me that sex for sex alone soon pales—it loses its pleasure. I think it is self-defeating behavior. The more a person does it, the less he is able to care, to give, and to share anything of himself. He becomes a modern Victorian who wants sex without falling into love—or into a relationship.*

Duane: *But sex without love is just a free-wheeling life style. What's so wrong with that?*

John: *Perhaps nothing—if that's what you choose. But I am saying that I don't see it working very well for many of those whom I have known. Many who try it discover that the risk of casual sex is the risk of becoming really involved. People like to think they can handle the emotional involvement by simply ruling it out—by refusing to become involved. Those who succeed may discover that a steady diet of this makes it difficult to ever build and nurture a meaningful, intimate relationship. Those who don't succeed at ruling out the emotional involvement often find that they are more deeply involved than they ever believed possible. This often happens in affairs where the couples do not intend to become emotionally involved—but they do anyway. This is also one of the dangers of open marriage—people don't mean to get emotionally involved but they do— and the end result is often pain.*

Duane: *So you're against premarital sex.*

John: *No! I am not against it—I am simply cautious about it. I think many people are taken back by the emotional involvement that can quickly develop—and they can't handle it—can't cope with it. I believe this is especially true in our culture where we have a time gap between physiological maturation and emotional maturation. Most males and females are physically ready for sex by age thirteen. But they aren't really ready for the emotional involvement until anywhere from say, eighteen to twenty-five.*

Duane: *Well, then, where do you really stand?*

Fran: *You seem to me to be hedging!*

John: *Okay. You want straight answers, so here goes. I am a situational ethic person. I believe "right," "wrong," "good," and "bad" are not absolutes but always relative—like greater goods and lesser evils. I believe the* *context, the immediate environment of the present situation, must always be taken into consideration. This holds true in extramarital sex as well as premarital sex. Further, I believe quite strongly that Erik Erikson is right when he places the developmental stage of identity before the stage of intimacy. If we feel fairly secure in knowing ourselves and in accepting ourselves—knowing our goals and what we want—then I think we have a much greater ability to be intimate, caring, giving, and sharing. I think many people are searching for their identity in sexual activity. This may be immediately pleasurable, but I don't think it holds up in the long run. Further, although I think that it is generally a bad thing to hurt ourselves or others, I prefer to emphasize the positive. I think one of the key issues in sexual ethics is whether or not our behavior represents a commitment to our own growth and to the growth of the other.*

Fran: *Your position upsets me. I think you're trying to ride both positions. Are you saying yes or no?*

Duane: *Right! You're riding the middle!*

John: *You think I'm hedging because I haven't backed up your positions. Okay. But maybe neither of you likes the idea of being responsible for your own actions. Duane wants no rules, and Fran seems to want everything spelled out.*

Duane: *Not me! I'll take full responsibility for anything I do.*

Fran: *So will I, but I still believe it's either right or wrong and it can't be both!*

Summary

The primary emphasis of this chapter has been on the relationship between sexuality and identity. A secondary theme centered around the relationship between sexual awareness and sexual ethics. A case was made for the position that our society has protected itself against anxiety over sexual matters by considering sex as a second-class facet of the individual. Sex has been treated as if it did not really exist. It has been considered part of the lower nature of men and women, as contrasted with the higher nature of the mind and the spirit.

As a result, most people are alienated from their physical and emotional sexuality. If we are to reclaim our sexuality, we will have to welcome this alienated portion of our beings into full fellowship and communication with the other parts of our beings.

Psychological identity was considered, as part of the problem and as part of the solution. *Identity* too often carries the implication that a mature person has a single identity—that each of us has only one real "me" and that any other aspects we may be aware of in ourselves are inferior or false. This belief, although powerful and popular, is destructive because it prevents us from acknowledging, knowing, accepting, and owning all of the many facets of our personalities. As long as any aspect is isolated and labeled as inferior or base, it stands little chance of being fully incorporated into a total self-concept.

Once we recognize sexuality as a first-class citizen within the total self, it can be dealt with. This will not happen, however, until a second falacious assumption is discarded. This second fallacy is the claim that if the individual incorporates sexuality into his self-concept, he will lose his sense of ethical direction—his morals will go "out the window." And so, we are told, if we allow ourselves to *feel* something, we will automatically *act* on what we feel. But this is misleading. If we are afraid of our sexuality it will exert more power over us than if we openly acknowledge it as a legitimate part of our humanity. Once we acknowledge and accept sexuality, we have the right and the responsibility to determine if, how, when, and under what conditions we shall express ourselves. Many people are frightened by this responsibility. It raises their anxiety to an uncomfortable level. Nevertheless, those who seek full self-awareness and self-acceptance must accept this responsibility. People who are genuinely comfortable with their sexuality do not feel they must suppress or deny their desires, drives, feelings, and fantasies. They know that they still have the choice as to if, how, and when they act on these feelings and desires. My contention is that this acceptance and self-imposed responsibility are necessary prerequisites for reclaiming our sexuality and for giving birth to our true selves.

Questions for Study

1. Is it possible for a person to own his sexuality and still abstain from sexual intercourse? Why or why not?

2. React to this statement: There is no such thing as a platonic friendship between a male and a female.

3. Do you agree that the only physiological differences between the male and female are the capacities to impregnate, menstruate, gestate, and lactate?

4. If a married person feels attracted to someone of the opposite sex, what are the possible ways of dealing with that feeling? Which do you think is best?

5. Discuss the "single-identity myth." How does this relate to sexuality?

6. When you read the dialogue at the end of the chapter, did you find yourself agreeing most with Fran, Duane, or John? Why? Role-play each character and see if any changes occur in your thinking.

Reading Suggestions

Sexual Myths and Fallacies by James L. McCary. New York: Schocken, 1971. Answers to often-asked questions about sexuality, sexual functioning, and abnormalities.

Getting Clear by Anne K. Rush. New York: Random House, 1973. Outlines methods of getting in touch with and accepting one's body; especially for women.

Human Sexuality by James L. McCary. New York: D. Van Nostrand, 1973. Thorough information on the physiological, psychological, and sociological aspects of sexuality.

Total Sex by Herbert Otto and Roberta Otto. New York: Peter H. Wyden, 1972. A program for developing sexual potential.

SIX
LOVE
AND ANGER:
DYNAMICS
IN
RELATIONSHIPS

**Love and Anger:
Dynamics in Relationships**

The Anger Taboo

The Conflict Taboo

Self-Awareness

Self-Disclosure

Summary

Questions for Study

Reading Suggestions

The Anger Taboo

Beth

Dear John,

Six months have passed since our counseling ended. I am writing because I want to tell you that I have finally learned how to express anger. We got to the point where our marriage was on the downgrade, and I really didn't care about much of anything. I kept my feelings to myself—thinking they would go away. But they never did—not for very long anyway. My mother and father were sick fighters. They used all kinds of maneuvers, from screaming and shouting to slamming doors and giving each other the silent treatment. I vowed I would not have their kind of marriage. I hated the very idea of anger—it was repulsive to me. So, you know what I did. I was the model wife. Whatever Sam wanted Sam got. I gave in to him on most everything. You name it—house, car, furniture, sex, friends, vacations—wow, did I ever avoid conflict. I suppressed my feelings on almost everything. And it worked fine for awhile. Then, slowly but surely, I began to have those queer feelings. They'd just come out of nowhere—feelings like wanting to run, or like wanting to cry and cry. Sometimes I had sensations like picking up a kitchen knife and wanting to stab something with it. One time I gave in to Sam on some little issue and all of a sudden I felt sort of nauseated inside, like I was sick in my stomach.

It's taken a long time to get from there to here but now I'm not afraid to express myself. Don't get me wrong, I still don't want the fight styles of my parents. But I have learned to respect anger as a genuine human emotion that can be expressed and handled in lots of good ways. First I had to see that anger was okay, that it was normal, that anger is a part of love and that it was okay for me to express my honest feelings. I had seen myself as a superhuman person of some sort—one who looked upon herself as everybody's nice "Miss Goody Two-Shoes," always ready to please, taking no thought for myself. It was very important to me that people see me as friendly, accommodating, and easy to get along with. Wow! How stupid can you get? I guess I was afraid that if I let my real feelings show no one would like me very much.

I have learned to own my feelings, whatever they are. I've learned to be assertive and aggressive if necessary. But the most important thing of all is that I feel fairly safe when I express my anger with Sam or the kids. I guess they've learned that I love them even though I get irked with them, and Sam has helped me by learning to fight fair. We both can deal pretty well with our feelings as long as we don't attack each other. You know what I mean—we express our own feelings first, then ask for input or reaction from the other. We also have learned that the expression of negative feelings can do a whole lot to increase our positive feelings.

Thanks for your help,

Beth

What is it about the negative emotions that makes intimate partners so afraid of them? Anger, resentment, disgust, disdain, hurt, bitterness, hatred—these are emotions that no one is immune to. Yet many people sincerely believe that these feelings should be handled by **suppression,** that they should be pushed downward and inward and swallowed.

There are two predominant reasons for suppressing negative feelings. One is sociological and the other is psychological. The sociological reason has to do with a cultural transmission of a taboo against the expression of anger. The cultural tradition has imparted the message that nice people do not show anger. Anger is wrong, bad, sinful, an indication that something is terribly wrong in a relationship, because in good relationships the partners do not feel anger. This tradition encourages a separation or alienation within ourselves, because we do not permit ourselves to be in touch with what we are experiencing. And so we deny a significant portion of our beings.

The psychological reason we are so afraid to deal honestly with negative emotions is that we feel insecure in expressing these feelings. The insecurity is caused by the unexpressed but underlying fear that if we let other people know what we are really feeling they won't love us any more. *Why Am I Afraid to Tell You Who I Am?* is the title of a book that speaks directly to this fear.[1]

suppression the conscious, intentional exclusion from consciousness of a thought or feeling.

When we were in diapers we learned to be afraid to display anger toward those on whom we were dependent for our sustenance. After all, we needed their nurture, their stroking, their feeding, and their caring. Karen Horney has pointed out that the most crucial struggle of our lives takes place at a very young age that most of us can no longer recall.[2] When the utterly dependent child has negative feelings, these are followed by anxiety. Terrified of opposing its benefactor, the infant represses its hostility. This leads to internal conflict and, hence, to anxiety.

Feelings of dependence, independence, incorporation, and individuation form the major schema of psychosocial development. When we become adults, the emotions and feelings that we experienced in early childhood often recur. This happens whenever a present event triggers a similar feeling experienced in the past. During childhood, when we felt anger toward someone we loved, we might have reacted by pouting or sulking or withdrawing. Now, whenever we feel anger toward someone we love, we react the same way we reacted then, by pouting or sulking. As a result anger is, still, too frightening and threatening to be dealt with, and so it is suppressed, displaced, or otherwise denied. Our primal fear is the fear of loss of love. We have great difficulty seeing that anger and love are inseparable, that both are necessary if we are to retain our dignity as unique human beings and our capacity to love. Jay Kuten has written of this paradox:

The fact is that were it not for this pattern, one of undulation, of change, of backing and filling, in our loving, no relationship, however apparently loving, would go anywhere. No growth would be possible in the two people or in the relationship that represents what is between them. Just as with individual development, where conflict and its resolution are a necessary catalyst for learning, so in couples and more extended involvements, the failures in loving, its lapses, its opposite, hating, are part of the yeast of growth.[3]

The Conflict Taboo

All interpersonal relationships are potentially conflict laden. A cultural tradition that, for whatever historical reasons, considers conflict morally wrong will encourage the suppression and **repression** of conflict and so lay a foundation for misunderstanding, resentment, anger, hostility, bitterness, hatred, and misplaced aggression.

Many cultures as well as our own endow conflict with moral or immoral connotations. I take the position that conflict is **amoral.** In other words, I see conflict as a neutral phenomenon. It is how one looks upon conflict and how one handles it that gives it a positive or negative value. Imagine a married couple socialized to believe that argument is wrong, that the voicing of disagreement is to be avoided, and that the essence of marriage is to create and maintain harmony at any price. This couple will probably claim that neither of them ever remembers an unkind word between their parents, and they will feel guilt that their own marital relationship is not beautiful or perfect. They will probably feel conflict and sense their underlying hostility, but they will not be able to do anything about it except be miserable, for, after all, conflict implies fighting and fighting is wrong! Perhaps the most unfortunate result of this kind of socialization is that the children of this couple will in turn be deprived of useful models of how to face and deal with conflict in a creative, growth-producing, love-filling way.

The root of this negative attitude toward conflict is the popular assumption that love is the polar opposite of hate. At times it may be. At other times the line between love and hate is very thin, and until the negative feelings are allowed expression there is a dwindling and erosion of the positive feelings. This leads many couples to conclude: "We feel nothing toward each other, neither love nor hate." Naturally, for when the negative is repressed the positive will be repressed also. "Our love has died" is an expression often heard by marriage counselors and psychotherapists. The experience of "dying love" is in part the experience of the denial of feelings, first the negative and then the positive. Rollo May has described this dynamic:

repression the involuntary and unconscious blocking of painful thoughts, feelings, or memories from the conscious mind; an ego defense mechanism.
amoral without moral implication; outside the bounds of that to which moral judgments apply.

A curious thing which never fails to surprise persons in therapy is that after admitting their anger, animosity, and even hatred for a spouse and berating him or her during the hour, they end up with feelings of love toward this partner. A patient may have come in smoldering with negative feelings but resolved, partly unconsciously, to keep these, as a good gentleman does, to himself; but he finds that he represses the love for the partner at the same time as he suppresses his aggression . . . the positive cannot come out until the negative does also. . . . Hate and love are not polar opposites; they go together, particularly in transitional ages like ours.[4]

The anger taboo and the conflict taboo are obviously inseparable. They are parts of the problem of dealing with one's negative emotions.

George R. Bach, who has written *The Intimate Enemy* (subtitled "How to Fight Fair in Love and Marriage"), has called attention to dirty fighters, sick fighters, fighting for intimacy, and training lovers to be fighters. Bach says:

Contrary to folklore, the existence of hostility and conflict is not necessarily a sign that love is waning. As often as not, an upsurge of hate may signal a deepening of true intimacy; it is when neither love nor hate can move a partner that a relationship is deteriorating. Typically, one partner then gives up the other as a "lost cause" or shrugs him off ("I couldn't care less"). Indifference to a partner's anger and hate is a surer sign of a deteriorating relationship than is indifference to love.[5]

Thus, indifference is often the polar opposite of both love and hate. Outright rejection is often easier to accept than being ignored or treated as though one were not there.

Clearly, then, the creative facing of conflict is an absolute necessity in marital relations. Previous generations embraced the ethical and moral concept of *honesty*. But one cannot help wondering how honest our ancestors, who took such great pain to avoid conflict, really were. Perhaps their dishonesty can be excused because they were socialized to believe that conflict was evil. Nevertheless, the avoidance of conflict is dishonest in interpersonal relationships.

Kathy and John's experience illustrates the effects of denial and suppression of negative feelings. Kathy and John had been married four years. They went to a counselor at Kathy's insistence.

Kathy and John

John: *I am afraid I don't love Kathy. I don't know how or why but the feelings I used to have are gone. I try to re-create them but . . . well, it just doesn't work. Sometimes I force myself to be loving but then it seems . . . like . . . pow! . . . she turns around and does something to really turn me off! One of these days I'm afraid I'm really going to unload on Kathy.*
Kathy: *Unload what?*
John: *Well, just . . . Oh forget it!*
Kathy: *No!* Unload what? *I suppose you think I'm just feeling good about you all the time. Well, I'm not! You've got me so mixed up and confused I don't know how I feel or what I think. Lately, you just make me sick— acting like a hurt little boy if you don't get everything your way, clamming up, pouting, and sulking.*
John: *You sure put your finger on it. How else am I supposed to feel when you put me down? You're the one who seems to have to get her own way. You act like no one can handle the money as well as you . . . You insist on doing things with your friends. You act like sex is a bore and you parcel it out like it was rationed. You undermine everything I try to do with the kids. The fact is, I think sometimes your judgment in handling them stinks . . .*
Kathy: *I suppose you're an expert!*
John: *I think you're too easy on them.*

And here we go with gunnysacking—the unloading of past grievances. At best, gunnysacking provides a release of pent-up feelings, an unleashing of the negative feelings that have been put down into the gunnysack for safekeeping, but that end up being used as ammunition at some later time. At worst, gunnysacking provides a decoy to get negative feelings out in the open, even if they are not the real cause of the present impasse. If Kathy and John are encouraged to unload on each other on deeper levels, they may succeed in getting at some of their real resentments. These negative feelings have been dammed up so long that the positive love feelings have diminished. No therapist would be surprised if at one of the next counseling sessions John would say: "I'm beginning to feel love for Kathy again. I don't seem to have as much resentment . . . and I'm not even trying to make myself be loving."

Self-Awareness

Probably the greatest threat to a vital, growing relationship occurs when one partner is hurt or threatened by the mate. The temptation is to protect oneself from further hurt. This is accomplished by shoring up the ego defenses, withdrawing ego investment, and generally taking steps to make oneself less vulnerable. But we should remember, "When we harden ourselves so that we are no longer vulnerable to *hurt*, we thereby harden ourselves to the effects of love and receptivity. We are too hard to receive love."[6] If we can see the wisdom and logic of this point of view, then we are ready to proceed to the question: How can we learn to express our real feelings?

The answer is two-fold. First, we need to become aware of our real feelings. And second, we need to learn how to express these feelings in a human, loving manner that is not devastating or even threatening to the mate.

Much has been written in recent years about self-awareness, primarily as the result of the human potential movement. Self-awareness is being in touch with your feelings, whatever these feelings may be. The basic rule is: "Feelings are neither right nor wrong—they simply are." How a person acts or fails to act on a feeling may be a matter of ethical choice, a question of right or wrong. The crucial point is that the feeling is not right or wrong—it is simply a part of you. It is something that is coming to expression within your being, within your body or your mind or both. Once we realize that feelings need not cause guilt, the ability to be in touch with feelings is enhanced. When we truly believe that it is all right to feel any feeling—that we are not subject to moral judgments because we have feelings—then and only then are we sufficiently free to experience ourselves and to become self-aware.

Relatively few people are aware of their authentic feelings. But once we grant ourselves permission to feel, there is no limit to the growth and self-development that can occur. Many people experience great anxiety and fright as they slowly grant themselves permission to feel. To feel what, you may ask? To feel joy, sorrow, hurt, disappointment, wishes, sexual desires, anger, pain, resentment, and love. To feel abandon and the satisfaction of commitment. To feel inner power and the futility of helplessness. To feel crushed dreams and unexpected pleasures. We live in a culture that teaches us not to feel these emotions. We learn to be schizoid—to be alienated from our feelings. We are a thinking culture, not a feeling culture.

I am not suggesting that we should denigrate the mind—disown it or reject its wise counsel. A mind–body **synthesis** is clearly called for. The mind, guided by ethical principles and standards, processes and evaluates data. The body experiences itself by permitting feelings to be received and felt. The body is the receptor organism of the impulses that permeate the being of the individual. As such, the body is a gigantic sensory mechanism that constantly transmits feelings, impulses, gut reactions, and fantasies to the mind. The mind processes, evaluates, studies, considers, and weighs: to do or not to do, to be or not to be, to act or not to act, to act this way or react that way, to seek advice or to handle it alone, to fight or not to fight, to accommodate or compromise, to erect barriers or to remain open to growth.

Self-Disclosure

Conscious disclosure of ourselves to others is partially dependent on self-awareness. And yet, ironic as it may seem, self-awareness is somewhat dependent on self-disclosure. (I am speaking about conscious processes

synthesis the combining of varied and diverse ideas into one coherent complex.

only; unconsciously we are continually transmitting nonverbal messages that reflect our inner feelings and state of mind.) Sidney Jourard says:

[A]nd it seems to be another empirical fact that no man can come to know himself except as an outcome of disclosing himself to another person. This is the lesson we have learned in the field of psychotherapy. When a person has been able to disclose himself utterly to another person, he learns how to increase his contact with his real self, and he may then be better able to direct his destiny on the basis of his real self. . . . self-disclosure, letting another person know what you think, feel, or want is the most direct means (though not the only means) by which an individual can make himself known to another person. Personality hygienists place great emphasis upon the importance for mental health of what they call "real-self being," "self-realization," "discovering oneself," and so on. . . . a self-alienated person—one who does not disclose himself truthfully and fully—can never love another person nor can he be loved by the other person. . . . Every maladjusted person is a person who has not made himself known to another human being and in consequence does not know himself.[7]

Jourard has successfully pinpointed the issue of the relationship of self-disclosure to self-awareness, and the related issue of mental health and wholeness. One of the tragedies of primary-pair intimacy is the lack of self-disclosure by the partners to each other. Is self-disclosure learned only through psychotherapy? In Chapters 11 and 12 I talk of marital growth groups, couples groups, and premarital groups as welcome techniques that facilitate the learning of self-disclosure and in-depth communication of emotion-laden material. Here, however, I want to focus on several techniques and exercises that are available to anyone.

If we assume that the anger and conflict taboos have been dealt with and the gates to self-awareness are at least opened a little, then what is the next step? To achieve self-awareness, you must be willing to make first-person (I) statements that reveal your state of being or frame of mind. You must be willing to share such personal data as where you "are coming from" and where you "are at." Frequently we are puzzled in everyday situations because we have no hint of the immediately preceding circumstances. We do not know where the other person has been (figuratively or literally). And so we do not know his mind set or frame of reference. No wonder we do not know where the person is—what he is thinking or feeling about himself.

Phyllis

I just came home that day—looked at him, and told him our marriage was over. He looked at me in utter amazement as if he didn't have the least idea what I was talking about. He knew what I had been feeling— and struggling with. He knew I believed in women's lib and that I was feeling really imprisoned by our marriage. He knew I thought marriage was created and maintained by a male-chauvinist philosophy.

What he didn't know (how could he—I never told him) was that I had just finished reading Jessie Bernard's book, The Future of Marriage,[8] *for your course and that it really turned me on. He didn't know I had been boiling inside myself because of our division of labor in our relationship. He didn't know I had been wallowing in self-pity for about three weeks. He didn't know I had just heard Betty Friedan on a cassette tape telling us that confrontation was necessary regardless of the hostility it aroused. . . .*

He didn't know where I was coming from and he didn't know where I was! How the hell could I have expected him to understand me?

This episode is probably repeated millions of times daily, not in content but in its dynamics: the expectation that the other person will somehow magically know my needs—where I am coming from, where I am going, and why.

But self-disclosure is more, much more. It is a leveling process through which we attempt to be congruent in our communication. Much of the time we are noncongruent—we feel one thing, think another, and say something else. When what we are feeling is in line (congruent) with what we are thinking, and this is in line with what we are saying, then we are congruent. At least we have a chance to send a clear message— without static or metacommunications (a message beyond the message

—one message between, within, or beside another). Have you ever noticed the "painted smile"? The smile that is a nervous habit? Often the painted smile reflects an uncertainty, a conflict, a contradiction, an insecurity, a desire to give a negative message in a sweet way. The painted smile is the very essence of noncongruence.

The leveling process requires a determination not to play games. It involves cutting through self-protecting cover-ups, rationalizations, and intellectualizations to impart to the other the way you feel, the way you think, or the way you see a situation. Because self-disclosure is usually a revealing experience, it is expedited when not hidden amid contradictory signals and stimuli. I am talking here about self-disclosure of feelings. We must make sure we differentiate between feelings and thoughts. If you can substitute the words "I think" for the words "I feel" and the sentence still makes grammatical sense, then probably you have not expressed a feeling.

1. I [feel] that spectator sports are not as rewarding as participant sports.

2. I [think] that spectator sports are not as rewarding as participant sports.

The sentence makes grammatical sense either way. Hence, it is a thought, not a *genuine* feeling. Try these:

1. I [feel] angry as hell.

2. I [think] angry as hell.

1. I [feel] warm and cuddly.

2. I [think] warm and cuddly.

1. I [think] I am [feeling] comfortable about the situation.

(This mixture of thought and feeling is sometimes appropriate.)

Generally, the words that follow are feeling words:

Negative	Positive
mad	glad
sad	happy
irked	good
scared	loving
crumby	warm
hurt	tingly
angry	inspired
spiteful	jubilant
cold	ecstatic
distant	sexy
rejected	sensuous
jealous	beautiful
numb	accepted
bitchy	close
picky	tender
anxious	whole

The leveling process requires a determined resistance to accommodation. Accommodation is not the same as genuine compromise, so essential to all human relationships. In a compromise, both individuals negotiate the issues, express their positions honestly, and are willing to give and take. In accommodation, one individual gives in to the other in order to placate, please, or appease. People often accommodate to their own peril. The individual who accommodates tends to obliterate his genuine feelings and thoughts in order to keep peace or to avoid conflict. People who are fearful of negative emotions and conflict are more prone to engage in accommodation, because it protects them from the anxiety of self-assertion and self-disclosure.

Self-disclosure is learned only as one is able to endure anxiety and discomfort. This is because it is a risk-taking behavior. We only take risks when we feel secure enough to withstand the counterattack of anxiety.

This is rarely accomplished in toto. Self-disclosure is risk-taking because the person has summoned enough courage to reveal his emotions. In secondary relationships this is uncalled for and usually unnecessary. But in intimate (primary) relationships it is the key to growth and joy, to spontaneity and vitality, to depth and meaning. This risk involved in self-disclosure is no small matter. Each person has his own private risk threshold—that point beyond which he will not go. Some people over-extend themselves and then retreat. Others retreat for a while to summon up new courage. The majority, however, will probably never experience the growth of intimacy, because they depend on a relatively low risk threshold to maintain emotional security.

Protection of the self against pain and hurt creates much of the dis-illusionment within marriage by blocking individual growth and growth of the relationship. The price of growth is the discomfort that results from having one's basic security challenged. Growth is facilitated by an open attitude toward anger and conflict, by the realization that any dynamic love involves acceptance of negative feelings. It further requires self-awareness and the ability to disclose one's innermost feelings to the intimate other. Without this ability there will be no risk-taking, and the partners will never experience the joy of knowing and being known.

Summary

The sociological basis for the anger taboo is the cultural belief that anger is always wrong and should remain unexpressed. The psychological basis is that we learned to suppress anger when we were very young because it was frightening to stand up against "the hand that feeds you." We were afraid to express ourselves because we were afraid of losing love.

The cultural belief gives people an excuse to continue in their refusal to express negative and potentially hurtful feelings. Unless and until we overcome the anger taboo, we cannot begin to learn self-disclosure.

Related to the anger taboo is the conflict taboo. This taboo says that fighting between a married couple is a sign of problems, that conflict indicates something is wrong in the relationship, that happily married people do not have conflict. As long as people believe that conflict is wrong there is little likelihood that anyone is going to succeed in helping them to express their true feelings.

When feelings are denied and suppressed there is an inevitable deterioration of the relationship, largely because the spontaneous good feelings are felt less and less. The positive feelings seem to fade away to the same degree that the negative feelings are denied or mishandled.

Once the anger and conflict taboos are overcome, the couple faces a new challenge—the challenge of learning to become increasingly self-aware and self-disclosing. Self-awareness is knowing who you are and what you are feeling. Self-disclosure is the process of communicating your feelings and information about yourself to the other person. I believe that increased self-awareness increases self-disclosure and that self-disclosure facilitates self-awareness.

The process of self-disclosure entails unlearning the habitual use of the second person pronoun—you—in expressing negative feelings. The you statements need to be replaced with first person (I) statements. These force the individual to express what he is feeling before he makes any attack on the activity of the mate. This approach does several things. It puts us in touch with our inner emotional state; it sets the stage for information-gathering whereby we can check out whether or not the situation is as we perceive it to be; and it enables us to deal with the problem situation rather than with the person. Few normal people enjoy being attacked, and when we use phrases such as "you are always doing that," we are attacking. When people are attacked, they usually jump to a defensive position. When that happens there is little chance for a constructive resolution of the conflict.

Questions for Study

1. Do you agree with Beth that anger is a part of love? Why or why not?

2. Discuss the sociological and psychological taboos against anger. In what ways have they affected you and others you know?

3. What is occurring when a married couple who have just exchanged many angry statements report that they feel more loving?

4. Using the list of feeling words, try to recall a situation in which you experienced each one.

5. What are the risks and rewards of self-disclosure? Evaluate them.

Reading Suggestions

Why Am I Afraid to Tell You Who I Am? by John Powell, S. J. Niles, Ill.: Argus Communications, 1969. A description of psychological games, ego defense mechanisms, and ways of dealing with emotions.

Coming Together—Coming Apart: Anger and Separation in Sexual Loving by Jay Kuten. New York: Macmillan, 1974. An analysis of the nature of amorous and sexual love; indicates the need for emotional boundaries as prerequisite for intimacy.

Pairing by George Bach and Ronald Deutsch. New York: Avon, 1970. Outlines skills for intimate relating.

The Intimate Enemy by George Bach and Peter Wyden. New York: William Morrow, 1968. A handbook for fair fighting between intimates.

The Transparent Self by Sidney Jourard. New York: D. Van Nostrand, 1964. A discussion of the need for self-disclosure in interpersonal relationships.

SEVEN
CONFLICT RESOLUTION: AN ENTRÉE INTO THE SELF

Conflict Resolution:
An Entrée into the Self

Intrapsychic and
Interpsychic Conflict

Transactional Analysis

Conflict Resolution: Adult-Adult

Dealing with Not OK Feelings

Marital Actualization
and the OK Child

Some Ground Rules for Fair Fighting

Conflict Defused but Unresolved

Summary

Questions for Study

Reading Suggestions

Intrapsychic and
Interpsychic Conflict

George and Betty

George and Betty have been going together for almost a year. Their relationship has been a deep and rewarding experience for both of them. Lately, however, George has become picky, hypercritical, and sensitive to things Betty says and does. George has decided to talk to a counselor about his relationship with Betty.

I don't know what it is, but everything she does bugs me. I get angry when she tries to plan an evening or a weekend. Then when she doesn't offer her opinions about what we're going to do, I feel she doesn't care. We're saving money for our marriage and then she comes up with expensive ideas on how to spend it. Lately, no matter what it is, I react negatively. The other day for instance . . . we were going for a walk downtown and she started window shopping—you know, saying how much she'd like this dress or that coat. I found myself getting critical and hostile. I felt like . . . well, like here was a person who was going to try to manipulate me. (Pause) A couple of weeks ago I wanted her to fuss over me a little. I had seen some girl really pouring a lot of love onto a guy and it struck me that Betty never fusses over me that way. So when I saw her I noted her reactions. She sure was a loser compared to that girl I had seen. And we argue a lot—no matter what we are discussing I end up disagreeing with her. You know—like if she says it's a groovy flick I'll take the opposite approach. If she thinks Vietnam is stupid, I find myself defending our commitment. . . . Yet I love her. I still want to marry her! Why do I keep reacting to her the way I do?

There is, of course, no simple answer to George's question. Every couple needs to work through their interpersonal reactions, and no relationship is entirely free of personality quirks or idiosyncrasies. However, it may be that George's basic conflict is intrapsychic, or inside himself. He reveals some contradictory tendencies. On the one hand, he fears being manipulated, but he is not altogether sure what constitutes manipulation by Betty. He wants to be fussed over, yet the result is that he creates a test for Betty, as if he says to himself, "I'll watch her every move and see how unsatisfyingly she responds." Of course, under these conditions, Betty can't do anything but lose. She doesn't know the name of the game George is playing. George finds himself opposing Betty, no matter what the issue. I would suggest that the main conflict is in George, not in his relationship with Betty. George has some deeply hidden anxiety and hostility. He is not nearly as autonomous and self-directing as he probably pictures himself. One possible explanation is that George is using transference; he is interacting with and responding to Betty as if he were still fighting his mother. George appears to be easily threatened by Betty and yet, at the same time, he looks to her for reassurance and overt displays of affection. Thus, George's problem is basically intrapsychic, a function of his personal development and environmental conditioning. The extent to which George understands and is able to handle his intrapsychic problems will determine the kind and quality of relationship he has with Betty or any other prospective mate.

Interpsychic or interpersonal conflict is a more obvious kind of conflict. It is this kind of conflict that has been regarded as taboo within marriage. According to this view, a husband and wife should not have conflict, even though familial conflict between parents and children is considered normal and acceptable. Even this conflict is not very comfortable for society; witness the labeling of intergenerational conflict as the generation gap. Could it be that the term *gap* is used to avoid the word *conflict?* And if it is a conflict, is it a conflict of drives and instincts, or is it a conflict of values, meanings, and purpose?

Interpersonal conflict may focus on trivial, inconsequential things, or it may focus on major issues. Within marriage, the little inconsequential things may serve as decoys for the actual source of conflict. Much of the pent-up hostility of marital partners is expressed in passive ways or is displaced to inappropriate objects. The designation *passive-aggressive* personality is given to those who aggress passively, perhaps by being unduly critical or by nitpicking. When aggressive, hostile feelings are displaced, we see a form of scapegoating. There is a well-defined pecking order in our society that designates the legitimate objects of our displaced hostility feelings. Neither displacement nor passive-aggressiveness need occur if we could take seriously the reality of conflict and learn to deal with it in mature and creative ways.

For lessons in "how to fight fair in love and marriage," as Bach puts it, the reader is referred to his book.[1] My intent here is to examine the nature of intrapsychic and interpsychic conflict and then to outline a system that will, hopefully, enable you to understand the nature of your intrapersonal and interpersonal communications. Only as a person understands the nature of his inner conflicts is he able to deal creatively with his interpersonal conflicts. The system I describe is called **transactional analysis.**

Intrapsychic conflict is conflict within the self that arises from our drives, instincts, and values pulling against each other. Classical Freudian psychoanalysis posits the fundamental conflict as one between the id and the superego. (Psychoanalytical and **neopsychoanalytical theory** developed since Freud has stressed the centrality of intrapsychic conflict as the essential dynamic of neurotic behavior. Intrapsychic conflict is one of the precursors of interpsychic conflict.) These two terms do not refer to phenomena existing within the self but are symbolic references to libidinous (instinctual) energy and the internalized voice of parents and society (conscience). Ideally, the ego is strong enough to be the arbiter between the id (seeking pleasure) and the superego (demanding perfection). The ego takes account of the reality of the core self of the person; the degree of strength and maturity of the ego determines the degree of control the superego is allowed to exercise over the instinctual libidinous drives. Frankl has pointed out that there is another kind of conflict besides this conflict of drives and instincts (which result in what he terms "psychogenic neurosis"). He suggests that anxiety ("noogenic neurosis") also arises from "conflicts between various values; in other words, from moral conflicts or, to speak in a more general way, from spiritual problems."[2]

---

transactional analysis a type of psychotherapy based on the study and analysis of the communication, metacommunication, and symbolic communication (transactions) between two people.
neopsychoanalytical theory expansion and reinterpretation of Freud's discoveries based on new empirical and clinical evidence; especially refers to the theories of Karen Horney, Harry Stack Sullivan, and Erich Fromm.

An internal conflict can focus on anything that encounters resistance when attempts are made to incorporate it or make it acceptable to the self. Since facing conflict creates unpleasant feelings of tension and anxiety, individuals develop conscious or unconscious methods of handling conflict. One method is to suppress it—that is, to consciously put it in the back of one's mind and deliberately decide not to deal with it. Repression, on the other hand, is an unconscious process of blocking out the conflict so that it does not come out into the open, into consciousness. However, material repressed in the unconscious still exerts a powerful influence on us, for repression can cause conflict to be disguised in the form of compulsions, obsessions, anxiety, and depression.

If a person is torn within, consciously or unconsciously, he will be unable to deal with conflicts on the interpersonal (interpsychic) level. People who have dealt successfully with their inner conflicts are able to address themselves to interpersonal conflict in a reasonably creative, autonomous, and spontaneous manner. Let us caution, however, that to experience internal conflict is to be human. There can be no counsel of perfection about our inner conflicts. Our humanity is such that we are capable of emotionality *and* rationality. We experience drives, desires, feelings, and pleasures; we also experience meaning and meaninglessness, value and worthlessness, intelligence and stupidity. Our intellect can serve us in conflict avoidance as well as in conflict resolution. For example, through *rationalization* one can refer to plausible reasons for his behavior and thus avoid facing the real reasons. Or a person can unconsciously *project* his own traits on another person so that he will not have to see them in himself. Or through *transference* an individual might transfer his feelings toward a significant person in his life (particularly parents) to another person. All of these are conflict-avoidance games we play with ourselves.

Now let us consider a method of self-study that may serve as a handle for creatively working through conflict. The underlying assumption is that conflict is a human reality, and as such it is amoral. As we become proficient in understanding and handling intrapsychic conflicts, we will be free to become equally proficient at understanding and working through our interpsychic conflicts.

Transactional Analysis

If marriage is to be thought of as a "human-actualizing contract,"[3] then it is important that both parties commit themselves, implicitly or explicitly, to the growth model of marital interaction and enrichment. Such a commitment implies a willingness to face conflict in a creative way. Transactional analysis is one method that may help us to do just that. It is a method for achieving self-understanding to further the process of growth toward self-actualization.

Eric Berne's *Games People Play* became a bestseller, but unfortunately its popularity seemed to be based on public fascination with the games rather than with the dynamics underlying the games.[4] Thomas Harris worked closely with Berne as one of the original members of the San Francisco Social Psychiatry Seminars. Harris' contribution to transactional analysis is entitled *I'm OK—You're OK*.

Psychoanalysis builds on concepts of energies in the self (superego, ego, and id). Harris names what he considers real parts of the personality—the Parent, the Child, and the Adult:

Continual observation has supported the assumption that these three states exist in all people. It is as if in each person there is the same little person he was when he was three years old. There are also within him his own parents. These states are audiovisual recordings in the brain of actual experiences of internal and external events, the most significant of which happened during the first five years of life. There is a third state, different from these two. The first two are called Parent and Child, and the third, Adult.[5]

The Parent is like a video tape recorder that recorded all the information available to it throughout childhood without editing, scrutinizing, or judging. Thus, the Parent is the "taught" way of life with which we were carefully indoctrinated during those early years, especially during the first five years of life.

The Parent is a huge collection of recordings in the brain of unquestioned or imposed external data perceived by a person in his early years, a

*period which we have designated roughly as the first five years of life.
. . . The name Parent is the most descriptive of this data inasmuch as
the most significant "tapes" are those provided by the example and pro-
nouncements of his own real parents or parent substitutes. Everything
the child saw his parents do and everything he heard them say is recorded
in the Parent.*[6]

The Parent is the source of rules, laws, standards, proscriptions, prescriptions, frowns, smiles, praise, approval and disapproval. According to
Harris, "The significant point is that whether these rules are good or bad
in the light of a reasonable ethic, they are recorded as *truth* from the
source of all security, the people who are 'six feet tall' at a time when
it is important to the two-foot-tall child that he please and obey them. It
is a permanent recording. A person cannot erase it. It is available for
replay throughout life."[7]

The Child is also a recording, which is made simultaneously with the
Parent recording. However, it is a recording of feelings—what the child
feels as he sees and hears, as he experiences, and as he understands or
doesn't understand. The child is two feet tall as he absorbs and responds
to his six-feet-tall parents. "Since the little person has no vocabulary
during the most critical of his early experiences, most of his reactions are
feelings. We must keep in mind his situation in these early years. He is
small, he is dependent, he is inept, he is clumsy, he has no words with
which to construct meanings."[8] If the Parent is the "taught" way of life,
the Child may be labeled the "felt" way of life. There are many positive
feelings that the child felt, which became the basis of his feelings of joy,
pleasure, happiness, and spontaneity. The negative feelings, however, are
the ones that seem to cause the difficulty:

*The predominant by-product of the frustrating, civilizing process is nega-
tive feelings. On the basis of these feelings the little person early concludes, "I'm NOT OK." We call this comprehensive self-estimate the NOT
OK, or the NOT OK Child. This conclusion and the continual experiencing
of the unhappy feelings which led to it and confirm it are recorded permanently in the brain and cannot be erased. This permanent recording is
the residue of having been a child. Any child. Even the child of kind,
loving, well-meaning parents. It is the situation of childhood and not the*

intention of the parents which produces the problem. . . . As in the case of the Parent, the Child is a state into which a person may be transferred at almost any time in his current transactions. There are many things that can happen to us today which re-create the situation of childhood and bring on the same feelings we felt then.[9]

The third intrapsychic phenomenon is called the Adult. The Adult is essentially our "thought" way of life, in that the Adult is like a computer that gathers and processes data fed through it by the Parent and the Child.

The ten-month-old has found he is able to do something which grows from his own awareness and original thought. This self-actualization is the beginning of the Adult. . . . Adult data accumulates as a result of the child's ability to find out for himself what is different about life from the "taught concept" of life in his Parent and the "felt concept" of life in his Child. The Adult develops a "thought concept" of life based on data gathering and data processing.[10]

The Adult does reality testing and probability estimating. He checks out the Parent data to see if they are valid or invalid, applicable today or outdated, and in this light he determines how to accept and handle the feelings of the Child. As Harris says, "the understanding of how the original situation of childhood produced so many NOT OK recordings of this type can free us of their continual replay in the present. *We cannot erase the recording, but we can choose to turn it off!*"[11]

Thus, the insight of self-understanding needs to be followed, sooner or later, by a conscious choice—a firm decision. Each of us must decide to live our remaining years under the tyranny of "shoulds" and "should nots," "dos" and "don'ts," "oughts" and "ought nots," or we must decide to put reason and feeling to work, forging a life style on the anvil of personal dignity and humanness.

Transactional analysis is a tool, a method of looking at the verbal and nonverbal transactions between people in order to determine where the transaction originated. Some originate in the NOT OK Child. Some originate in the Parent. Hopefully, most transactions originate in the Adult. If a person had unpleasant feelings as a child of being rejected

or criticized, it is not at all unlikely that in his grown years he still cannot handle rejection or criticism. The old feelings—or recordings—play
their old familiar tune: We would say his NOT OK Child is "hooked."
Our children ask us, after we have given an authoritative pronounce-
ment on the acceptable limits to length of hair, "Who put that into your
head?" We may discover, after careful examination and self-scrutiny,
that we are dispensing archaic Parent data that has not been analyzed
by our Adult computer. By the same token, we may feed into the computer "I don't like long hair! I was raised differently! I guess I'm a little
old-fashioned! Nevertheless, the standard will be this: If you want to
wear long hair then I expect it to be combed and clean." In this case, although the child may not feel he has won anything, the transaction is a
result of his father's using his own Adult computer, rather than blind
repetition of archaic (and maybe faulty) Parent data.

Transactional analysis is a method of introspection that can serve as a
framework for a great variety of psychological and therapeutic theories.
Furthermore, the method advocated by Harris makes it possible to discover one's own games and to consciously choose the Adult position. *This
is not easy to do.* Nevertheless, when we realize that the NOT OK feelings
will never be erased, but that as adults we can refuse to listen to them,
then the game-playing strategy can be discarded. Harris says:

*The only way people get well or become OK is to expose the childhood
predicament underlying the first three positions. . . . it is essential to
understand that I'm OK—You're OK is a position and not a feeling. The
NOT OK recordings in the Child are not erased by a decision in the present. The task at hand is how to start a collection of recordings which play
OK outcomes to transactions, successes in terms of correct probability
estimating, successes in terms of integrated actions which make sense,
which are programmed by the Adult, and not by the Parent or Child,
successes based on an ethic which can be supported rationally.*[12]

Slowly, our Adult will discover that we need not go through life trying
to bandage up our wounded NOT OK Child. Instead, we can use what
Parent and Child data we decide is meaningful, relevant, and appropriate
after we have put it through our Adult computer.

Conflict Resolution: Adult-Adult

The tension between the NOT OK Child and the Parent is usually, in one way or another, the root cause of intrapsychic and interpsychic conflict. NOT OK feelings take the form of insecurity, inferiority, helplessness, worthlessness, shame, doubt, and guilt. NOT OK-ness is, as Harris has pointed out, the inevitable result of early childhood and the dependency it implies. The intrapsychic conflict which the NOT OK person experiences is a continuation of the struggle to achieve self-trust and autonomy. In this connection, Horney has pointed out that when a person fails to learn self-trust and consequently lacks autonomy, he will likely move toward others, trying to win their praise, approval, and affection, taking great care to conceal any resentment or hostility.[13] He is afraid of rejection or rebuff, and hence is overly sensitive to the remarks and opinions of others. The NOT OK Adult (translated to Horney's terms) may move "against others" instead of "toward" them, putting himself one-up and adopting a manipulative, controlling stance so that he can exercise power over others. A third tactic may be to move "away" from others by seeking solitude as a haven of security from the risks of intimacy. Horney notes that everyone uses these three patterns and that the healthy person keeps all three in balance while the neurotic usually leans heavily on one of the three to the exclusion of the other two.

Transactional analysis can help the Adult to see and feel his NOT OK Child at work. Once we learn to see clearly the Parent and Child working within us, we can consciously decide to disallow the Parent and Child recordings. This, however, is an Adult decision. When the Adult is in control of the situation, the transaction may include updating Parent and Child data. The Adult does not need to play games that in one way or another (one-downmanship, one-upmanship, escapism) are calculated to control and manipulate others. In his book *Man, the Manipulator*, Everett Shostrom talks about "Top-Dog" and "Under-Dog." Shostrom makes the same point—that we assume these positions in order to manipulate and control others.[14]

The challenge in transactional analysis is to pinpoint the origin of a thought, a feeling, or a communication. If the point of origin is in our

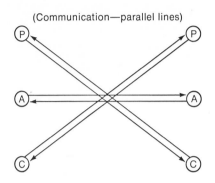

Figure 7–1
Complementary Transactions

Parent or Child then we can see it, identify it or label it, and proceed to consciously move into our Adult by updating the Parent or Child data to determine if it is relevant today. If it is not, then the Adult acknowledges it to himself; if it is relevant, then the material still needs to be analyzed by the Adult computer and placed into proper perspective. The situation may call for the Adult to face the conflict using clear communication directed to the Adult of the other person, whether the other person is a parent, a spouse, or a friend. If this is done, the chances for a resolution

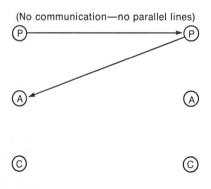

Figure 7–2
Noncomplementary Transaction

of the conflict are increased. Conflict resolution is possible only when the Adults of both people are communicating. If I direct my communication to the Child of another person, and if that Child responds to my Adult, we do have a complementary transaction. But conflict resolution will be difficult, because the Child is not able to handle conflict as the Adult can. It is the Child that is so easily threatened.

If the transaction is not complementary—that is, if the Parent addresses the Child and the Child responds to the Child, there is a breakdown of

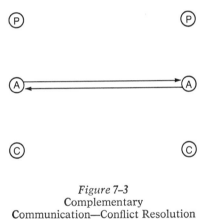

Figure 7–3
Complementary
Communication—Conflict Resolution

communication. Figure 7–1 illustrates complementary transactions among the Parent (P), Child (C), and Adult (A) of two people. Complementary transactions always have parallel lines (communication); noncomplementary transactions do not, as illustrated in Figure 7–2. Effective conflict resolution, however, requires not only parallel lines but parallel lines between Adult and Adult (see Figure 7–3).

Dealing with Not OK Feelings

Most people deal with their Not OK feelings by playing games. Each game has some sort of emotional payoff, usually hidden or implicit. The more common games include: "Mine is better than yours," "If it weren't for you," "Ain't it awful," "Look what you did to me," "Look what you made me do," and "Look how hard I tried." In addition to these games, we often resort to other maneuvers, ploys, displacements, and compensations to make us feel OK. Spending sprees (the purchase of something we do not need or even want but which, for the moment, makes us feel better), drinking, eating, sleeping, taking drugs, having sex, flirting, participating in sports—can all become mechanisms to enhance beaten down self-feelings. We all need diversions and interests, and the healthy, growing person will welcome a variety of such experiences. There is, however, an emphatic difference between the compensation-oriented person and the growth-oriented person. Individuals who are growing have abandoned short-cut methods to psychic security and instead permit themselves to find authentic roots for a positive self-concept. The foundation of OK feelings is in the self-feelings—how I feel about being me. When we choose to stop listening to the negative tapes of the past and begin to acknowledge our present strengths, assets, and talents, we may be quite surprised. The tragedy is that we live under the influence of past "curse" messages. Yes, you may have been awkward and unlikable at age nine or thirteen—and you learned that people thought negatively about you. But is this true of you now, today? Have you been living your life on the basis of information that was true then but is wholly inaccurate and untrue now?

It would be reassuring to most people if we would prescribe a guaranteed method for developing positive self-feelings. But there is no therapy or program or ritual that can do for you what you must do for yourself. There is no escape from the work, the pain, the effort, the commitment, and the agony of growing up into authentic autonomy and selfhood.

Marital Actualization
and the OK Child

In marital conflict the Parent or Child often takes over, and

the whole marriage is shattered when imperfections begin to appear. Marriage is the most complicated of all human relationships. Few alliances

can produce such extremes of emotion or can so quickly travel from pro-
fessions of the utmost bliss to that cold, terminal legal write-off, mental
cruelty. When one stops to consider the massive content of archaic data
which each partner brings to the marriage through the continuing con-
tribution of his Parent and Child, one can readily see the necessity of an
emancipated Adult in each to make this relationship work.[15]

Transactional analysis could be a most effective tool in helping to bring about self-actualizing marriage, because the Not OK Child is the source of most illegitimate needs that individuals bring to relationships. The roots of marital disillusionment can be traced, in part, to failure to use the Adult computer when confronted with legal, moral, traditional, and societal expectations of marriage. The socialization of the young is a Parent function, and much of that teaching applies to masculinity/femininity expectations and husband/wife roles. The data absorbed by the Child may be valid or invalid, moralistic or rooted in carefully considered values. The reaction of spouse to spouse often never gets beyond the Child-Child stage of communication, as each spouse tries to get strokes from the other or to play a game of one-upmanship. The desire for romantic love may well be the crying of the Not OK Child seeking new promises of affection. This happens because the Not OK Child has consistently allowed other people to do the "valuating," the placing and ascribing of value and worth upon the individual.

Self-actualization would seem almost impossible if we had no way to get in touch with the sources of our feelings, reactions, attitudes, and behavior. The Not OK Child is wallowing in deficiency needs; being needs can be met only by those who make a conscious decision to embrace the "I'm OK—You're OK" position. The neurotic need for affection, about which Horney writes, is the Not OK Child asking for strokes by playing various games and employing various strategies and maneuvers. The Not OK Child may also employ sex as a means of obtaining strokes. However, such acting out of feelings of anger, hostility, resentment, and aggression in the sexual sphere is a very questionable type of human sexuality.

When the spouses can interact with each other on the "I'm OK—You're OK" basis, they are free to work with Adult data rather than with archaic Parent–Child data. They are free to deal with present reality unhampered by past Not OK feelings. Communication often takes place between the Parent of one spouse to the Child of the other spouse. Growth-producing communication should be between Adult and Adult. Indeed, Adult-Adult communication is an absolute prerequisite for a self-actualizing marital relationship, at least as a basic life stance. Obviously, no one can speak as an Adult all the time; there will be times of backsliding and momentary returns to the Parent and Child positions.

Only when human beings are free to be themselves, free from the tyrannical Parent which beats upon and threatens the Child, can they have an actualizing marriage. Freedom *from* is a prerequisite for freedom *to*. We cannot be what we are until we are somewhat at peace with what we were. Actualizing selves are not paragons of perfection. They are human beings who seek to express and fulfill their humanity.

Two self-actualizing people will not automatically have a self-actualizing marriage, but the prerequisites are partially met. Marriage, even with self-actualizing partners, requires a certain amount of role definition and clarification. Male and female role models from the early years may return to plague the partners; this is to be expected. Idealized self-images and idealized spouse images often need to be exposed and frankly labeled. The premise still holds, however, that until we are free from the archaic tyranny of the Parent and Child, we are not free to be ourselves.

Some Ground Rules for Fair Fighting

Six basic principles are axiomatic in handling negative emotions and conflict.

1. The individual must make a firm decision to negotiate as the Adult rather than as the Child or the Parent. All fighting (interacting, arguing, conflict resolution) will remain woefully ineffective until this most basic decision is made. There is no way the Child can truly negotiate because it is usually feeling hurt or threatened. And the Parent tends to defend the archaic positions of the past, making it almost impossible to move beyond a rigidity and arbitrariness that impedes the responsible sending and receiving of feelings and messages.

2. We must avoid statements that leave the other no room to move around. No one likes to be attacked! No one enjoys being backed up to a wall or being put in a corner with no space for dignified response. Negotiation is the tool of compromise and resolution. What many people call negotiation is not negotiation but ultimatum and counter-ultimatum. When we allow no room for authentic communication, we have effectively obliterated the other—we have put the other in the Child position because we have assumed the Parent position.

3. In our highly competitive society, we are all socialized to winning and losing. But when one wins and one loses, both lose. In an intimate relationship, the after-conflict feelings are crucial. Whoever wins may feel good, or guilty. Whoever loses may feel defeated—stamped down, rejected, manipulated—or strangely, he may feel good because once again he had had it demonstrated that he is a loser or a victim. Because it is the two partners, the winner and the loser, who form the relationship, the relationship also suffers—and usually more than we recognize. Good feelings and bad feelings become enmeshed. Resentment is bound to result— and feelings of hurt and futility.

Once we succeed in dealing with feelings by becoming self-aware and self-disclosing, by leveling and permitting ourselves to accept our vulnerability, then we are able to place the health of the relationship above the individualized fact of winning or losing. When we see clearly that the relationship always loses when winner is pitted against loser, we can begin to commit ourselves to authentic negotiation instead of allowing ourselves to be manipulated into accommodations or frontal attacks.

4. Never say yes if you mean no, and never say no if you mean yes. Any reservations should, if at all possible, be stated at the time of the response, not later. Grave harm is done by premature accommodation, and also by false representation of one's true feelings and thoughts. Here again, we must have at least some awareness of what we are really feeling. I have observed that a common reason people give for being dishonest (that is, for not saying what they really feel or think or want) is that they want to protect the other person from being hurt. To this I can only reply that people often find that, whenever they protect someone they care about, the situation becomes worse rather than better. We need to ask ourselves: Who are you really trying to protect, the other person or yourself? Often it is yourself. A great deal of dishonesty that ostensibly occurs in an effort to prevent pain actually occurs as we try to protect and shield ourselves from the agony of feeling our own pain, fear, fright, shame, or embarrassment. Thus, such dishonesty is a maneuver that effectively inhibits growth of the self, the partner, and the relationship.

5. Avoid attack. The threatened self (the Child in us, the source of dependency feelings and excessive feelings of jealousy) is likely to spring to the attack. As I noted in the previous chapter, "you" statements are often implicit or explicit attacks. "You make me angry." "You made me do this." "You always act that way." "You never apologize for anything." I counsel against attack, because attack puts the other person on the defensive. Rare is the person who does not become defensive when attacked or accused. If, however, the person who is taking the initiative uses "I" statements and tries to recognize his own feeling, the entire issue is put in a fair and manageable perspective.

She: *You belittle me. You put me down. Every time I say something you have some way of canceling it out.*
He: *You're damn right—because your ideas are stupid! You haven't had a good idea since you were born.*
She: *I feel very badly when everything I say is rejected.*
He: *I don't mean to reject you. I sometimes think you don't really grasp the problem I'm dealing with.*

You may wonder if this small distinction is important. After all, is it not true that the charge still stands? Yes, the charge still stands, but it does not demean the other person's humanity and dignity. This is of great importance in conflict situations, because the possibility of negotiation depends largely on the absence of defensiveness. Raising an issue, airing a criticism or complaint, stating a hurt or a deeply felt grievance—these can always be done honestly and forthrightly if we allow the other to respond with dignity and fairness. This is rarely possible in direct attack, because an attack usually puts the partner on the defensive. And once we become defensive, either the Parent or the Child takes over and the battle is on.

If we take the time to recognize and accept our feelings, and then to raise the issue of the other person's behavior in a given situation, we enhance the possibility of effective communication. We may still end up being hurt or angry, but that is all right because these are honest feelings. We express our feelings and invite the other to hear us out and then to respond.

None of this will work if the fighters are triggered by a hidden agenda or are engaged in intrapsychic conflicts. Then no fair-fight rule will help, because the real problems are imbedded within the personalities of the fighters.

This ground rule has a corollary: Focus on the feeling first, then on the behavior that seems to be related to the feeling. Do not focus on the other person—only on the problem. Obviously, this is more easily said than done. But usually it is a productive method of approaching a threatening or touchy issue.

6. Always employ a checking-out technique. Ask the other person whether your perception of them or of the present situation is accurate. In other words, check out your perceptions, impressions, or feelings. If in doubt, ask.

He: *Dear, I sense you're angry as hell about something—is it me?*
She: *It's not you—not really.*
He: *Then what is it? Is there anything I can do?*
She: *Yes. Just leave me alone.*
He: *Okay. Yell if you need me.*

Assuming she means what she says, he can now leave her alone, trusting that whatever is upsetting her does not involve him. If, however, ground rule four has been broken (never say no if you mean yes) she will probably resort to increased passive-aggressive behavior. And that will probably lead to an explosive outpouring. "What the hell is wrong with you, you know damn well what I'm upset about, at least if you really loved me you'd know!" And we're off and running.

There are other ground rules that might be helpful. But too many rules block effective use of the basic ones. There is no substitute for reality-testing. Dealing with actual interpersonal conflict is the *only* way to learn to fight fairly and constructively. And the only way to discover the validity and helpfulness of these ground rules is to test them.

Conflict Defused but Unresolved

Conflict resolution requires a relationship between mates who are basically in the "I'm OK—You're OK" position and are communicating with the Adult components of their personalities. Yet even a complementary transaction between Adults is no guarantee that a given conflict will be resolved. There are times when the partners can proceed no further. If the unresolved conflict is being handled by Adults, and if the source of conflict is sufficiently important to each person that living together is no longer feasible, then sometimes divorce is the only alternative, even with Adult people.

If the conflict is not resolvable and if it is defined as not being of absolutely crucial importance, then two Adult people may simply have to accept their inability to resolve that particular issue. At least the conflict is defused. Stalemate need not be harmful providing the conflict has been adequately dealt with. The danger of unfaced conflict lies primarily in the process of conflict denial, suppression, or repression. In these situations, the conflict cannot be defused because it is not being treated on the Adult-Adult level. Denied and displaced conflict tends to create anger, hostility, resentment, anxiety, depression, and aggression. Defused conflict, although not resolved, at least loses its potential to be destructive in a hidden way. It is always the repressed and the denied that comes back to drive the person; unresolved conflict, once defused, has little power to harm if the partners are able to accept the stalemate in a mature, Adult-Adult manner.

Summary

This chapter emphasizes that conflict-handling is the most important skill in the total communication process. There are two kinds of conflict, intrapsychic and interpsychic—within the self and between two people. Intrapsychic conflict can be the cause of interpsychic conflict. Whenever one has disharmony or a raging conflict within oneself, this internal frustration is bound to carry over to interpersonal relationships. Much interpersonal conflict is an acting out of internal contradictions and anxiety.

I have described transactional analysis as a helpful approach to handling both kinds of conflict. Transactional analysis (TA) is a system of personality dissection in which the individual is seen as a mixture of three basic ego states—the Parent or "taught" way of life, the Child or the "felt" way of life, and the Adult or the "thought" way of life. Our communications to others originate from these three ego states. Those originating from the Child are the most revealing of our feelings. Those originating in the Adult are the most revealing of our morals and manners. The goal of TA is to help people see through these ego states and to learn to consciously decide to allow the Adult ego state to dominate and control. The Adult can choose to allow the Child to operate, or it can choose to allow the Parent to operate. In either case, however, the Adult serves as the final arbiter. The Adult—the mature, autonomous self—expresses the legislative, judicial, and executive functions of the personality, gathering data from both the Parent and the Child and then taking appropriate action after careful assessment of the total situation.

TA deals with both intrapsychic disturbance and interpsychic disturbance. It insists that we get in close touch with the maneuvers and ploys of our own Parent and Child. The constant instructing, admonishing, warning, and threatening Parent messages join forces to make the Child feel Not OK. We can exercise some power over this internal process by gaining insight into how the Parent and Child control us and then by making a conscious choice to place the Adult in control. In doing this we disengage ourselves from the destructive portion of the Parent and Child messages.

The primary goal of TA in dealing with interpersonal and intimate relationships is the establishment of a relationship in which the partners operate on an Adult-Adult level, rather than on a Child-Child, Parent-Parent, Child-Parent, Child-Adult, or Parent-Adult level.

Some conflicts cannot be resolved. It is possible for all interpsychic conflict to be faced and dealt with. This defuses the ability of suppressed conflict to work underground by driving us into passive-aggressive and other dirty-fight styles. If two people, dealing with the conflict in an Adult-Adult manner, are unable to arrive at an honest solution, fairly negotiated, then they will need to decide whether they can live with their differences or if the differences are serious enough to warrant separation or divorce.

Questions for Study

1. Do you agree that only when a person understands his intrapersonal conflicts can he deal with his interpersonal conflicts effectively? Why or why not?

2. Can you identify the thoughts, feelings, and mannerisms associated with your own Parent, Adult, and Child ego states?

3. Try to remember some instances when you or others have played the games described in this chapter. Identify the emotional payoff in each situation when the game was played.

4. Do you believe that when a person says he does not want to hurt another, he is really trying to protect himself?

5. Change this attack statement into a more effective sentence beginning with "I": "You are a rotten bastard."

Reading Suggestions

Born to Win by Muriel James and Dorothy Jongeward. Reading, Mass.: Addison-Wesley, 1971. A basic outline of transactional analysis and a discussion of gestalt experiments.

I'M OK—You're OK by Thomas Harris. New York: Harper and Row, 1967. Transactional analysis explained and applied to life situations and human institutions.

Games People Play by Eric Berne. New York: Grove, 1964. Psychological games described and analyzed in the terminology of transactional analysis.

Man the Manipulator by Everett Shostrom. Nashville, Tenn.: Abingdon, 1968. A theory for understanding the self and intrapsychic conflict.

Be the Person You Were Meant To Be by Jerry Greenwald. New York: Dell, 1974. A tool for self-understanding in the here-and-now; uses gestalt terminology.

EIGHT
BINDS AND UNBINDS: UNLEARNING AND RELEARNING

Binds and Unbinds:
Unlearning and Relearning

Binds and Double Binds

The Growth Bind

The Double-Standard Bind

The Sex-Role Bind

The Couple Bind

The Ownership-Fidelity Bind

The Good Girl-Bad Girl Bind

The Love-Is-Limited Bind

The Future-Security Bind

Summary

Questions for Study

Reading Suggestions

Binds and Double Binds

David's Journal

Slowly I felt our lives narrowing. We invested in each other and I continually tried to content myself with my chosen profession and my chosen wife. I felt lonely because Jenny didn't share my restlessness. She is a practical, functional person—matter of fact, solid. She always was so sure—she knew what she wanted and she was content. Looking back now I see how much security that attitude gave me—how I sapped strength from it, and how it makes my present situation so painful. I was the thinker, the philosopher, the dreamer, the poet. Oh yes, I was the moralist too. Then the affair happened. I went all the way in every way. I mentally invested my ego in her. My soul came alive. I was no longer atrophying. But the affair meant pain, and more anxiety—deceit, and guilt, and even distrust of my new love. The affair came to light and the day of reckoning was upon me. I was scared to death. I still loved my wife—more than I knew—she gave me some kind of queer sense of security. I chose Jenny, and together we rebuilt. She was more open to me now! Sex was great. Past resentments melted away. She accepted my thoughts and feelings and restlessness, even if she wasn't where I was in her growth. Good times—reinvestment of my ego in her. Life is great—life is being alive.

And now, you know what comes next. One day a reunion with Jenny's old class chums. Fine! And several days later, out of nowhere, Jenny's saying, "I could be completely comfortable having a sexual relationship with Jerry. I have fantasized it! What would you think?" "Fine," I said, as my legs started to tighten and my pulse stepped up its beat. "I'm so glad you've had the feeling!" And part of me was telling the truth. I was glad! But within hours another part of me had taken command. I became furious at the thought, angry at myself for urging her to be open, angry at her for daring to have such a feeling. Jealousy pervaded me. No way could I share my beloved with another man. Just the thought "his penis in her vagina!" I'll go out of my mind!

Days go by, and the time is spent in thought—and in pain. I feel self-disgust! Now I can really laugh at myself. "Here you are old boy, alive and aware and committed to growth and openness, for others, for me. But you goddamn bastard—not for your mate. I hated myself with a pure hatred. My security system had been taken away from me—my little blanket had once again been yanked away from my clutching grasp. "How could you do this to me? Jenny? How could you?" I know what I'll do— I'll set up my defenses. Oh! Stop it David. Who are you kidding—allow yourself to feel the hurt and the pain. Allow her the freedom you have wanted for yourself—allow her the dignity of having the same feelings you demanded she accept in you.

Oh wow! I hardly believe myself! In the hour of testing I flunked but good! I see more clearly now the frightened child, the scared little boy, petrified by the possibility of love lost, of meaning gone, of abandonment. Feel the pain—experience the vulnerable wound—don't further deny your own humanity. Now reexamine yourself—your whole self, your whole life. Were you right or were you wrong?

And so here I am. I grew in my mind. I searched and dreamed and reached out to life—and then one day I was faced with the cruelest self-deception of all: "I have not grown in my guts." My learning is academic, not visceral. To grow in the mind but not in the gut is worse than not to grow at all!

Binds and double binds may be illustrated by using the ideas of approach and avoidance. When we are disposed to approach someone or something we usually do so, unless there is a stronger force within us that influences us to avoid the person or situation. Then we are in an approach-avoidance situation. The stronger force will win out at that moment. Sometimes we may have to choose between two attractive alternatives— this is called an approach-approach situation. When we are asked to choose between two undesirable alternatives, we are in an avoidance-avoidance situation. If a person is caught between two alternatives, we say he is in a bind. The feeling of being caught refers to possible rewards and punishments that may result as a consequence of the choice. When the choice of either alternative will result in negative and undesirable consequences, we say that the person is in a double bind, inferring that he cannot possibly win. The situation has already determined that the person must lose.

The only real difference between a bind and a double bind is that the double bind leads a person beyond a feeling of simple frustration, restriction, or restraint caused by the need to make a decision and into a feeling of futility caused by the realization that no matter what he chooses he is a loser. He is damned if he does and damned if he doesn't. When we are in a bind we can choose to act to unbind ourselves. When we are in a double bind there is no hope of resolution. Notice that many childhood situations are double binds, because the child is placed in a position where he cannot possibly win.

David is in an approach-avoidance situation. He is in a bind. In his mind he wants an open, honest, and permissive marriage. He despises his own conduct and dependency. Yet he is frightened and threatened by the prospect of acting on what he thinks he wants.

I will discuss several kinds of binds in this chapter. Sometimes the culture puts us into a bind. Often, however, we put ourselves into a bind. First we will examine the growth bind, because it is so crucial to the establishment of a durable relationship.

The Growth Bind

The growth bind is made up of two opposing forces. The attracting dynamic is the appeal to one's desire for self-fulfillment and self-actualization. This dynamic relates to the quest for being, aliveness, spontaneity, vitality, and wisdom. The opposing force is the quest for security, the desire to maintain the status quo. Any change is threatening, even if the change is only contemplated. The body seems to resist change because of a need for certainty. And so man seeks absolutes, finality, answers, and a wedding service that exacts the promise of love and fidelity "til death do us part."

Each individual also wants to be secure about his identity. Identity is partly a function of our roles as males and females, husbands and wives, fathers and mothers. The growth bind occurs because every step in growth is accompanied by some corresponding change in the individual's security system. Likewise, any change within one person in a relationship produces a change of some type in the other person. And that change may be discomforting or painful.

Those who seek to grow are threatened by the risk of the loss of people, values, and things they hold to be precious or important. Yet, as David's situation portrays, not to grow may be an even greater risk. David's basic dilemma is typical of growth-oriented people. He is anxious for growth. But when the growth opportunity occurs, he is tempted to choose security.

I know of few growth-oriented people who have not, sooner or later, encountered a moment of terrifying dread. When that happens, the growth that has been gained through pain and self-discovery is threatened and the individual is terrified at the prospect of what he may lose. This is temporarily immobilizing, and may even make the individual dysfunctional. Most people who have doggedly fought their way to this point are only temporarily paralyzed. They pause to breathe in new courage and new determination to continue. The growth-oriented person may make mistakes, but he will weave those mistakes into the fabric of his growth.

Learning on the gut level is not easy. If we are to avoid binds, we need to unlearn many of the directives, preachments, and exhortations with which we have been socialized. To unlearn is to externalize; to learn is to internalize. We must externalize all the unproductive and self-defeating beliefs and attitudes that we have internalized since birth. Then the new learning, the relearning, or the new internalizing can begin. Actually, learning and internalizing are constantly interwoven, because the old is easily washed away as the new comes along. Some individuals find that they must firmly establish the rationality of their new position before they can even consider expurgation of old beliefs and ideas. And even after a new approach has been learned, and confirmed in the mind, it may not be truly internalized—integrated into the being and accepted in the gut. This is because internalization is an emotional rather than an intellectual process.

The Double-Standard Bind

A double standard is any situation in which one behavioral response or stimulus is acceptable for one partner but not for the other. Western tradition has long embraced different standards for women and men regarding sex mores, sex behavior, and marital obligations. If we are to free ourselves from the powerful influence of that double standard, we must be firm in our beliefs about this complicated and controversial issue.

Not all people believe that the double standard is wrong. The Judeo-Christian tradition has long been the strongest force opposing a single standard of sexual equality. According to the double standard, the female is supposed to be subservient to the male. The male derives his authority from his supposed strength and superiority. Regardless of how we may wish to interpret biblical accounts, the cultural tradition has evolved from them. If a person genuinely believes in the cultural tradition, then he will not see any problem with this double standard.

The problem develops when we wish to be done with the double standard but discover that, when face to face with it in operation, we are not as far removed from it as we had thought. Many males insist on their right to sexual activity before marriage, but they consciously or unconsciously look for a "good" girl to marry. In many societies men are expected to "sow their wild oats," but no such expectation or privilege applies to women. Married males are permitted flings, affairs, flirtations, nights out, and lunches with female office workers, but the female is denied these activities. Some men say they accept similar behavior in women, but I have known few who accept such behavior in women to the extent that women are expected to accept it in men. Why is the male so easily threatened? Perhaps the answer is found in the sex-role bind.

The Sex-Role Bind

With rare exceptions, the roles that men and women play in society have been determined by the very fact of gender at birth. Males are socialized to become the protectors, the breadwinners, the providers for the mate and children. Females are socialized to be the homemakers, the bearers of children, the givers of love and nurture to the husband and offspring. The sex-role bind occurs because individuals—both male and female—are capable of a wider variety of roles than the narrow sex roles that society has prescribed for them. "Male" and "female" are not "either/or" concepts; in fact, masculinity and femininity are poles of a continuum, and each individual has both masculine and feminine characteristics in his or her personality.

Biologically it is a certainty that only males can impregnate, while only females menstruate, gestate, and lactate. While the question of sex roles is still very much subject to debate, it seems likely that most other male/female differences are due to role learning rather than inherent physiological differences. In a society where sex roles are rigidly defined, there is bound to be a great deal of frustration for those individuals who wish to engage in behavior which is culturally limited to individuals of the opposite sex. In the United States today we are beginning to see both men and women engage in many roles that were formerly restricted to one sex. A recognition of individual needs and abilities is the best solution to the sex-role bind.

The Couple Bind

This is the bind of which Nena and George O'Neill have written in their book, *Open Marriage*.[1] The *couple front* is the tradition, based on societal expectations, that says a married couple must (or at least should) have mutual friends, preferably other couples of about the same age. Friends of the bride, both male and female, are now excluded, as are friends of the groom, both male and female. Further, the couple will like the same things, think somewhat alike, and pursue similar interests. They will go to social events together, not alone or with a companion other than the spouse, and especially not with a companion of the opposite sex. In all matters the couple will present a united front to the outside world, even though they may be feeling quite separated or alienated.

These restrictions demand behavior that obscures erosion of marital vitality. The couple bind is one of the greatest enemies of dynamic intimacy, because this conformity to the standards of couple unity and social propriety excludes so much of the real live world. Commonality of interests within marriage is important, but it is not nearly as important as the romantic marriage-manual approach would have us believe. Vitality is a function of being open, alive, and receptive; decay and apathy are the results of being closed off. As the O'Neills point out, the only foundation

for openness is a trust that is not a negative threat. "You won't do anything to hurt me" is an implicit threat. "I trust your commitment to your
own growth, to my growth, and to the growth of our relationship" states
a positive trust based not on prohibiting negatives but on the very
essence of love—the well-being of the other. There will be pain and
hurt. The episode at the beginning of this chapter illustrates well how we
can learn on the mental level but not on the emotional, gut level. The kind
of trust the O'Neills speak of is a trust that takes time to learn and often
is painful. But it is a trust based on positive affirmation rather than on
negative proscription.

The Ownership-Fidelity Bind

Implicit in the marriage customs of our culture is the idea of possession
or ownership of the mate. This is a logical outgrowth of the feudal concept of the female as chattel (property), just as land is a possession. The
concept has evolved into the belief that she belongs to him and he belongs
to her. The O'Neills point out that a simple change of prepositions can
make a big difference. He may belong *with* her but not *to* her; she may
belong *with* him but not *to* him.[2] But they are talking about belonging
with, not in terms of the couple front, but in terms of a mutual choice of
primary-bond partner.

The concept of ownership leads us into a security based on prohibition
rather than on positive commitment to the other's welfare. We learn
security from mate possession because from birth we have been taught
that possessions provide security. And it is only a small emotional step
from physical possession to emotional possession—from owning things to
owning people. We would be wise to remember that people are for loving
and things are for possessing. But many of us have been socialized to
believe that things are for loving and people are for possessing. The very
essence of love, as set forth by Fromm, Horney, and May, is the desire to
impart the self to the other, to give rather than to take.

Fidelity is a concept that has taken on an almost totally sexual connota-
tion. It is but a small step from the chastity belt to the legal emphasis on
infidelity as the prime abrogation of marital trust. In many cultures,

extramarital sex has constituted infidelity. However, when there is a consensual agreement about extramarital sex, it is not infidelity. Furthermore, and by far the most important point, infidelity refers to more than extramarital sex. The husband and wife who stopped any meaningful communication years ago are unfaithful. The partner who withdraws into a private mental chamber is unfaithful. Unwillingness to listen, to commit oneself, to explore, to relearn, to attempt to understand, to learn to fight fairly, to learn to express negative feelings constructively, to become self-aware and self-disclosing—these are all acts of infidelity. The physical definition of infidelity is one of the cruelest and most deceptive beliefs our culture embraces regarding marriage.

The Good Girl-Bad Girl Bind

Good girls are for marrying. Bad girls are for sexual fun. Everyone knows that! Males know it and have lived by it emotionally for generations. It is this belief that prevents many females from accepting their sexuality. They have learned their lessons well—good girls do not enjoy sex. If you enjoy it, there is something deviant about you. Your husband will not trust you. He will be suspicious and doubting. Much as he would enjoy having a frolicking good time in bed with his wife, he knows—because he has been thoroughly conditioned—that any wife who will do that is practically a harlot. Indeed, another name for this bind is the madonna–harlot syndrome—that phrase polarizes the ideas of good and bad in a more dramatic and poetic way. The madonna symbolizes sexual innocence, and the harlot is historically the fallen woman. (Of course, there are no fallen men—that old double standard again.)

The effects of the good girl-bad girl bind are devastating to many marriages. When sex as intimate fun and communication is lost, sex often becomes only a physiological release for the male and even less for the female. Orgasm for the female is of no importance. Soon the male experiences his mate as boring, nonstimulating, and passive. He experiences occasional impotence and worries about it more than he will admit. With a decrease in sexual interest (to protect himself) comes a general decrease in vitality, including diminished enthusiasm for the life and growth of his marriage. An affair may or may not be in the offing. Another man's wife or a pickup or a prostitute will not find him impotent! And another woman's husband may find his lost potency with the first man's wife. All four will have been victims of their guilt, their beliefs, and their inability to learn the truth about human sexuality.

The Love-Is-Limited Bind

Many people believe that love is like money—the more you spend the less you have. Each individual has only so much love to give. (If parents believed they had a finite amount of love to give to their children, each couple would have only one child.) Freud is partly responsible for this limited view of love, since his view of narcissism was based on the idea that self-love precluded love for others. It is fair to say that Freud was opposed to self-love because he believed this reduced the amount of love available for others.[3] But is love like that? Is love so limited? Americans are socialized to believe that love is like a dollar and that the entire dollar should be spent on the mate. Society says that you cannot love two people at once. But love is not finite or measurable. The individual's ability to love is limited only by such factors as time and energy.

The romantic tradition claims that love is not truly love unless it is intense, exhausting, and exclusive. I believe that love based on libido, eros, philos, and agape can exist in varying amounts for more than one person at a time. The primary-pair bond, if it is to be cultivated, nurtured, and enriched, requires a sizable investment of time, energy, and self. Thus, the question is not, "How much love is there to give?" but rather, "How much commitment and investment can one person bring to his love relationships?" (If I have seven children, I cannot possibly give each one as much individualized attention as I could give each of three children.) Love is both the feeling and the expression of that feeling. In a conjugal or marital relationship there grows over time a deep and solid bond of love that strengthens and enriches the partners as they pursue their daily lives, even when they are not experiencing amorous attraction.

This same point is of vital importance in learning to deal with anger and other negative emotions. "I know I love you. I have loved you beautifully and genuinely for eleven years. But right now I don't *feel* very loving. I am tired/worn out/preoccupied/angry at you." One's love for another person may take many forms and be expressed in many ways. When romanticizing Americans claim that it is possible to love only one person at a time, they are almost always referring to "falling in love"— to feelings of deep emotional abandon and desire for total fusion with the other. This romanticized love requires such a total self-investment that there is usually little time or energy left for any concurrent love. When the O'Neills speak about love relationships outside marriage, they are emphatically not referring to such a romanticized (and usually destructive and escapist) type of love. The following statement makes this point very clear:

Despite our tradition of limited love, it is entirely possible to love your marital partner with an intensely rewarding and continually growing love and at the same time to love another or others with a deep and abiding affection. And this extra dimension of love feeds back into the love between the partners.[4]

The Future-Security Bind

The final area of unlearning and relearning has to do with the human desire for guarantees regarding the future. There is something pervasive about man's quest for certainty, for absolute assurance about the future as well as the present. Think about the traditional wedding service and its binding words, the promise to love "until death do us part." How can a person of sound moral character promise to love someone even into the distant future? Is this not asking both to prostitute themselves by extracting a promise that they may or may not be able to keep? If the promise were to "work at this love" or "to commit oneself to the nurturance of this love," then I would have no quarrel. But a promise about one's future feeling of love seems to me to be something we may not be able to deliver. If our premise is accurate, as stated earlier, that we are the ones who kill love, marriage, and sex, then it is foolishness to expect these words of future promise to mean anything.

But, of course, we are really not practical people. When it comes to love we are motivated by a desire for reassurance. We want the security of knowing that we will feel the same about each other in ten or thirty years as we feel right now. We want to freeze the present moment so that it will last and endure forever, as if that were the only way we could experience the validation of the present. The basic dynamic is not love as much as the desire for security. We want to believe that we can count on this present feeling in all future circumstances. "Validate me and promise never to change." This is impossible. Further, the effort to keep the promise not to change would have a disastrous effect on growth and on life. The promise is self-defeating because it encourages behavior that fosters decay and apathy. And such a promise encourages marital partners to take each other for granted, although nobody likes to be taken for granted.

I do not deny the need for a deep emotional security. All of us would like to feel more secure than we do. But the absence of change does not provide security. If I ask another person not to change, I am creating a false security. In his search for ultimacy, man attempts to transform less than ultimate objects into ultimate objects. Not only is this the precondition of idolatry, it is in fact the making of the other person into some sort of god—the essence of idolatry. The net result is to dehumanize the other, for neither is allowed to be fallible or to grow. And am I fostering my own dependence on the other person? David's dilemma (at the beginning of this chapter) was his conditioned dependence on the promise of another human being. When the promise fails—when the person on whom I make such demands and from whom I try to draw an irrational amount of emotional security develops his self-awareness and humanity—then I experience a traumatizing loss of security. The only workable answer to the future-security bind is to diminish the demand for security obtained from others. Rather, we should each strive for authentic intrapsychic growth. Irrational dependence on external objects will not do for us what we have not been able to do for ourselves.

This is not to deny the value and validity of an authentic faith in God or in an eternal mind or spirit. It is to say that we must accept anxiety as part of our lives. If we believe that creation is good, then we can find strength in our innate abilities to cope with our anxieties and our problems and to live vigorously in the present. We can trust that when tomorrow becomes today, the same inner resources will enable us to endure and grow. There is a "wisdom of insecurity," as it were. Paul Tillich suggests, in *The Courage to Be*, that it is only as we learn to take our insecurity into ourselves—as a fact of our existence—that we can truly unlearn the crippling and self-destructive dependencies.[5]

Summary

This chapter considers some of the more powerful beliefs and practices we use in destroying love and killing marriage. One of these is lack of commitment to growth. A basic principle underlying the growth process is that mental acceptance of change is a necessary but not sufficient precondition of change. There must be a corresponding emotional growth.

The double standard, while honestly preferred and embraced by some, tends to dehumanize both males and females because it endorses different ethical-moral standards for the sexes. Once again it is the security payoff to the male that keeps the double standard alive. Until the male is able to part with the security he has experienced, there will be little real change and growth regardless of how much he mentally disapproves of the double standard.

The sex-role bind is akin to the double standard bind in that sex-role differences paved the way for two standards of sexual ethics. The solution to these binds is the recognition of a wide variety of needs and abilities by individuals of both sexes.

The couple bind is the subtle assumption that marriage requires both the fact and the appearance of togetherness, combined with a denial that friends of the opposite sex are necessary to meet basic needs that the mate can fill only partially. We are narrowed by our lack of exposure to friends of the opposite sex, but the couple can break out of this restrictiveness only by learning a new dimension of trust and commitment.

The ownership-fidelity bind is related to the couple front. Fidelity is defined as sexual ownership of the mate's body. The payoff of a restrictive definition of fidelity is an increased sense of security. As long as our inner sense of security is based on prohibition and ownership of the mate, rather than on positive commitment to the growth of the self, the mate, and the relationship, there will be no opportunity to learn a new sense of trust.

The good girl-bad girl bind is a dilemma for both males and females. The male has learned that "good" girls are preferred as mates while "bad" girls are preferred as sexual partners. This prevents the male from encouraging his mate to become sexually alive. The female has learned that she is not to be sexually aggressive. She is not to be antisexual, but she should not give the appearance of being overly interested in sex. This bind increases the distance between the sexes, further alienating and separating them from each other. It also perpetuates the old definitions of trust and ownership.

The love-is-limited bind restricts the ability to give as well as to receive love. As long as we believe that love is a limited commodity we are reluctant to seek out new friendships, to part with the couple front, and to reexamine the possessive aspect of the traditional concepts of fidelity and trust. One result is an increase in the expectation that the mate will satisfy all needs.

The future-security bind exacts the promise that the love of the partners for each other will not change. I question the right of any human being to make such a far-sweeping promise. The quest for security is again the prime motivator. We derive our security from a promise not to change rather than from a commitment to our mutual well-being as individuals.

Questions for Study

1. Referring to David's journal, point out the different types of binds that his statement reflects.

2. Is it ever true that not to grow may be a greater risk than to grow? Give examples.

3. In what specific ways has the double-standard bind and the sex-role bind affected your life?

4. Explain the thinking that underlies this statement: He may belong *with* her but not *to* her.

5. Among the students on your campus, is the good girl-bad girl bind prevalent?

6. React to this statement: "Love based on libido, eros, philos, and agape can exist in varying amounts for more than one person."

7. Is it unrealistic to promise to love someone forever? If so, how does that fact affect the love relationship and the institution of marriage?

Reading Suggestions

A Guide to Rational Living by Albert Ellis and Robert Harper. North Hollywood, Calif.: Wilshire, 1961. Presents a theory of rational thinking; includes a method for overcoming past influences and irrational beliefs.

Open Marriage by George O'Neill and Nena O'Neill. New York: M. Evans, 1972. Describes a new style of marriage; includes an analysis of the sex-role bind and the couple bind.

Premarital Sexual Standards in America by Ira Reiss. New York: Macmillan, 1960. An historical analysis of contemporary sexual standards, including the double standard.

The Future of Marriage by Jessie Bernard. New York: Bantam, 1972. An analysis of the past, present, and future of marriage; includes a thorough description of the sex-role bind.

3

FOCUS ON THE FUTURE: WHERE WE MAY CHOOSE TO BE

NINE
A
NEW WAY OF
BEGINNING:
TRIAL
MARRIAGE

186

**A New Way of Beginning:
Trial Marriage**

Marriage in Two Steps

Trial Marriage vs. Cohabitation

Does Marriage
License Sex?—or Children?

Advantages and
Disadvantages of Trial Marriage

The Trial: Where Are We Going?

Taking Premarital
Sex off Its Pedestal

Summary

Questions for Study

Reading Suggestions

Marriage in Two Steps

Joanne and Randy

I've started writing several times and have had to stop myself after several pages. It's been impossible for me to condense all my thoughts on "Why I'm happy we've lived together." Tonight I thought of a new approach—"Why I think we've lived together happily"—so I'll give that a go now.

There are several things vital to our relationship, which is now over a year old. Foremost is honesty. We are totally open and honest about what bothers or upsets us and so we avoid pent up emotions and resentment. We have very open lines of communication.

Randy and I have remained completely independent financially. We split rent and groceries down the middle. All purchases for our apartment have been made separately. This type of independence is very important to me. I would hate to ever feel tied to someone because of money.

Also, Randy and I respect and like each other and try to be considerate of each other's feelings. Our love developed after we were living together and is still growing. By living together we've avoided a lot of romantic crap and have really gotten to know each other. Randy put it concisely: "Living together eliminates illusions." We have carried on as individuals. We have separate as well as mutual friends. And we have many separate interests. After Randy and I had lived together for a year, a friend at work asked me if I had a boyfriend. It made me feel good. It's a very small community and she even knew Randy.

Through all this we have grown very close and are now planning our futures together. We think we'll make it.

I will outline the concept of trial marriage as advocated by anthropologist Margaret Mead, and then will discuss changes, alternatives, and deviations from her prototype.[1] Mead envisions two kinds of marriage: individual marriage and parental marriage. Individual marriage would "be a licensed union in which two individuals would be committed to each other as individuals for as long as they wished to remain together, but not as future parents. As the first step in marriage, it would not include having children."[2] Mead says that the obligation would be an ethical one, not an economic one. That is, if the relationship broke up neither spouse would be able or expected to claim support from the other. The legality of the relationship would be formalized in a "registration" of the union with the civil authorities. "Individual marriage . . . would be a serious commitment, entered into in public, validated and protected by law and, for some, by religion, in which each partner would have a deep and continuing concern for the happiness and well-being of the other."[3] If the individual marriage proved to be untenable and unfulfilling, the original contract allows either partner to terminate the relationship without stigma. In other words, divorce in the first step of marriage would be very easy and totally nonjudgmental.

The second step of marriage, termed "parental marriage" by Mead, must be preceded by individual marriage. "Every parental marriage, whether children were born into it or adopted, would necessarily have as background a good individual marriage. The fact of a previous marriage, individual or parental, would not alter this. Every parental marriage, at no matter what stage in life, would have to be preceded by an individual marriage."[4] Parental marriage would anticipate a lifelong relationship. Failing that, it would be terminated by a divorce, but a divorce more akin to a court decree than by individual choice as in individual marriage. (In other words, divorce in parental marriage would be a serious matter and would be subject to legal codes and procedures. This is not to say, however, that today's divorce procedures would dominate, for there is much in current divorce practice that is cruel, hypocritical, unjust, and punitive.)

If a couple decided to move from an individual marriage into a parental marriage they would obtain a license and, with or without formal ceremony, define the nature of their mutual commitment to each other. Because parental marriage involves broader responsibilities, commitments, and obligations, the decision for transition from individual marriage to parental marriage should be deliberately thought through, without haste or pressure, and unaffected by romantic overtones or unrealistic expectations. Herein lies the chief justification for marriage in two steps. The individual marriage provides a lengthy period in which the couple can learn new roles, gain marital identity and experience, and shed unrealistic expectations and idealizations.

According to Mead, everyone would benefit from such an arrangement: the couple themselves, the children *not* born to the individual marriage, the children who are born to the parental marriage, the society, and the members of the society who support the welfare programs, mental health programs, and correctional programs. Marriage in two steps also strikes at the heart of the abortion issue by answering "yes" to the question "Does not every child have the right to be wanted, loved, hence, invited into the life process?" The "yes" answer is found in the fact that a child is born only when its parents have already entered the second stage of marriage and have a reasonable basis for predicting a mature relationship with favorable prospects for happiness and stability.

In our society it is considered blasphemous, when discussing the coming of new life, to focus on what is best for the parents. Society seems to say that the unborn child should be considered above all else. I have no quarrel with those who say that the child should be considered above all else. I just point out that in considering the child above all else it may be that the greatest mercy we can show the unborn child (a zygote—containing only the potential for human life and personality) is to allow it not to be born. The entire issue of when life begins has never been settled, and it is likely to remain forever unsettled. Perhaps the most we can say is that there is a cellular birth, a physiological birth, a psychological birth, and a sociological birth. An academic or philosophical discussion of these approaches to birth is of little help in dealing with the emotional issues. The vitally important point is that when a child is born to parents who want the child, who have persevered through the adjustment process of individual marriage, and who have established a marital relationship based on mutuality of affection, concern, respect, and meeting of needs, the promise for the child's future is infinitely brighter. The *greatest gift* that can be given to a newborn is a home with a *father and mother who are reasonably secure and happy in their relationship with each other.*

The legal-ecclesiastical establishment may reject Mead's proposal totally. However, trial marriage is not really a debatable future option; it is a present reality, *except* for legal and ecclesiastical endorsement.

Trial Marriage vs. Cohabitation

Although it is unlikely that two-step marriage will become common in the near future, it is entirely probable that within several decades 5 to 20 percent of the population will have practiced it. However, trial marriage is not to be confused with cohabitation or casual living together arrangements. Eleanor D. Macklin has defined cohabitation as sharing "a bedroom and/or bed with someone of the opposite sex (to whom one was not married) for four or more nights a week for three or more consecutive months."[5]

Cohabitation differs from a trial relationship in several basic ways. First, cohabitation implies absolutely no commitment to the future. It is not an experience designed to reveal an answer to the question, "Should we get married?" Even though cohabitation may evolve into a trial marriage (or vice versa), it is not to be considered the same thing. Second, cohabitation is primarily a living arrangement, while a trial marriage is additionally an attempt to build a more enduring relationship. Thus, in a trial marriage the partners must come to terms with conflict and negative emotions, and they must develop in-depth communication skills. These things may happen during cohabitation but there is no urgency. Third, a cohabiting couple need have no commitment to each other. A trial couple does share at least a limited commitment to each other and to the relationship.

Contrary to Macklin, I believe that cohabitation may include weekend living together arrangements, occasional sharing of quarters, or a day-in, day-out sharing of bed and board. There are some relationships that, strictly speaking, are neither cohabitation nor trial marriages. I classify these as nonlegal marriages or extralegal unions. They include couples who choose to share their lives with each other but are opposed to the institution of marriage and its legalization, couples who choose on ideological grounds to live together but not to marry.[6]

Does Marriage
License Sex?—or Children?

We are continually faced with trends that lead to utopian answers as well as trends that cling to age-old traditions long after the symbolic meaning of the traditions has been lost. Is it not logical and reasonable, then, to seek to deal with changing times and traditions in the most responsible way possible? In a bygone day people were taught that marriage licensed sex. Many people (far too many, one suspects) married so that they could have sexual relations. To marry in order to have sex is a questionable motivation; we can only hope that young people have many better reasons for getting married.

Malinowski, in a cross-cultural study of marital customs, wrote: "Marriage cannot be defined as the licensing of sexual intercourse but rather the licensing of parenthood."' In Western tradition, however, marriage became the means for controlling the sexual desires of men and women. Coitus was acceptable only within marriage, and so a premium was placed on virginity. Sex became a reward for the patient male suitor, rather than an authentic expression of affection between two people. This helped strengthen the double standard of sexual behavior as well as the notion that proper and decent young ladies abide sex but do not enjoy it.

The trial marriage Margaret Mead has described is an attempt to solidify the marital–familial system within our society. Trial marriage fits with the belief that legal marriage is of primary importance as an institution because it creates a structure for the birth, nurturance, and socialization of children. Every known human society has had some interest in the mating activities of its young people. Society is not particularly concerned about individual happiness. But it is concerned about the role of the individual in transmitting the mores, customs, and traditions of the society. The state is really interested only in its own survival.

I believe that legal marriage can do far more than provide a structure for the socialization of the young. Legal marriage is, in fact, productive of stability and deep emotional security. Nevertheless, whether legal or extralegal, any primary bond requires a commitment based on faith and trust—a commitment to nourish and cultivate the relationship. We shall consider this relationship more fully in Chapter 11. For now, let it be said that trial marriage is not a shortcut to sexual access nor need it be an indiscriminate method for avoiding personal responsibility. On the contrary, in terms of responsibility to oneself, to one's mate, to one's unborn and born offspring, and to one's society, it would appear to be a far more responsible process for establishing permanent marriages and families than now exists. Trial marriage need not be rationalized on any theological presuppositions, and for this reason stands a better chance of widespread acceptance.

Advantages and Disadvantages of Trial Marriage

The advantages of a trial marriage can be described briefly: (1) Sex is deidolized as an area of human expression (this thought will be developed in greater detail later). (2) The responsibility for trying to find honest answers is expressed in the experience of conjugal living rather than in well-intended but often irresponsible promises about the future state of one's emotions. (3) Conception is delayed until a child is welcomed into a healthy relationship. We cannot ignore or deny that brief marriages that produce children are emotionally costly—to the children, to the parents, and to the society. (4) A long-term commitment is delayed until the partners have a reasonable storehouse of practical experience in meeting each other's needs and engaging in constructive handling of conflict—experience that could not be acquired in a traditional engagement period. (5) The partners have the opportunity for a dignified dissolution of the relationship without agonizing (and culturally transmitted) feelings of guilt and failure that are harmful to the self-concepts and self-worth feelings of the partners. (6) A trial marriage is an opportunity for in-depth personal growth based on the experience of a shared life style. This growth can occur even if the trial relationship should be dissolved. Many young people value this experience, even when the trial ends in separation.

Trial marriages also have disadvantages: (1) There is the constant danger that one or both partners will leave the relationship as soon as the first real conflict surfaces. That would deny both of them the opportunity to learn the skills of conflict resolution, negotiation, and compromise. There is also the danger of avoiding the experiences of pain and vulnerability. (2) One failure or successive failures in trial relationships can have very negative effects on the self-concept and feelings of self-worth. Separation counseling can help the partners achieve an honest assessment of the good and bad experiences within the relationship, and can help them arrive at a realistic evaluation of the total experience in terms of their emotional growth.

The following statement was written by a college senior who had kept a journal during the period of her trial marriage. At the time of the trial relationship she was twenty years old and her partner was twenty-two. Her statement is included here to give the reader a glimpse into a real trial relationship.

Vicki

We were to have been married in August, but the date was postponed indefinitely. I wasn't as sure as he of marriage, so since we both were to attend summer school, we rented a house together for two and a half months. Now, eight months later, I can look back through the journal I kept of those days and congratulate myself for having the courage to enter that trial marriage. Quickly, all the disillusionments of the early months of marriage set in—loss of romantic feelings, squabbling over everything, mutual feelings of being taken for granted, and sex becoming part of a daily routine. It was a highly emotional time for me, as I swung from great joy and tenderness to awful depression over what seemed such a failure—us. My predominating emotion was the sense of being trapped, of finality. One day in my journal I complained that I felt possessed, and longed for an "open-ended relationship. What I've got instead seems closed, and is pushing me down a narrowing funnel toward a wedding ring." Even on the "good" days when I thought maybe we could make it work, I called my feeling "resignation." I was trapped by love and a "duty" to return that love. Now I can see that my trap was partially self-made by my own emotional needs and insecurities.

Our house shook with conflict—over how to fry bologna, when to feed the dog, the dishes, sex—anything! Much of the conflict stemmed from the final uncovering of our true attitudes toward ourselves, each other, and life in general—but the fights were usually about the little surface annoyances. Communicating the real gripes was very difficult. Did I love him intellectually as well as emotionally? Why did I resent him so much —was he too dependent on me? At the time, I was too involved to sort out all the problems; I only felt the disappointments. We had friends, a newlywed couple, who were experiencing the same things. I'm so glad that mine was only a trial marriage because if I had been chained by a ring and a license, I don't know how I could have handled the intense disillusionment, the unavoidable conviction that we had made a mistake.

At the end, he left town as planned, and two months later I found strength to break our engagement. Now I see that not only were we not right for each other, but also that it was not the right season of my life for the responsibility of marriage—I still have much growing to do before I will be ready. As far as the ethical question of what we did, I do not see how we could have chosen a more moral action. We accepted our responsibility to ourselves, our possible children, and to society by trying to ascertain whether we could build a fruitful marriage before we made a final commitment. If we had married instead, and if it had lasted, I think we would both be very unhappy right now. Even my parents, who were understandably upset at first, now agree with me and share my happiness at having avoided a costly mistake.

My trial marriage was a time of dreaming, planning, fighting, and crying —a very painful time; but I know that I will never marry anyone until we have seriously tried our marriage on for size first.

The Trial: Where Are We Going?

In earlier eras the betrothal became the accepted pattern, and in more recent times the engagement. Similarly, trial marriage will probably gain definition and structural form through an evolving process, with innovations along the way, until a cultural pattern is established. What seems to be evolving is an alternative to traditional marriage based on a two-step

marital commitment. In the trial marriage, the first step is a trial relationship unburdened with legal, financial, or child-related matters. The
second step is akin to traditional marital definitions, responsibilities, and
patterns. If the legal-ecclesiastical establishments do not endorse this
change in marital patterns, or at least seek to deal with it in an honest,
forthright manner, the trend will undoubtedly continue without them.
Marriage in two steps will become an accepted alternative to marriage in
one step despite the societal-cultural traditions. This is not to say that a
majority will be following this pattern within two or three generations.
The movement is a college-population phenomenon and it may be that
even after several decades only 10 to 30 percent of the population will
have participated in a two-step marriage.

I am not advocating a permissive and irresponsible sexual expression.
Rather I am suggesting that the most beneficial trial marriage would be
based on this rationale: "We love each other, we have serious intentions
and wonderful dreams; we have a bond of affection and a commitment of
ourselves. We will live together, faithful to each other's humanness, sharing ourselves—our resources, our minds, our bodies, our beings. We will
face conflict and differences, and we will use these as instruments for
growth and fulfillment. If, after we have lived this way for a while, we no
longer feel we can make it together, we will part. Hopefully, we will know
when to seek the help of a friend or counselor as we evaluate our feelings
about our relationship. We may not part—we may simply remain this
way for a longer duration. We may, however, conclude that we wish to
share our lives in a growth-producing commitment and provide children
with the love we experience in our own relationship. Whatever our decision, we will be authentic and responsible to ourselves, to each other, and
to the offspring we choose to have or not to have."

Clare and Ron

*I have wanted to speak with you before, but now my situation is some-
what resolved. I am twenty years old (almost twenty-one) and was engaged to be married for one year. I say "was" because our relationship
ended almost a month ago. Ron and I met during my freshman year of
college, but started dating at the beginning of my sophomore year. By*

April of that year we were engaged. Last summer he moved to my city and was staying at my parents home. After one week, we decided to move out and live together. My father took it very hard—he didn't think it was proper. But we loved each other and genuinely wanted to see what trial marriage would be like.

The first week or so, it was exciting to have our own place to come home to. We both worked full time, so we didn't see each other during the days except for weekends. At dinner time, I would cook, and we'd sit down and eat and talk of our day's activities. At night we often went out, and occasionally friends would visit us. Actually, it was a very good living arrangement. We weren't ashamed because we loved each other and even after the initial excitement wore off, it was still a healthy living situation. Ron and I shared in all the household activities, including doing the dishes, the wash, taking out the garbage, shopping for groceries, and paying the rent. In the two months we lived together I learned so much. It wasn't at all like a dating relationship, or even like seeing each other every day at college, or even like sleeping over at one's boyfriend's room. It does something psychologically. We knew we had nowhere else to go, it was our home, together. All the pretenses are shed. The good grooming and the always "kept" appearances fade away. I think we became much more real, in-depth people to each other. We fought more than before, but conflict was handled in a healthy way. We just had more occasions for genuine disagreements. But we also became more intense, more emotional, and more vulnerable. At times it was frightening.

When the school year began we lived in different dorms, and the fighting became the overriding focus of our relationship. We continued to grow, but we grew apart. It is ended now, but I have no regrets about the past. I know I learned so much from such an intense relationship. I feel I am a fuller person for it.

Where are trial relationships and cohabitation going? Where are Clare and Ron now? Our society seems to be entering a stage in which there is increasing honesty about human intimacy. There appears to be little or no change in the desire of young people for meaningful primary relationships, but does appear to be a significant change in what they are willing to settle for in a relationship. Sex, virginity, and sexual experience are of less importance to today's young people than to those who are now in their forties, fifties, and beyond. Today many young adults believe that the primary evil is not sex before marriage but inauthenticity—superficiality, pretense, and hypocrisy. Increasing numbers of today's young people want dynamic marriages, healthy interaction, and a monogamous life style within which they can commit themselves to their own growth, the growth of their mates, and to the growth of the relationships.

Taking Premarital
Sex off Its Pedestal

There are those who, because of their own beliefs and upbringing, will condemn trial marriage in any form. These same people will be equally adamant in their opposition to any premarital sexual relationships.

I believe that sexual relationships prior to marriage can be extremely harmful or beneficial. In an age and in a society that has made sex into the greatest idol of all time, it seems to me that the sooner sex is demythologized the better. If sex is taken out of the back seat of the car or out of the dorm room and is placed in the context of two people living together and sharing the facilities of a twenty-four-hour, day-in, day-out living arrangement, then sex is permitted to take its rightful place in the totality of the interpersonal relationship.

The worn-out phrase "But you wouldn't buy a pair of shoes without trying them on!" is as inept and misleading as the moralistic "sex is dirty" attitude. Often "the shoe is tried on" in a context of romantic unreality, and that leads the couple into a situation where disillusionment after marriage is far more likely than it would have been without premarital sex.

Bill and Jean

Bill is twenty-three years old. He has never been married but was involved in a trial marriage that ended after four months.

"I don't understand it," Bill said to the therapist. "I thought everything would be great. Jean and I went together for about a year and we really hit it off. We did all kinds of things together. I could hardly stand to be away from her and I looked forward to every time we could see each other. Of course, we got close and we had a great time sexually. At first she was reserved but slowly she began to open up and relax. I swear, everything was wonderful. I didn't even think about anyone else—she was it. Even when I was away from her I couldn't imagine myself wanting sex with anyone else. I wanted to get married but . . . well, she wanted to try living together for a while. I kept fighting it by saying I didn't see what there was to gain—that we were like old married people anyway. She really surprised me—wanting a trial marriage kind of thing. Well, anyhow, I agreed and we got an apartment. For several weeks things were fine—but not for long. I don't get it yet—all I know is when we started living together everything was spoiled. Boy, next time I won't try any of that trial stuff—it doomed us. We started fighting—really sort of picking at each other, blaming each other for little things, getting on each other's nerves. She claimed I was closed minded—that I was old-fashioned in the way I wanted to be the protector and the head of the house—you know, like I should let her make the decisions. I suppose I could have taken some of the changes but not the sex one. Boy—how could such a wonderful thing become so dull so fast? All of a sudden it was—like—well, like warmed-over coffee. Before it was exciting and full of challenge—and I really could hardly wait to give myself to her—and man, I mean 'give' because it never was just a physical thing with us. . . . But, it all went! Here we were living together and what should be the greatest thing became the worst."

Bill, hopefully, will one day welcome another trial, but right now he's doing the best thing possible—starting to take a long look at the relationship with Jean. He does not realize now that the trial marriage saved both of them from the worse fate of entering marriage thinking everything would be just as it was before marriage. In the trial, many things presented themselves as problems to Bill and Jean. However, nothing seemed to bother Bill quite as much as the sexual comedown. There is much that Bill and Jean could have learned. Nevertheless, Bill and Jean, since they decided that they couldn't make it together, did themselves, their unconceived children, and perhaps their future mates and their future children, a real favor in entering a trial relationship.

But did sex before marriage hurt Bill and Jean? Yes, it did. Not the sex they had within their trial, but the sex they had before their trial—the sex that was wrapped in moondust. When sex is part of a highly romanticized relationship, there is a dangerous tendency for the partners to pretend to please and enjoy, to impress and score points. This is a form of dishonesty that is destructive if it continues. But it is not likely to continue when sex is part of daily, routine conjugal living. This was what led Bill to ask, "How could such a wonderful thing become so dull so fast?" There is a world of difference between the sexual experience of a trial relationship and the sexual experience of the infatuation between two people who are not living together. Each individual has the right to choose both or neither. But we cannot honestly say that there is no difference between the two.

A last question remains: What about sexual exclusivity in a trial relationship? For those who define their relationship as sexually exclusive there is no problem. But what about sexual permissiveness for those who do not define their relationship as sexually exclusive? There must be mutual agreement about sexual exclusivity or permissiveness in a relationship. A meaningful, intense relationship, characterized by mutuality in total commitment to the well-being of each other, is not likely to be strengthened or enhanced by sexual relations beyond the relationship during the early, intense phase. On the contrary, such relations may dilute and undermine the oneness and the integrity of the relationship. A less intense relationship could well be enhanced by sexual relationships beyond the dyad. This is not a question of what is good or bad, right or wrong, moral or immoral. It is entirely a matter of responsibility to oneself and to the other. Some may protest that, ideally, the relationship should not need such a protective definition. Nevertheless, our society seems to persist in socializing people who are not secure enough to cope with the stress of extramarital sex, especially during the initial, intense phase of a relationship.

Summary

This chapter has emphasized the advantages and disadvantages of trial marriage. Using Margaret Mead's concept as a prototype, I have suggested that any trial relationship must fit the needs and situation of the couple. People do not adapt to a specific brand of trial marriage but rather trial marriage must be adapted to the couple. Distinctions between trial relationships and casual cohabitation include: commitment to the future and to discovering if the relationship has a reasonable chance of success; concentration on the working through of conflict; and a concern about the goals and expectations the mates have for each other. Cohabitation need not involve any commitment beyond the present. Another type of relationship, which technically is neither a trial marriage nor cohabitation, is the extralegal union that will always remain extralegal because the partners are opposed to legal marriage.

Trial marriage encourages premarital sex and discourages parenthood during the trial period. This is in line with Malinowski's famous dictum that marriage is not for the licensing of sexual intercourse but rather for the licensing of parenthood. I believe that trial relationships may help decrease the percentage of marriages that end in divorce. Legal marriage is postponed until the couple are reasonably secure in their relationship, at least secure enough to welcome a child into the union, if children are desired.

Specific advantages of trial relationships include: the deidolization of sex; the straightforward approach to the question of how well suited the partners are to each other and to the dyadic relationship; the postponement of conception until the relationship is reasonably sound; the withholding of long-term commitment until the wisdom gained in daily living enables the couple to understand their expectations of each other; the opportunity to learn constructive methods of facing and resolving conflict; the opportunity for dissolution of the relationship without guilt or a sense of failure; the opportunity to grow through the experience of a shared life style; and the opportunity to begin the second step of marriage with reasonable assurance that a sound foundation has been established. The chief disadvantages include: the possibility that the partners will abandon the relationship at the first signs of trouble, thus failing to come to terms with the conflict; the possibility that one or both partners will abandon the relationship when they are feeling pain and hurt, thus preventing themselves from experiencing their vulnerability to each other; and the danger that successive failures in trial relationships will contribute to increased feelings of worthlessness.

Trial relationships are not acceptable to some because they include pre-marital sex. I believe that premarital sex, within a trial relationship, can increase the chance for marital joy and stability. It is my view that far too many young people enter marriage without sufficient understanding of what they are doing. Many young people have fantastic expectations of marriage and romanticized notions about what love is able to do. And many of these same people believe they need no preparation for marriage except love and good intentions. Trial marriage may be the most effective marriage preparation because it allows each couple to learn by experience without the responsibilities of children and a legal commitment.

Questions for Study

1. Do you think Mead's system of individual and parental marriages will ever be practiced by most people? Why or why not?

2. Have you known couples who were living together? Do you see differences between their relationships and the relationships the author describes?

3. Referring to Vicki's journal, evaluate her trial marriage on the basis of the advantages and disadvantages of trial marriage that are presented in this chapter.

4. React to this statement: "The primary sin is not sex before marriage but inauthenticity, superficiality, pretense, and hypocrisy."

5. "I believe that sexual relationships prior to marriage can be extremely harmful or beneficial." Use the case studies from this chapter and other examples that you know of to illustrate this statement.

Reading Suggestions

The Family in Search of a Future edited by Herbert Otto. New York: Meredith, 1970. An examination of life styles of the future, including Mead's proposal for marriage in two steps, cluster marriage, and permissive monogamy.

Becoming Partners by Carl Rogers. New York: Dell, 1972. A description of the "new" marriages, including cohabitation.

Intimate Lifestyles edited by Joann Delora and Jack Delora. Pacific Palisades, Calif.: Goodyear, 1972. Readings on the various emerging life styles, including cohabitation.

"Trial Marriage: Harnessing the Trend Constructively" by Miriam E. Berger. *The Family Coordinator* 20 (January 1971): 38–43. The evolution, advantages, and difficulties of trial marriage.

"Living Together: An Alternative to Marriage" by Ludith L. Lyness, Milton E. Lipetz, and Keith E. Davis. *Journal of Marriage and the Family* 34, 2 (May 1972): 305–311. A research article about the problems and satisfactions of "living-together" couples vs. "going-together" couples.

TEN
RIGOR MORPHIS: ALTERNATIVES AND OPTIONS

206

Rigor Morphis:
Alternatives and Options

Emerging
Nontraditional Mating Patterns

Monogamy with
Extramarital Permissiveness

Progressive Monogamy

Group Marriage

Communal Families

Cluster Marriage

Mate-Swapping

Comarital Union

Meaning, Value, and the
Ethics of Extramarital Sex

Summary

Questions for Study

Reading Suggestions

Emerging
Nontraditional Mating Patterns

Louise and Jamie

I would say it all started in our fifth year of marriage. It was the second marriage for both of us and believe me, we both wanted it to work. We had both been single awhile since our first marriages ended and we both were reasonably sure that we could make this marriage work. Things were fine for awhile. We were alive and bursting with talk. Sex was great. Then, sort of suddenly, I had the desire to flirt and look around. I had one or two quickies but they were disappointing, to say the least. It was then I made up my mind that I was going to come clean and tell Jamie what I was feeling. I felt very strongly that deceit was wrong for us—and yet I wanted both of us to have an openness in outside relationships.

Jamie about flipped. It turned out that he too, had had some secret relationships, but he was afraid to tell me about them. He agreed with me that openness was better and so we agreed to try it that way. We would tell each other what we were doing and reassure each other if we needed it. We were determined to avoid the destructiveness of secrecy and cover-up. Jamie had trouble every time I told him of any attraction I had. He would get angry, as if he was terribly jealous and threatened—and he still was saying nothing to me about his affairs. Then one day he told me he was ashamed of himself because he was still afraid of telling me about his feelings and activities. He said he had gotten so used to deceptiveness and cheating as a way of life that it was hard for him to be honest.

Well, things did get better. We wanted to find another couple that we could be intimate with, but no luck. That's hard to do. So we each went our own way, being honest but not flaunting our activities in each other's faces. The danger was that we could get too emotionally involved or else get involved with others who really weren't good partners because they had too many problems of their own at the time. I blew my stack one day because Jamie was not able to see the danger of his being with a gal whose marriage was washing out from under her.

The truth is, I enjoy the companionship and the sexual loving but I still detest the fact that we are each with separate interests. I still want another couple—maybe even a group marriage—but at least comarital sex where we can have friendship among the four of us. That way there would be openness and togetherness—we could grow together. I still have the feeling that separate affair-type relationships are destructive, even if they are out in the open, simply because they take us in different directions. There's nothing really to share! We just seem to stand still. I don't like that.

Many people say the traditional monogamous marriage has rigidified into unworkable expectations and roles. Thus, I have coined the term *rigor* (a state of rigidity in living tissues or organs that prevents response to stimuli) *morphis* (from *morphic*, pertaining to form) to refer to structural rigidity within the marital relationship.

Many of those who find the marital relationship and its legal and ecclesiastical traditions in a state of rigor morphis are seeking viable alternatives. This rigidity is a reality for many, and they have chosen to cope with it by experimenting with new life styles and mating patterns. In this and the next two chapters we consider various ways of dealing with rigor morphis.

Louise and Jamie have experienced affairs, then consensual sex in which they granted sexual permissiveness to each other. Louise was open to the possibility of a group marriage, but she confided that her real preference was for a comarital relationship. This is a form of "swinging" that includes psychic friendship and intimacy.

Before we look more closely at these options, a word of caution is called for. Seidenberg has suggested that truly distressed people will find very little joy or fulfillment in the nontraditional arrangements, such as trial marriages, affairs, swinging, switching, and group marriages. He maintains that you cannot deal with long-term personality problems by using a new panacea.[1] I tend to agree with him. The O'Neills are very careful to point out that the most important goal of the open marriage is the growth of the primary-pair relationship, and that all outside activity is carried on in this context. In my private marriage counseling practice I have witnessed many couples who wanted to use an open marriage as a means of patching up their differences. My experience with these couples is that it rarely works. The primary relationship needs remedial attention, or one or both partners need private counseling or psychotherapy.

Monogamy with Extramarital Permissiveness

What is viewed by one culture or era as new often is, in reality, quite old. Thus, many "emerging" marital patterns are simply reemerging. The first option, monogamy with extramarital permissiveness (or permissive monogamy), is a cultural reality even without legal sanction. George P. Murdock has estimated that only 5 percent of the societies on the face of the earth—and the United States is part of that 5 percent—make no legal provision for sexual intercourse outside of marriage.[2] As noted in Chapter 1, the ancient Hebrews disapproved of adultery, yet there was concubinage and harlotry. To the Hebrews, adultery was sinful not so much because of sexual betrayal but because it involved taking something from another person. For example, Canaanite women who were the bounty of war were acceptable sexual partners for married Hebrew men. David's sin with Bathsheba was his taking of what rightfully belonged to another. Indeed, David solved that dilemma by military manipulation.[3] Further, the Hebrew patriarchs Abraham and Jacob had offspring by their wives' maids.[4]

Edward Hobbs has pointed out two traditions of marriage—marital permanence and **sexual exclusiveness.** The American way is to destroy marital permanence whenever the principle of sexual exclusivity is broken. Various states have laws that permit divorce only on the grounds of adultery. Hobbs complains that we destroy the nest in order to maintain the code of sexual exclusivity, thus undermining the stability of the family structure as the pivotal security source for the maturation and socializa-

---

sexual exclusiveness the practice of confining one's sexual activity to one and only one mate, as opposed to sexual permissiveness which allows one to have sexual liaisons with other partners as one chooses.

tion of the young. For this reason, Hobbs suggests that our values are backward—that instead we ought to preserve the marital union and permit sexual relationships outside the union. In effect, this arrangement would amount to a utilitarian marriage with sexual freedom for both partners. *"Thus, we are in the process of abandoning the permanence of marriage, while maintaining* (in law and in principle, even if less in reality than ever before) *its sexual exclusiveness.*[5] Indeed, this alternative is already very popular in the United States. Basically, it is one answer to the question, "Can marriage be a vital, loving, interpersonal relationship and still be sexually permissive?" For many, it cannot be both. Hence, rather than stand on sexual exclusiveness at the expense of marital and familial breakup, the stand is taken on familial unity at the expense of sexual permissiveness.

Hobbs' stand in favor of familial stability over sexual exclusivity seems to make sense in view of what is known today about child development and the importance of security and love needs. But we must also ask about the effect of sexual permissiveness on the solidarity and emotional health of the marriage. People will point to personal experience and come up with both answers. Some will say that "sexual permissiveness has little harmful effect; it is growth-producing." Others will say "it has a very negative effect; it is destructive to mutual trust." Any workable answer must hinge on one's recognition that there are two basic types of "permissive monogamy."

The first type, which I call "utilitarian," describes the couple that chooses to remain together despite the fact that much of their positive emotionality has been lost. As Cuber and Haroff point out, these people may once have had a very vital relationship but now it is devitalized.[6] Under these circumstances, each partner decides individually whether or not to engage in intimate relationships (both psychic and sexual) with others. Such marital partners have given up the possibility of building mutual love but still cooperate in the working partnership of maintaining a home.

A second type of permissive monogamy has been receiving a great deal of attention in conjunction with the concept of open marriage, as described by Nena and George O'Neill in their book of the same name. The O'Neills point out that the important hallmark of open marriage is not sexual permissiveness but the commitment of the couple to maintain a mutually satisfying growth relationship. Partners in an open marriage seek vitality and dynamic understanding. Thus, the emphasis is taken away from the societally prescribed, role-oriented marriage contract and placed instead on an open contract created by those living under the contract. In order to achieve a nonpossessive, nonjealous, nonmanipulative, and nonintrusive relationship with each other, such traditional words as trust and fidelity are given new meaning. Trust, as commonly used, can be a negative dare ("Just try to be unfaithful!") or a threat ("I'll never forgive you if you betray my trust"). There is a more open trust that can have more positive effects. If the partners trust each other to be open and honest in their total relationship with one another, they can give each other the freedom to be a human being instead of a role performer and an expectation meeter. In such a relationship the traditional vow of fidelity is out of place, because it is demanded as part of a closed, non-freedom-giving contract. Infidelity would equal mistrust or broken trust. Ironically, the expectation for sexual fidelity to one's partner, based on trust as a threat, may destroy the very relationship it was intended to protect. Recognizing this, proponents of open marriage consider intimate friendship with opposite-sexed friends outside the marriage a permissible norm. Intimate friendship may include sexual and psychic intimacy, or it may involve only psychic intimacy. Whether or not partners in an open marriage actually become involved in intimate friendships is up to each couple. The important point is that the *freedom* and the *right* to do so are *inherent* to the open marriage and are not considered to be an abrogation of trust or fidelity to one's mate.[7]

Progressive Monogamy

Another alternative to marital rigor morphis is called "progressive monogamy," "serial monogamy," or "monogamous polygamy." Here we have the very eventuality that Hobbs warns against. In principle, there is sexual exclusivity to one's *present* mate, but the marriage is severed in favor of a more promising one at any time. Naturally the family unit suffers. The children may have a father and several stepfathers, a mother and several stepmothers. In practice, however, many of these relationships do not begin until the youngest child has left home and the nest is empty.

Progressive monogamy is a fact of life today. Even more, it is a *legal* fact and a culturally approved fact, even though many disapprove of it and condemn it. The chief negative effect on the individual who marries and divorces several times seems to occur toward the later years of the life cycle. A backward glance may lead to feelings of remorse, dread, emptiness, loneliness, and despair as people fail to see meaning, purpose, richness, and depth in their past. Progressive monogamy may provide the basis for many intrinsic marriages, each with its own value. Nevertheless, the extrinsic value that can come from the total configuration allowed by a sustained relationship is often lacking. The inability to sustain a meaningful one-to-one relationship over a long period of time may be totally unimportant to many people until they enter the later stages of the life cycle. The study of aging (gerontology) may provide us with insight into the relationship between value-filled permanent liaisons and the self-concept in one's later years.

Howard

Howard retired a little over six years ago. He was married four times. He got married for the first time at the age of 20, and the marriage lasted seven years, ending in divorce. Howard had three children in his first marriage. His second marriage was at age 29 and it lasted for two years, ending in the death of his wife in an auto accident. His third marriage, at the age of 32, produced two children and lasted for eighteen years. This marriage ended in divorce due to what his wife called "cruel and premeditated adultery." Howard's last marriage took place when he was 55 and lasted until a little after Howard retired; his wife and he agreed that the relationship had run its course after twelve years. Howard is now talking to a counselor:

"I'm having trouble understanding myself—or life—or something . . . I go from feelings of joy and happiness to states of despair and depression. Seems like everywhere I go I'm getting some kind of message that life has passed me by. I don't know . . . it's just . . . nothing adds up. Here I am, retired, some money—enough to live without too many restrictions—and all I can think of is how I messed everything up. Oh,

not really messed *everything up but unable to build anything permanent. My kids, well—I'm close to one daughter and occasionally I see one of my sons: The other three I haven't the foggiest! And . . . and that isn't right! Been married four times—big deal! What's it all mean now? Adds up to nothin'. I get a little sex every now and then—but even that's a lot of nothin'—no one really cares—no feelin'—just ass, that's all it is. I think life's a dirty deal—all that talk about retirement being the best time of life—let me tell you, it stinks . . . I keep looking back, thinking about Jean—she's the one who got it in that accident. Well, I keep thinking—if only Jean had lived—she and I could have made it together. Then, the more I think about it, the more sure I am that it wouldn't have mattered if she had lived—it still would have ended in failure. (long pause) . . . I had fun with all of my wives for a while . . . then, well, you know I just couldn't stand them any longer. Honest to God, the other day I saw a man about my age and I envied him—there was his wife and I guess his son and a couple of grandchildren. . . . He seemed contented—you know—maybe not overwhelmingly happy, but contented—like his life had added up to something—like it counted. Then all of a sudden I had this feeling in my stomach—sort of an ache, and then I felt nauseated— like I was vomiting part of myself up."*

It is interesting that Howard did not sense unhappiness or self-disgust until later in his life. It would be a fair assumption that there were many good things about each marriage and that each relationship had a lot of intrinsic meaning. The void which has come into Howard's later life is not so much the void due to the loss of a beloved person but rather the void of realizing he has been unable to create or to preserve a configuration of lasting value to him. No meaningful thread tied all the separate relationships together into a meaningful whole. Even Howard's five children lacked a place in the overall picture. While there is no doubt that much of Howard's problem has been in Howard himself for many years, he was able to defend against the emptiness until his later years. No longer able to do so, he views life in a cynical way.

Group Marriage

A third alternative has been known traditionally as "group marriage," implying a communal living arrangement. However, not all communal living arrangements imply group marriage. An increasing amount of research is being done on group marriage. The following statements come from Larry and Joan Constantine, who are among those who have contributed to this research:

As researchers studying multilateral marriage (often called group marriage) we find ourselves in contact with developments at the very edge of marriage and family relations. Multilateral marriage is an essentially egalitarian marriage relationship in which three or more individuals (in any distribution by sex) function as a family unit, sharing in a community of sexual and interpersonal intimacy. We feel that the multilateral marriages we have studied over the past year, and related phenomena with which we have had contact, are definite precursors of a significant new social process. . . . [M]ultilateral marriage, though a promising growth-oriented form of marriage, is itself a structure limited to a relative few.[8]

Benefits of group marriage may include greater latitude in individual growth and self-actualization, variety in sexual relationships and patterns, reduced living expenses and correspondingly less tension and anxiety over financial problems, several parent figures for children, and in-depth interpersonal sharing. Disadvantages may include jealousy, possessiveness, disagreement about forced choice vs. free choice in sexual matters, unequal distribution of work and financial responsibility, differing beliefs about socialization and parenting of the children, and the handling of conflict. There are also the ongoing problems of societal pressure, community relations, and economic survival.

Historically, there has been distinction between group marriage and polygamy. *Polygamy* is a general term that takes two forms: *polyandry* in which one wife has two or more husbands, or *polygyny* in which one husband has two or more wives. Group marriage, on the other hand, is usually considered a combination of both forms of polygamy. Polyandrous unions have been more common in hunting and fishing subsistence economies. The several husbands are home at different times. Usually, but not always, the polyandrous society desires a low birth rate because of the scarcity of items necessary for survival. Thus, a wife has sexual relations with several husbands but the biological facts limit her childbearing to only once every nine months. Polygynous unions have been more frequent in agriculturally based economies in which a higher birth rate is desirable. Polygyny, while often considered the norm of the culture, is usually an economic status symbol since few of the males can actually afford more than one wife. Economically successful males are expected to take more than one wife.

Thus, a group consisting of three people would formerly have taken one form of polygamy but now would probably be a multilateral marriage. Because polygamy used to come about out of economic necessity, and because previous economic limitations no longer apply in our culture, it is probably safe to say that people are getting married today for less immediate reasons—to satisfy needs higher in Maslow's hierarchy, the psychic needs. Polygamous unions require harmony, not psychic intimacy. Today's multilateral marriages seek psychic intimacy in addition to harmony and economic benefits. Further study of multilateral marriage is needed, especially to discover the minimum, maximum, and ideal sizes of the group. Additionally, very little is known about the longevity and durability of such unions.

Communal Families

Communal families are considered a fourth alternative because they may or may not include group marriage. The historical Oneida Community, under the charismatic influence of John Humphrey Noyes, is a prime example of communal living which was also group marriage. The kibbutzim (communal farms) of Israel are not thought of as group marriages, but they are communal families. The settlement at New Harmony, Indiana, during both the Rappite and the Owenite periods, was communal in its life style, yet it did not include group marriage.

Utopian experiments, including the early Communist familial experiment in the USSR (1918–1936) have not fared well over time. The Oneida Community endured for thirty-four years (1846–1880). The kibbutzim would appear, from the perspective of history, to be the most successful communal enterprise. "The history of the Kibbutzim dates back to the 1880s when a group of Russian Jews established the first agricultural collectives in what, at that time, was Palestine."[9] Leslie says that by 1936 there were 47 kibbutzim in Palestine, and by 1948 when the state of Israel came into being there were 149. In 1954 the number reached 227.[10] The test of time is one, but only one test. The kibbutzim have been constantly changing and evolving, and it seems, at this writing, that they will endure in one form or another for some time to come.

Communal experiments have been regarded as utopian because they usually seek, in one way or another, to cope with the world by withdrawing from society. Thus, although they may differ in form, they usually have in common a disaffection with the traditional patterns and mores of the society. There is either a feeling of societal disillusionment or rebellion against traditional authority. There is sometimes a religious assumption that becomes the motivating factor in the communal establishment; other communal societies have been based on political presuppositions.

Common problems facing communal societies include child care and nurturance, educational provisions, economic subsistence, sexual privileges and mores, internal discipline and government, external relations with the community, and the ordinary problems of day-to-day interpersonal relationships.

In the United States there has been a notable growth in communal living establishments, and many include a variation on the theme of group marriage. The prospects for the successful endurance of these societies appear to be slim. What is probably happening, and will continue to happen, is that people who are dissatisfied or disillusioned, with traditional marital patterns or with the American society, will continue to form new unions and living patterns. Some of these will endure. Those that do will probably have fairly strong organizational structures and procedures. The less attention to structure, discipline, procedure, and continuing governing patterns, the greater the stress placed on the individuals. Nonselective membership and the lack of internal control will likely combine to end many such experimental arrangements.

A review of earlier experiments leads one to be extremely cautious about high-sounding predictions. Small group marriages of the multilateral type will probably become the favored organizational pattern for those who seek more satisfying sexual expression. These smaller multilateral marriages will probably require constant turn-over and adaptation if they are to survive. If problems relating to child care, sexual expression, jealousy, interpersonal rivalry and competition, and group discipline can be handled in imaginative and creative ways, the possibility for success in particular instances will be enhanced.

A survey of current and historical communal experiments reveals six basic factors that seem to indicate the likelihood of success or failure, depending on their presence or absence in the group. These are: (1) charismatic leadership, (2) strong internal organizational structure, (3) subsistence beyond the land—that is, some enterprise that produces an abundance of a product that can be used in barter, (4) a religious, political, or philosophical commitment—any idea, vision, or dream to which the communards commit themselves, (5) a careful selection of members, and (6) satisfactory group communication, including self-criticism and open handling of conflict and anger.

A careful study of the Oneida Community founded by John Humphrey Noyes reveals five of these conditions. The sixth, strong internal organization, was present but flawed. Noyes failed to provide a mechanism for succession to leadership. This omission became a key factor in the community's demise.

If we look at past marital arrangements and the dynamics that motivate people to consider such living arrangements, we see the need for caution in predicting the future of such arrangements. I would hazard the guess that at most 2 or 3 percent of the population may eventually be attracted to such marital and familial structures and that group and communal arrangements are not really options for the overwhelming majority. The people who have the highest degree of personal maturity and the highest degree of self-actualizing ability seem to be the ones who, if they were ideologically committed to the concepts of group marriage or communal living, could contribute significantly to their success. Paradoxically, however, these people appear to be the least interested.

Cluster Marriage

A fifth variation in family structure is known as cluster marriage. Margaret Mead has described this pattern as a cluster of families, each of which retains its identity within the cluster; there is no common occupational or economic base. According to Mead,

There would be in each cluster some families, some childless married couples, older and younger, some individuals not yet married, some working or studying and some retired, some with strength for energetic play and talk with children and some very fragile persons whom even children could help care for. . . . Some things would be owned personally; other necessary resources would be owned and used within the larger group. . . . Nor should families and individuals make long-term commitments to membership. It is necessary, I think, for people to keep the sense that they are free to change and move.[11]

The cluster family pattern is designed to help overcome the isolation and alienation experienced by many nuclear families now that the extended family of prior generations no longer is typical, if indeed it ever was. Feelings of aloneness, isolation, and alienation motivate people toward structural changes that may help to overcome these barriers and provide an enriched style of daily family living. Frederick Stoller outlines some of the specifications of such a cluster group, including a circle of families, regular and frequent meetings, reciprocal sharing, exchange of services, and extension of values.[12] Such a cluster group would require physical proximity, probably a neighborhood. Families could buy homes in a given block or subdivision; they could build, buy, or rent an apartment house. Each family would live apart, yet physically adjacent or otherwise close to other families in the cluster.

Under discussion here . . . is a different arrangement in which families have consistent alternatives before them: to share or to hold to themselves. To have never known privacy is, of course, to be robbed of the experience of separateness. However, to have never known the experience of openness and sharing is to be denied the possibilities of interchange with others. Exclusive adherence to either one of these polarities can only be impoverishing; the individual is faced not with a choice but with a limitation. The intimate family network, therefore, stands for a diversity of experience, a moving between privacy and sharing rather than the exclusive reliance upon one or the other.[13]

Again, it seems likely that a relatively small percentage of the population will be able to create, organize, and sustain such an arrangement. As a deliberately chosen life style, the cluster depends on too many contingencies. Such clusters do exist, but they have usually evolved *spontaneously* in subdivisions and housing complexes as intimate friendships have developed and the style of interfamilial interaction became a value for the cluster of families involved.

Mate-Swapping

The sixth type of nontraditional pattern is the phenomenon known as mate-swapping, or "swinging." In this arrangement, people exchange partners for sexual purposes. There may or may not be other commitment or sharing. Mate-swapping is not usually considered to imply any communal or group marital arrangement. It can be completely spontaneous or well organized. Mate-swapping clubs advertise in magazines, tabloids, and newspapers. The larger clubs may have regular meeting times with planned games and agenda leading to "orgies." Rules explicitly require total involvement and acceptance of each member of the opposite sex as a partner. The number of mate-swapping clubs increased until about 1972. Mate-swapping is confined largely to the middle class.

Two couples with mutual interests may have partner exchanges on a regular basis. Advertisements are often used to bring such couples together. "Swinging" has advantages that group marriage does not have, and vice versa. Advocates of group marriage point out that there is a total commitment by members of the group to each other and to the marriage and that there are rewards to be found in interpersonal sharing, communication, and a life style devoid of routine, boredom, and loneliness. However, I cannot help wondering to what extent group marriage is a rationalization for desire for sexual variety. If this is so, then mate-swapping would appear to be a more honest endeavor than multilateral marriage. Mate-swapping keeps the nuclear family intact. And because the husband and wife are both involved, no stigma is placed on either partner. Further, advocates of mate-swapping claim that feelings of jealousy may be nonexistent or minimal and that if any incompatibility or dissatisfaction exists, the relationship one couple has with another can be easily terminated.

Comarital Union

A seventh alternative is a comarital relationship, which is a mixture of multilateral marriage and mate-swapping. A comarital relationship is not a multilateral marriage because there is no organic union of the resources of the two couples. Nor is it mate-swapping because the couples in a comarital relationship want a total interpersonal relationship, not just a sexual relationship. Comarital relationships are probably more common than generally realized. Couples who have been friends for many years may learn to love each other in sexual as well as psychic ways. Bruce is an example of a person who has, at least for the present, rejected extramarital sexual relationships which are not part of a co-relationship.

Bruce

My solution is a—well—sort of an in-between compromise. I said I wanted sex outside marriage, and I said I wanted my marriage to be a vibrant and alive marriage. I concluded that the only way to achieve both of these goals with minimal threat to the marriage was to: (1) do everything openly, and (2) do everything together. Eureka! Comarital sex! Very difficult to achieve—a couple with whom you can enjoy the dignity of a meaningful relationship, share a loving affection, and experience the fun and pleasure of sexual warmth. For us the couple was right there. A lot needed to be done to cultivate them, to build trust and security, and to live with our own experiences. Nevertheless, this kind of relationship could be totally open to both of us and we would be involved in it together. We could learn together and grow together. The structure for building mutual trust and security was before us. I felt exhilaration! I had gotten honest about what I really wanted most, and she had done the same. I think under these conditions it would be wrong for me to have other sexual relationships—at least I sense that they could be very destructive to our comarital relationship.

Meaning, Value, and the
Ethics of Extramarital Sex

I have outlined the more daring and far-out kinds of alternatives. What, if anything, do these life styles have to do with meaning and purpose in our daily lives? What is the value and purpose of sex? Obviously, people like it and anticipate it, enough to create situations in which sex can be enjoyed with more than one partner.

I noted earlier that sex is a pleasure in and of itself and that this intrinsic pleasure is its own meaning with its own value. I further noted that there can be added value and meaning if a number of values are congruent and form a configuration that imparts a meaning to a whole that is greater than the sum of its parts. Each individual holds several values, and each value is intrinsically meaningful. As long as values do not conflict, they can complement each other and form a configuration in which the whole is greater than the intrinsic meaning of any of the individual parts.

There is little question that value trade-offs need to be arranged if a configuration including extramarital sex is considered desirable. Or one may deliberately trade off opportunities to have extramarital sexual relations (of the sexual or erotic types) in order to preserve the value of a configuration. Countless men and women make this trade-off, and countless others do not. Still others have, at one time in their life, failed to make a trade-off and opted instead for the intrinsic meaning resulting from an experience with an extramarital partner only to discover that there was a weakening of the extrinsic meaning which the marital relationship had provided.

Sexual ethics can be seen as the value relationships and value hierarchy set up by each couple. Commitment, trust, sex, and marriage will be totally unacceptable for many people because they do not hold the particular configuration to be of value. Others will opt for utilitarian marriages in order that a partial congruency may exist, even if not a fully satisfying configuration.

Albert Ellis, writing on the pros and cons of adultery, suggests that the person who has established a marital relationship of value and meaning may hesitate before entering an adulterous relationship because adultery implies an adulteration, or a diluting, of something containing value.[14] An extramarital relationship may dilute the primary relationship and weaken the configuration of value and meaning.

Let us consider as illustration the various possible sexual responses, attitudes, and desires of married people. One couple's configuration

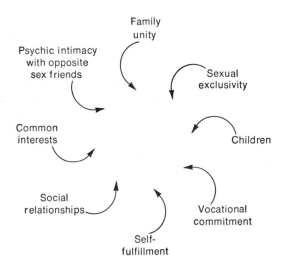

Figure 10–1
A Configuration of Congruent Values

might consist of valuing sex as fun and intrinsically enjoyable, with great value placed on such other factors as fidelity to one's mate, interpersonal trust, firm commitment, and the feeling of love as embodied in acts of caring, sharing, and facing conflict. The configuration might or might not include children, with or without some shared assumptions about how the children are to be cared for and socialized. All of these parts may be intrinsically valuable, but a greater (extrinsic) meaning comes from the fact that the values are not in conflict (congruent) and work with each other in the total configuration.

Figure 10–1 represents a life situation in which all of the values are congruent. The total congruency eliminates severe strain or conflict and allows a configuration of value to be formed that is extrinsic to every one of the individual values but that, nevertheless, gives an added meaning to each of the individual values beyond their intrinsic value.

Another couple's configuration might represent sex as intrinsically valuable but consider freedom more valuable than fidelity or monogamous exclusiveness. Whether or not these values are congruent would depend

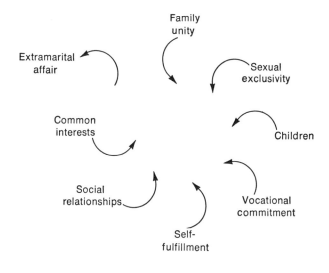

Figure 10–2
A Broken Configuration
—One Noncongruent Value

on such factors as whether both spouses held these beliefs or whether one spouse held different values. For example, it would hardly be congruent for a husband to embrace freedom in sexual contacts for himself and deny equal freedom to his wife.

Figure 10–2 might represent the value configuration of this couple, with one noncongruent value damaging the configuration. The noncongruency of a single value is sufficient to put the configuration into disharmony and dysfunction.

Figure 10–2 illustrates the situation portrayed in the following dialogue between Mike and Sally.

Mike and Sally

Mike and Sally are in their middle forties. Mike is an engineer in a small industry. Mike and Sally have been married for 24 years, and neither had been previously married. They have four children, ranging in age from sixteen to twenty-two. Mike and Sally are in marital counseling together.

Sally: *"I've thought a long time about what I'd say to you [the counselor] when I first came to you—but now that we're here I don't know how to begin. . . . It all seems so jumbled . . . like . . . like the bottom has fallen out of our marriage. We were so happy—at least I thought so—but now this! I knew Mike was restless but I never dreamed he would actually . . . actually . . . (pause). How could he do this to me? We've had arguments and differences, sure—but nothing to cause any serious barrier between us. Just the other day I was talking long distance to my sister and I was telling her how Mike and I valued all the different things we enjoy in life—the kids, our home, our interests—but now. . . . Oh, how can I ever face her after saying that. I guess I'm more angry and hurt than I am jealous. I trusted him. He always seemed to enjoy sex with me. He teased me once in a while—but I enjoyed intercourse . . .*
Mike: *I think you're overdoing this, Sally! Look, I'm not leaving you or anything like that. I told you I was sorry. We do have a lot going for us— do you honestly think I don't care about you or the kids?*
Sally: *How could you?*
Mike: *I told you I was sorry. What more is there to say? It was just a physical thing. I don't have any feelings for her.*
Sally: *God, don't tell me that—it just makes the whole thing worse.*

The dynamics in this broken configuration are many and varied, and include suppressed conflict and repressed anger. Nevertheless, there is no reason the preexisting configuration cannot be restored. When a relationship is defined as being built on mutual trust, there can be no painless way to deal with the consequences of broken trust. If Mike were pressed he would probably not deny that the extramarital experience was indeed pleasurable. In this particular marriage, however, Mike's activity has created a rupture in a meaningful configuration. In our terminology, intrinsic pleasure with a third person has temporarily destroyed the extrinsic meaning and value of the sexual relationship within the marital dyad.

Figure 10–3 represents another life situation in which all of the values are congruent. Although the values are contrary to those of the previous illustration, they are congruent. Because they are not in conflict and are jointly held, the configuration is unimpaired.

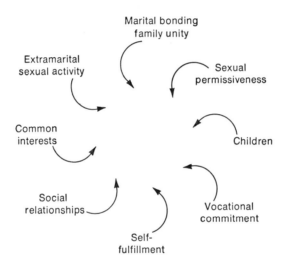

Figure 10–3
A Configuration in Which Extramarital
Permissiveness Is a Congruent Value

The reader will note that whether an extramarital relationship will rupture a meaningful configuration depends on the perceived value of the sexual relationship and the agreed upon definition of the marital relationship.

As noted earlier, sex is often used as a means of warding off anxiety and filling the emptiness of the existential vacuum. This orientation often proves to be self-defeating, because the value of sexual pleasure is considered in isolation and is not related to other meaningful constructs in one's life. I have stressed that sex is indeed meaningful pleasure but that when this particular meaningful pleasure is in congruence with other values and other meaningful constructs, a configuration of meaning is formed that is not only much greater than the sum of its parts but is the essence of a meaningful existence.

Different life styles and cross-sexual living arrangements need not be endorsed or approved by all (or even many) to be of value and meaning to the participants. If we believe in the right of others to do their own thing, as long as all participants act voluntarily, then the current experimentation in mating is welcome and healthy. Carl Rogers, commenting on the explorations and experiments of the modern day, says:

To me it seems high time that here too we begin to move into the twentieth century. It is high time that we recognize and respect the fact that quite revolutionary as well as evolutionary experiments are a fortunate, not an unfortunate, aspect of our cultural life. Can we accept the fact that here too the name of the game is change, and that we are desperately in need of just such a revolution in the area of living partnerships and family life as has taken place in industry, agriculture, flight, space, and all the other aspects of life? Can we respect our explorers? This is the great question we face. And if we did, what would we do?[15]

Summary

Alternatives to monogamy, excluding the nonmarital life style, include two kinds of permissive monogamy—utilitarian and open marriages. Utilitarian marriage is one that is maintained even though the emotional attachment has waned. There are many types of open marriages but all are based on the enduring bond of the husband-wife relationship. In open marriage, the primary-pair bond is the central focus. Primary commitment is to the mate.

Progressive monogamy, or serial marriage, refers to a vital or intense primary relationship which, when the emotional attachment wanes, will be replaced with another vital or intense relationship. Progressive monogamy is legal. It is a well-established life style for countless people in American society.

Group marriage, increasingly known as multilateral marriage, is technically a marriage between one individual and at least two others within a group. Group marriages are usually communal arrangements in which resources are pooled. Communes are not necessarily group marriages. The kibbutzim are communes without group marriages. The Oneida Community was a very large group marriage that was also communal.

In cluster marriages and cluster families, the autonomy of the individual marriages and families is preserved without any communal or structural organization that requires total sharing of resources. A cluster is a grouping together, usually in fairly close geographical proximity, of several marriages or families that desire psychic intimacy and interpersonal closeness. The cluster may be considered as a non-bloodline replacement for the extended family and is sometimes referred to as an *expanded family.*

Mate-swapping or "swinging" may or may not be akin to open marriage. "Swinging" is a particular type of consensual sex wherein the marital partners give their consent to each other to engage in extramarital sex. The variety of extramarital sexual relationships ranges from very closed affairs to group sex and swapping clubs. Consensual agreement between the marital pair is also known as *comarital sex.* A special type of comarital sex occurs when one married couple shares sexual intimacy with another married couple. This implies the swapping of mates rather than a four-person, group sex situation, although some foursomes prefer the group approach. This bilateral comarital relationship should not be confused with group marriage, nor should it be concluded that this is the ideal type of open marriage.

The ethics of extramarital sex are viewed as being the private concern of consenting adults. The basis for the sexual ethic is the degree of value and meaning that such relationships bring to the participants. When the several intrinsic values are not in conflict, they not only yield their own value and meaning but also form a whole that I have called a configuration. A configuration of values, in which several values are in reasonable harmony with each other, is capable of giving not only intrinsic meaning but also extrinsic meaning. This is because the unity of the configuration conveys a greater meaning than any of the individual parts. However, if any of the individual values is in conflict with the other values the person holds, the configuration is broken, at least until the conflict is removed or otherwise dealt with.

Questions for Study

1. I have suggested that couples in problem-oriented marriages are not likely to find solutions in the nontraditional mating styles. Explain why this may be so.

2. Referring to Hobbs's theory of the two traditions of marriage—marital permanence and sexual exclusivity—what social and personal conflicts might arise?

3. Evaluate the alternative mating styles in this chapter, listing the advantages and disadvantages that you see in each style. Pick the one that is most acceptable to you.

4. Referring to Figure 10–1, design your own configuration using the values that are important to you. Are any of your values in conflict?

5. Carl Rogers says of sexual and social experiments: "Can we respect our explorers? And if we did, what would we do?" Answer this question by discussing legal, social, economic and attitudinal changes that might result.

Reading Suggestions

Group Marriage by Larry Constantine and Joan Constantine. New York: Macmillan, 1973. An extensive examination of present-day, multilateral marriages.

Beyond Monogamy edited by James Smith and Lynn Smith. Baltimore, Md.: Johns Hopkins University Press, 1974. Readings on sexual alternatives in marriage, including comarital sex.

The New Communes by Ron E. Roberts. Englewood Cliffs, N.J.: Prentice-Hall, 1971. Studies of various types of communal living, in the past as well as the present.

Renovating Marriage edited by Roger W. Libby and Robert N. White-hurst. Danville, Calif.: Consensus Publishers, 1973. A series of readings on alternate sexual life styles.

ELEVEN
MAKING IT TOGETHER: GROWTH FROM WITHIN

**Making It Together:
Growth from Within**

To Kill a Marriage

The Residual

What Price Fulfillment?

Action Plans

Summary

Questions for Study

Reading Suggestions

To Kill a Marriage

Diane

Dear Mr. Crosby,

I heard you speak on TV the other day about how we kill marriage and sex. Two years ago I would have laughed at what you said. Now I am crying. You are so right. I killed my marriage—my man, our fun, our kids. I didn't just kill it gently—I strangled it. I never cared about sex one way or the other but I'd do it two or three times a week just to keep him satisfied. But I treated him like an animal—I never put myself into it. I always assumed we were the way we were supposed to be for people our age, you know, let the younger ones have fun but it's too late for us. Not just in sex but in lots of little ways we lived the life of "quiet desperation" you talked about on TV. Do you know we haven't really said anything to each other of any meaning in years and years. Did you see that movie, "Lovers and Other Strangers,"—where the old man asks who's to be happy in marriage? That's the way I felt. I had resigned myself to boredom and drudgery and dullness. I wasn't terribly unhappy, just sort of a slow infecting type of misery. I'm not blaming my husband either. He tried earlier to be exciting—he would take me out and encourage me to do all kinds of things. I don't think he's been unfaithful to me, but looking back I wouldn't blame him. You said unfaithfulness can be in different ways than sexual and that puzzled me but now I think I see what you meant. I've been really unfaithful because I haven't done hardly anything in all our married life that would be called creative or spontaneous. Now it's too late—we're in our early forties and . . . well I was wondering if we could get into one of those marriage growth groups you mentioned?

Too late? No, not at all. In fact, the best time to begin is when you are motivated by a feeling of self-disgust. Diane's life can be very different very quickly, but she must be willing to look at some of her attitudes and change some of her behavior.

I have often pondered the question: What is the difference between a rut and a groove? I think it is the difference between losing variety and making constructive use of routine. A rut is negative in that variety and spontaneity have been choked to death; a groove is positive as long as the routine and the ordinary are continually used as springboards into experiences involving variety and spontaneity. People who wish to deny the need of routine and the ordinary may find fulfillment in one of the emerging marital patterns, but they probably will not find it within traditional monogamy. Two people cannot live together over a long period of time without coming to terms with the routine and the ordinary. The only option (but a most important one) available to couples who commit themselves to a monogamous, sexually exclusive union is the option between the rut and the groove.

Diane and her husband were in a rut of great length and depth. They never learned how to redeem the ordinary or to use any other positive means to make themselves attractive to each other. This probably happened because both of them were dead to themselves. Our attitudes toward our mates can readily be a projection of our own feelings of futility and despair.

I have also wondered how hard a task it would be to create in people a totally negative attitude toward marriage. If someone were to appoint a presidential commission on "how to destroy marriage," I could offer some cogent suggestions on strategy. The first maneuver should be to use the mass media to condition people to believe that change and variety are wrong and to be resisted at all costs. Such a step would allow cultural traditions and patterns, myths, and taboos to be absorbed into a rigid form and function within marriage. Isn't it true that we often commit "maricide" and "familicide" the very instant we say "I do"? Oh, not intentionally, but in a rather subtle, sneaky way we conclude that since he or she is now mine there is no need to continue to score points—no need to be creative, imaginative, spontaneous, or interesting. Many promising relationships begin to die when the relationship becomes legalized—not because a legal bond works some sort of deadly witchcraft but because legalization becomes an open invitation to take the partner *too much* for granted. Our second suggestion on how to kill a marriage is therefore, "Take each other for granted—always."

There is no doubt that marriage should provide a couple with a haven in which they can bask in the luxury of not having to put on false pretenses for anyone. This freedom to be oneself provides the joy of being taken for granted, of being loved (agape) "in spite of" one's faults, idiosyncrasies, and hang-ups. Yet there is something in us that does not like to be taken for granted, even though we may persist in defending our right to take the other for granted. To be taken for granted is both a relief and a threat; it is both a security and an insecurity; it is both a joy and a peril. Thus, a delicate balance must be maintained in a marital relationship. Agape must never be too much out of balance with philos and eros. (In-spite-of love must be balanced with friendship love and physical, passion-filled love.) Whenever equilibrium is upset, it is probably because one or both partners are demanding the right to take the other for granted while claiming that it is not the other's prerogative to take him for granted.

Frank and Sarah

Frank and Sarah have been married for two years. They have one child, a daughter, age eight months. Sarah and Frank have come to a marriage counselor because they feel they are at an impasse in their relationship.

Sarah: *He just doesn't pay any attention to me. No matter what I do or how hard I try to carry on a conversation, he ignores me. He comes home from work and hardly even says "hello." I tried getting dressed up in the late afternoon but he never noticed. When we eat he is silent. When we go out in the car he's silent. Even when we are angry about something he remains uninvolved and unemotional. It's like I'm married to a machine. If only he would acknowledge that I'm alive!*

Frank: *Sarah makes it sound as though I'm a criminal. Look, I need peace and quiet when I get home from work. All day long I've been selling —sell, sell, sell—and it feels damn good to just turn it off. If I can't relax in my own home where am I ever going to be able to be me? I never did talk much—socially I mean—and if you ask me, Sarah is just making a lot of fuss about nothing. I love her, but that doesn't mean I have to keep on courting her—like I was still trying to impress her.*

Sarah: *If you love me why don't you ever show me?*

Frank: *Show you! I work hard for us. What do you call working five days a week going from customer to customer? Of course I love you, but that*

doesn't mean I have to go around proving it by saying nice things all the time. If you only knew how much I have to sell myself in order to get an order you wouldn't be talking that way.
Sarah: *Well it's no joyride taking care of Judy all day long either. All day I care for her, do laundry, cook meals, clean house; and you act like it's too much work to talk to me.*

This is a classic situation, portrayed in magazine articles, cartoons, and TV shows. The situation will be accentuated if either partner is especially dependent, because the dependent personality relies on affirmation from others, especially the spouse, for his self-esteem. Even without personality problems, this situation can be destructive if either partner has special legitimate ego needs which only the spouse can fill. For example, Frank's job requires him to be outgoing, aggressive, alert, and "a nice guy." Frank may normally be some of these things some of the time, but he finds it fatiguing to be all of these things all of the time. Consequently, it is natural that he would relish the idea of coming home to peace and solitude. However, Sarah's situation is the reverse, and it is one shared with unknown thousands of young mothers. Sarah has been living in a child's world all day, and she anticipates an exchange of conversation with her husband—even if the exchange is small talk or an abbreviated account of the day's events. Sarah yearns for this verbal sharing; Frank can't abide it.

Thus, we have two normal people who both need to be taken for granted in some ways; but Frank is taking Sarah for granted in a way that fails to take into account her basic need for human warmth and adult companionship. Sarah, on the other hand, has failed to understand Frank's needs after a long day at work. Experiences in role-reversal, or in a modified role-reversal, could probably help Frank and Sarah develop increased empathy for the situation of the other. Role-taking, in which husband and wife practice adopting the other's point of view, can often serve to temper the excessive or unrealistic expectations a couple has of each other. A child can often upset the balance of a relationship also, and Frank's and Sarah's daughter may have made them more sensitive to being taken for granted. They are probably going through a reorientation stage since their child has necessitated a new daily life style for Sarah and may be an ego threat to Frank. It is well established that some new fathers are threatened by their children because father is no longer number one. While most men negotiate this adjustment quite well, it is unusual for a new father to admit that he feels displaced and taken for granted when a child appears.

The rut that Frank and Sarah find themselves in brings us to the third suggestion I would make to the presidential commission: Create a cultural milieu in which no one is rewarded for creativity and imagination. Once we convince people that deviation from the traditional role assumptions and marital expectations is wrong, risky, and unnecessary, we can then quickly proceed to the marriage funeral. The rut will become unbearable. I suspect that such a commission would suggest that imagination be checked permanently at the door before the marriage ceremony takes place.

Answers to the following questions would indicate that the presidential commission had been highly successful. Answers implying "seldom," "a long time ago," or "we never would" indicate a rigidity in marital roles and a successful campaign to destroy marriage.

When was the last time the couple was separated for at least several days? When was the last time the husband stayed home with the children while the wife went away? When was the last time the couple went away together, leaving the children with a sitter, alone if older, or with friends? Where did the couple go? A nearby motel for overnight? Away with another couple?

How often are the traditional roles of male and female reversed? When did he last cook dinner? Or clean house? Or go to his child's teacher's evaluation conference instead of his wife? When was the last time the couple had sexual intercourse someplace other than in the bed the couple ordinarily sleeps in? Outside? In the living room? On the floor? (The sexual technologists have a good point when they lash out at our sexual rigidities and suggest positions in intercourse, changes in technique, and exploration of intimacies beyond coitus.[1])

When has the couple varied the time of sexual intimacy? Must it always be evening, or morning, or on certain nights of the week? When has the couple last reversed the so-called traditional sex-roles in which the male is always active and the female passive? (A passive male and an active female may be a welcome relief and change for both.)

How many couples have ever seriously attempted to learn transactional analysis? How many married couples or families use transactional analysis to cope with the conflicts, changing moods, and everyday situations in family life?

This discussion presupposes a motivation to change, to grow, to explore, and to enrich and enliven. Once a couple agrees to give up the defense mechanisms and safety devices that they have used to avoid intimacy, there is no limit to what can change, with or without outside help. Most people feel that change is dangerous and risky, and so they gravitate to the security of the mundane and the habituated behavioral patterns that are so comfortable. Any couple can learn to work together, without the benefit of an organized enrichment, growth, or counseling group, to change and improve their marriage. Indeed, transactional analysis is emphasized in this book because anybody can learn it. This has been shown with children, older people, and the mentally retarded.[2]

Two married people can also learn role-taking in a matter of minutes—that is, he plays the wife and she plays the husband. Couples using this format can deal with many conflicts and can explore many feelings. When one person tries to think and feel himself into the role of another, his understanding and empathy will increase. Further, when I watch another person play my role, I am bound to get insight and find myself reacting in interesting ways. Others who know us deeply and intimately can give us a glimpse of how we come across to others—they can give us feedback.

Feedback in human relations can be either divergent or convergent. Divergent feedback is a communication (verbal, written, or symbolic) we usually do not want to hear. Convergent feedback is welcomed because it agrees with our self-images. Role-taking can drastically reduce the divergent feedback and increase the convergent feedback, because it can help one "feel into" the other person and learn to change one's attitudes and behavior. More positive feelings (positive feedback) are bound to result from new insights. Role-taking can also help us cut through idealized images of the self and the other by forcing us to see ourselves as others see us. Since idealization obscures a realistic acceptance of one-self and of others, role-playing can help us to learn authentic self-acceptance and acceptance of others.

Role-playing can also help a husband and wife uncover some of their traditional expectations. Thus, a fourth suggestion that the presidential commission should implement is to mount an attack on those who would test traditional male-female and husband-wife roles. The commission should demand role rigidity and a strict sex division of labor, duty, and responsibility. This would guard against honest self-examination of role expectations which can often change a conflict-ridden, rut-oriented marriage into a growing relationship. A husband may relate to his wife for ten years on the mistaken assumption that because his mother starched his shirts and cheerfully made a career of housekeeping and mothering, his wife should also be contented to stay at home as sole housekeeper. Similarly, a wife may expect her husband to be domineering and sole breadwinner like her father was, even though she may consciously dislike her father or bear animosity or resentment toward him. Such role expectations, which are deeply embedded in cultural and religious traditions, often provide fertile ground for manipulation of the mate.

A government effort to rigidify traditional husband-wife, male-female, father-mother, and parent-offspring roles would go a long way toward killing the potential of monogamous unions. Whenever either partner fails to measure up to the sacred institutionalized expectations of the other, feelings of hurt, anger, resentment, and hostility are likely to run rampant. Thus, a fifth suggestion might be, "Create a national climate that encourages perfection and harmony." The mass media could create the illusion that happy, successful marriages are those in which there is no conflict and everybody is improving day by day in their quest for perfect relationships.

Analysis of happy, vital marriages often reveals a total absence of perfectionism and a total acceptance of each other despite character defects, personality flaws, and hang-ups. *Perfection* and *lack of conflict* may prove to be the most reliable predictors of *unsatisfactory* marriage. Perfection

is blatantly nonhuman and stupid, and lack of conflict indicates a fundamental dishonesty through denial of feelings.

A final suggestion for our commission (the reader can carry on from
here) is to create a marriage ritual law that prescribes phrases of the
wedding ceremony that make the marriage contract forever nonnegoti-
able and nonamendable. Such a nuptial requirement would prevent the
constructive orientation that Sidney Jourard describes as "serial polygamy with the same spouse." By serial polygamy Jourard means the re-
invention of marriage by the same husband and the same wife. Impasse
is struggled with; the old union dies, and a new union is born—between
the same two people.[3] The fallacy in traditional marital relationships has
been the assumption that people do not really change. Most individuals'
core personalities are relatively consistent over time, but it is also true

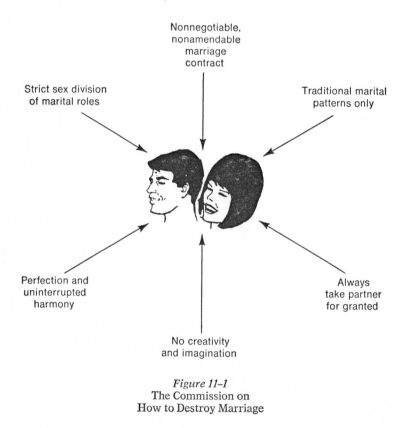

Figure 11–1
The Commission on
How to Destroy Marriage

that we are always changing, growing, reverting, regressing, progressing, or discovering. It is totally unrealistic to think that two adults should be confined to the (implicit) contract they both agreed on at the time of marriage. What Jourard calls reinventing marriage is perhaps better described as redefining, re-creating, or revitalizing the present relationship. Redefinition (by that name or any other) needs to take place if the marriage is to be a self-actualizing experience for both spouses. Redefinition is an ongoing occurrence; the two partners are committed to the fulfillment of each other and to the fulfillment of their relationship.

Redefinition springs from a certain set of values. If the highest values held by a couple are aliveness, creativity, authenticity, vitality, health, lovingness, intimacy (sexual and spiritual), and productivity, then redefinition will come as naturally as day and night. On the other hand, if the most basic values are loyalty to past tradition, conformity to societal expectations, ancestral beliefs and mores, and the authoritarian triad of obedience, respect, and duty to one's parents, then redefinition will be difficult at best.

Throughout these pages I have stressed the principles of growth, self-fulfillment, self-actualization, and self-realization. There is no reason why married couples need to settle for a watered-down version of monogamy —for a lifeless, joyless, dull relationship.

The Residual

What remains after we have torn down our defenses in a marital relationship? What is left on which to build? The residual remains after the tearing-down process has taken from us our defense mechanisms and our safety devices. The residual is the foundation beneath the taboos and myths in which we took refuge; it is the sperm and ovum which united to conceive the marriage in the first place. Many marriages have far more going for them than the partners permit themselves to see. People seem to celebrate failure and divorce by pointing out the things that went wrong—the incompatibilities, the impasses, the drudgery, the disillusionment. Yet at the conception of each union there are legitimate hopes, dreams, and possibilities, trust and love, commitment and spontaneity.

What is love's legacy? What is the residual we seek to uncover and re-create? To what do we seek to give vitality and fulfillment? The question may be approached in several ways, but the underlying assumptions are much the same. Monogamy as it has evolved in our society has tended to work against the development of individual potential; it has tended to create rigidity, joylessness, frustration, monotony, boredom, hostility, anger, and a pleasureless sexuality.

Perhaps the initial step in the direction of change is to opt for a con-tinuing revision and updating of the marital contract. Herbert Otto has spoken of the "New Marriage," which is a framework for developing personal potential.[4] In another article Otto asks, "Has Monogamy Failed?"[5] Both articles are variations on the theme of monogamous marital enrichment:

Has monogamy failed? My answer is "no." Monogamy is no longer a rigid institution, but instead an evolving one. There is a multiplicity of models and dimensions that we have not even begun to explore. It takes a certain amount of openness to become aware on not only an intellectual level but a feeling level that these possibilities face us with a choice. Then it takes courage to recognize that this choice in a measure represents our faith in monogamy. Finally, there is the fact that every marriage has a potential for greater commitment, enjoyment, and communication, for more love, understanding, and warmth. Actualizing this potential can offer new di-mensions in living and new opportunities for personal growth, and can add new strength and affirmation to a marriage.[6]

Virginia Satir has also spoken to the issue of "Marriage as a Human-Actualizing Contract.'"[7] Another way of presenting this view would be to advocate the ongoing process of redefining the relationship. There are times when marriages peak; there are times when these same marriages are void of vitality and joy. The wedding ceremony can be an open in-vitation to decay and stagnation, simply because the two people now legally possess and are possessed by each other. Duty, responsibility, and obligation, however important and necessary, can sound repressive and are often the causes for loss of spontaneity in marriage.

Growth centers and organizations for actualizing human potential have sprung up all over the United States.[8] The basic purpose of these centers is to help individuals and couples break out of the binds that constrict full self-expression. In order to do this there must be a willingness to experience some discomfort as one permits the breaking down of barriers and defenses against intimacy. Reawakening of the senses, openness to others, spontaneity in self-expression, and honesty in interpersonal relationships are encouraged, usually in a group context.

The history and background of such centers is a story within itself. Here I want to suggest that traditional monogamy is still the marital pattern chosen by the vast majority within our society and that much can be done to revitalize and to actualize the marital relationship.

Yet in defining marriage as a "human actualizing contract" it is all too easy to fall back into the same trap as before—the trap of excessive and unrealistic expectations. Just as romantic and societal expectations often lead one to post-honeymoon disillusionment, so also expectations regarding marriage as the heart-bed of psychic intimacy may lead a couple to discontent and disillusionment. Is it possible for a couple to have peak intimacy experiences day-in and day-out? If the answer to this question is "no," why do we conclude that something is wrong with the marriage? Richard Farson has pointed out that discontent in good marriages arises from several sources, including heightened expectations about sexual and psychic intimacy, comparison with other marriages, and comparison of the marriage with itself in its better moments.[9] Farson says that "probably the most important source of discontent is the comparison of the marriage with its own good moments in the present. . . . These peaks, however, are inevitably followed by valleys. Couples lucky enough to have these moments find themselves unable to sustain them, and, at the same time, unable to settle for ordinary moments. They want life to be a constantly satisfying state. But to be a constant state, to avoid the valleys, it is necessary to eliminate the peaks. . . . Good marriages are not like that, but the price they exact in depression and pain is high."[10]

If the residual, the core of the marriage, is to be secured and cultivated, it must be tempered with realistic expectations—expectations that are in line with what we know about human life through experiences and the testimony of others, including historical and literary confirmation. For example, when Farson speaks of peaks and valleys, he is giving witness to a basic human experience. An idealistic person might say, "Why? Why can't life be filled with peaks?" A pessimistic person may claim in the name of realism that Farson is wrong because "life is basically valley after valley with no peaks."

We cannot secure our residual, let alone cultivate it, until we are able to see through the self-destructive tendencies born of unrealistic expectations. As illustration, consider the rather common occurrence of a meeting between two strangers on a bus or plane. In a matter of an hour or two, such relationships often develop deep-felt emotions and problems in one or both of the travelers. A common reaction to such an experience is the wish that one could attain and remain in such an intimate level with one's own spouse. But is this a realistic expectation? Can a married couple live day-in and day-out in such an emotionally charged manner? In the majority of bus or airplane experiences, the two people involved will never see each other again . . . and they know it! And if, perchance, they do meet again, the odds are that any effort to re-create a semblance of the intimate moment of the past will end in frustration and disappointment.

Thus, the residual has great potential only if it is intellectually and emotionally placed in a context of balance and perspective. If variety is a desirable quality in human experience, then it follows that we would do well to welcome variety in the range and type of marital relationships as well as in any particular relationship. A couple may achieve a great deal of variety in their sexual relationship, but even this desirable quality will not fill the need for variety in meeting other basic needs.

The residual is, in short, more than enough to sustain the great majority of monogamous and sexually exclusive marriages providing the residual is placed within a configuration of congruent life values and goals. Once the romantic expectations disseminated by the media and the conditioning process of socialization are seen through and placed in perspective, there follows the challenge of seeing through the double bind created by unrealistically expecting our mates to fill all our basic human needs. Let us hope for meaningful peak experiences between husband and wife, yet without either feeling guilty or apologetic about the transitoriness of such experiences. In a very real sense they are meaningful *because* they are transitory.

There are those who will claim that the residual can survive only if the marriage includes the standard of sexual permissiveness. The argument is advanced that if we embrace the value of psychic intimacy with people other than the spouse, we should also embrace sexual intimacy with people other than the spouse. That may be true for some people. I do not think it is either necessary or logical. What is often desired in sex is an affirmation of the self by the other. It is no more logical to conclude that psychic intimacy must culminate in sexual intimacy than it is to conclude that sexual intimacy must culminate in psychic intimacy. A fair statement about the relationship of psychic and sexual intimacy seems to be this: Sometimes and in some situations psychic intimacy progresses into sexual intimacy and in other situations psychic intimacy is destroyed by sexual intimacy. Sexual intimacy often creates only an illusory facsimile of psychic intimacy; that is, when one fails to experience psychic intimacy he deludes himself into believing that sexual intimacy will be an effective substitute.

What Price Fulfillment?

Fulfillment is costly, for both the individual and the marital relationship. The price is paid in the form of pain and discomfort, the slow process of learning new patterns, the break with security mechanisms, or the parting with games and strategies calculated to manipulate or dominate the other.

The growth toward maturity, toward self-acceptance, toward learning to deal with conflict, and toward unlearning standards of perfection exacts a toll from those who would build on the residual in their quest for marital fulfillment within a monogamous relationship. Maturity is required to make it together, to see through the illusions of romantic, societal, and parental expectations of marriage.

Marital fulfillment requires, probably above all other qualities, the grace of self-acceptance. The self-accepting person is the one who is best able to recognize his own foibles and hang-ups without becoming defensive or unnecessarily compulsive in compensating for them. Consequently, he is most free to analyze societal and cultural data and to consciously decide his own level of contentment or discontentment. There is little doubt, either experimentally or clinically, that the self-accepting person is best qualified to accept others, most especially his mate.

The myth of conflict-free interpersonal relationships has been treated in an earlier chapter. Suffice it to reiterate that acceptance and confrontation of conflict are essential requirements for human growth and development. Once we accept conflict as an amoral fact of life, we are in a position to be done with old patterns and voices that told us we would not be loved if we expressed our deepest and innermost feelings. In dispelling one myth, we run the risk of falling prey to another myth—the myth that all conflict is resolvable. It is not! To believe otherwise is to add to one's own level of discontentment.

Perhaps the greatest price to be paid in building on the residual is the death of perfection. I can hear murmurs and protests to the effect that this villain was put to death years ago (or at least several pages or chapters back). Maybe so. Likely not! The perfectionist tendency has been reinforced by one's family, competition with siblings, the educational establishment (nursery through postdoctoral), the mass media, and the ecclesiastical establishment. Perfectionism may have been conquered in one or several areas of one's life without having been recognized in one's marital expectations. The purists will maintain that to settle for anything less than perfection is a cop-out or a compromise. Yet perfection and the perfectionist fallacy have, in my opinion, been among the greatest curses mankind has suffered. The fallacy of perfectionism is its tacit promise that we will one day be satisfied, when at last we reach the coveted goal. If the perfectionist claims he is realistic and that he knows the goal is unattainable but that the meaning is in the striving, he deceives himself precisely because he is unable to live in the present. How can he? He does not accept the present without superimposing his own qualifications and improvements. He is then thrust into the future—where all perfectionists dwell—and hence, happiness itself becomes part of the future illusion.

Perhaps the price of fulfillment can best be described by people who are endeavoring to pay it.

Gene and Dorothy

Gene and Dorothy have been married for five years. They have two daughters, ages two and one-half and four. Gene is self-employed as a proprietor of a sporting goods store. Dorothy is not gainfully employed. Gene and Dorothy record their own story a year after the conclusion of a marital enrichment therapy group in which they participated for twelve weeks.

Gene: *I find it hard to think on paper. The past two years have been a whirlwind. First, I was convinced our marriage was a big mistake. I was positive another woman would be much better for me than Dorothy. I have no idea of which "other woman"—I just had the constant thought that there must be a better match available somewhere and somehow. Then I reluctantly joined the enrichment group. I hated it at first. I went more out of appeasement and curiosity than for insight and enrichment. The first couple of meetings left me cold. I know I had a chip on my shoulder. I was critical of everyone in the group, which made me feel quite superior. At the fourth meeting Dorothy put herself in the center ring. I thought, "Oh boy, here she goes in her 'Let's get Gene' game." She didn't. Instead she talked only of her own problems she had been struggling with and how when she was starved for intimacy she would shut people out. I don't recall much else except that whatever she said changed my attitude toward the whole enrichment group. I no longer felt defensive or superior. Slowly I began to participate in the discussions and exchanges. It was very uncomfortable at times, especially when the group members moved in on me and pinned me up against the wall. I guess one thing led to another and I began to get introspective. Then for a while I withdrew into myself. I felt scared and tense. A few more weeks and I began to look forward to the weekly session. My feelings about Dorothy were different now. It wasn't any great turnabout or electrifying romantic episode, just a warm feeling within myself toward both me and her. Somehow I knew that I had been kidding myself about making it with someone else. Sure others might attract me, but now I began to feel that if I couldn't make it with Dot I probably could not make it with anyone. I also began to feel happier within myself, sort of like "a welcome home to me by me."*

The year since has not been easy. Many times I have felt despair. It used to be I never felt despair—I guess because I ran away from it. My feelings toward Dorothy have been deeper than ever although, and I can't make much sense of this, we seem to fight a lot more. I express my feelings and so does Dot. This isn't very comfortable. Sometimes things get worked out. Sometimes they don't. I can only say that even though we fight more there is something better between us than ever before.

Dorothy: *It is a strange feeling to put something down on paper that you have carried around within yourself for so long. I don't know where to start. I was becoming more and more dissatisfied with my marriage. Everything seemed to be turning in on me. I felt Gene no longer loved me or even cared. The two girls seemed to occupy most of my time and for a while I guess I escaped unpleasant feelings by concerning myself exclusively with them. The more I allowed the girls to possess me the more I felt resentful toward them. I became depressed and irritable to such an extent that I started to look for help. That's how we eventually ended up in the enrichment group. Gene was against it from the start, but I sensed that unless we did something it would all break up anyway.*

The group and I got along fine for a while. I really ate it up. It was obvious that Gene didn't share my enthusiasm. About the fifth or sixth week I started to sour on the group. I felt they were merciless toward me; I felt attacked and I wanted to get out. About the same time Gene started to show signs of interest in the whole thing. So there we were, me against and him for! One night I really opened myself up only to be criticized instead of pitied. It took awhile, about three weeks, for me to look at some of the things people had said to me. More than anything I was wanting group support for my self-pity. They would sooner crucify you than give you pity. My resentment grew worse until one night I told the group how I resented their not giving me pity. Someone in the group looked me straight in the eyes and said: "Pity! Why do you insist that we feel sorry for you?" I started to cry and, of course, I had no answer. When the group ended, I felt about half. It was Gene who benefited most from the group. Since that time things have been better. I seem to be able to live with myself now without being so uptight and depressed. I can't say that the situation has changed any: Gene still works long hours and the girls are still very demanding. Yet there is a difference. I no longer resent the situation, you know what I mean—Gene, his job, the kids, the routine. I don't like lots of things, but I no longer hide my frustration or pretend to myself that someday everything will be different. It's easier for me to express myself to Gene, and when the girls expect too much of me I no longer feel guilty about drawing a line. I have learned to ignore some of the housework that used to bug me, and I've become interested in antiquing furniture, of all things. I believe in our marriage more than ever, but it's not a blind belief. I guess what I'm trying to say is that life is better for all of us even though we have the usual stresses and strains. I guess I grew up a little and now I don't need to escape into my "self-pity chamber" as I've come to call it.

The above statements illustrate the necessity for the death of perfection. The perfectionist fallacy leads couples to expect the impossible of each other and thus to deny each other's humanity and personhood. As reflected in their forthright honesty with each other in conflictual situations and in their efforts to cut through some of their divisive tactics, Gene and Dorothy are beginning to mature in their relationship. The price of fulfillment does not seem to be cheap; the way is sometimes quite painful and usually uncomfortable. Yet those who travel the road seem to return a unanimous verdict that the price is well worth it.

Action Plans

There are no panaceas that will guarantee you a vital marriage in five easy lessons. But there are creative steps that can be taken by those who are serious about building a new relationship on the residual.

Behaviorism as a psychological theory holds that our behavior changes when we succeed in establishing new patterns of acting and being for which we are rewarded or reinforced. It might prove very useful to translate behavioristic psychology and behavior modification techniques into action plans. An action plan chooses a small, manageable piece of everyday behavior and then works on that behavior for a given period of time. Positive feedback from the partners regarding how they receive the new behaviors in each other establishes a payoff, or reinforcement, for new behavior. We can proceed from one action plan to another, building on the good effects of the earlier ones that are still being carried out.

The following action plans have been used successfully by various couples who committed themselves to the process of learning new kinds of positive behavior.

Give each other one constructive, genuine compliment a day.

Set aside a talking time each day. Begin with fifteen-minute segments. Keep the kids away. Have cocktails or other refreshment. Nourish each other. Listen and respond. Be alive.

Hold each other in a warm embrace for five minutes each twenty-four hours. Don't talk. Feel the messages. Communicate nonverbally.

Surprise your lover with some special favor, gesture, or gift once a week. We all like surprises.

Take over one chore of the other and do it well once a day.

Take a shower together before making love, the next five times. Lather each other. Play together.

Set aside thirty minutes once a week to do nothing except physical pleasuring of the partner. Insofar as you can, do everything for which the partner expresses a desire.

Lose weight. Begin by losing two pounds a week.

Learn a sport together. Get serious about it. Allow it to sap some of your excess energy.

Choose a new leisure time pursuit—gourmet dining, dancing, or bridge, for example.

Open yourselves to new friendships. Be assertive. Invite that couple over for dinner.

Pursue new individual friends. Both partners should talk, listen, give, and take, separately to new friends. Then be open and have something new to share with your mate. New relationships can enrich you, and that makes you a more interesting mate.

Make yourself take that honeymoon weekend. Make it a time to enjoy each other without outside distractions.

Males only: Forbid yourself ejaculation during a lovemaking session. See how far you can go without orgasm. You may drive yourself wild in sheer excitement and anticipation.

Females only: Think of yourself as a seductive tease. Allow yourself the continuing experience of turning your mate on.

Read and talk about The Joy of Sex *by Alex Comfort,* More Joy in Your Marriage *by Herbert Otto,* Couple Therapy *by Smith and Phillips, and* We Can Have Better Marriages *by David Mace.*

Level with each other:

   5 times: I feel bad when you..............

   5 times: I feel good when you............

   5 times: I wish you would................

   3 times: I see your strengths as...........

   3 times: I resent you because............

   3 times: I spite you by...................

   5 times: I love you because..............

   5 times: I love you in spite of............

These are only a few of the limitless number of things that can be tried immediately. Do they sound silly? Ridiculous, perhaps? Try them anyway—for only as you learn to quit running down marriage and take a few risks with your mate will you begin to experience some change in the way you *feel* about your lover, and about your life together.

Summary

One of the most important themes of the book is developed in this chapter: we are the ones who kill marriage. There may be much about marriage as an institution and about the socialization process to criticize. But there is no escaping that we have the most destructive influences on our marriages. We take our mates for granted. Spouses consider each other as possessions. Partners fail to be imaginative in communication and lovemaking. We expect perfection from ourselves and our mates. We have unrealistic expectations. And we fear conflict, change, and growth.

Marriage can be a means of continuous growth for both partners. It is an opportunity for experiencing life in a shared relationship that is vital and spontaneous. If this is to happen, both partners need to be willing to risk becoming adventuresome and imaginative. The residual—what remains after the fantastic expectations, the taboos, and the illusions are dispelled —provides the married couple with a foundation on which they can rebuild. The rebuilding process necessitates the redefining and reinventing of marriage so that the couple can create for themselves the conditions and understandings under which they wish to live.

Building on the residual further entails the ongoing motivation to cultivate the relationship by being alert to possible growth and enrichment opportunities. The price of marital fulfillment is expressed less in dollars than in energy. There is simply no way a vital relationship may be maintained without an investment of one's time and energy. Unfortunately this is the greatest stumbling block to vital marriage. Too many people honestly believe that marriage is "doing what comes naturally," that they do not need to invest themselves in continual cultivation of the relationship. This naive, romantic view still persists in our society, masquerading under the guise of the "love is all we need" myth. If we are to have fulfilling relationships, we must learn new ways of handling conflict and of dealing with feelings such as hurt, pain, and anger.

A technique of behavior modification was suggested as a means for changing the marriage relationship. Action plans are designed to change small slices of behavior. It was suggested that commitment to action plans will help us as we seek to learn new patterns of relating. The way we act with and toward each other has a powerful influence on how we feel about ourselves, each other, and the relationship. If we passively wait for our feelings to change before we attempt to change our behavior, we may wait forever—with increasing disillusionment. If we are willing to take the risks of changing our behavior, we are likely to rediscover and recover the joys of intimacy.

Questions for Study

1. Referring to Figure 11–1, describe specifically how each of the principles will destroy marriage.

2. How can role-playing and role-taking be utilized to improve a marriage?

3. Explain the thinking that underlies the concept of serial polygamy with the same spouse. Do you think it is a workable concept? Why or why not?

4. I have posed the question: "Can a married couple live day-in and day-out in such an emotionally charged manner?" Answer this, drawing on experiences and observations from your own life.

5. Devise your own action plan, designed to benefit the relationship you are now involved in.

Reading Suggestions

The Joy of Sex by Alex Comfort. New York: Simon and Schuster, 1972. A handbook for playful, joyful, sexual loving.

More Joy in Your Marriage by Herbert Otto. New York: Hawthorne, 1964. New ways of thinking and acting to give life and increased vitality to marriage.

We Can Have Better Marriages If We Really Want Them by David Mace and Vera Mace. Nashville, Tenn.: Abingdon, 1974. Describes the companionship marriage, which is designed to bring couples closer together in intimacy and creative sharing.

Couple Therapy by Gerald Smith and Alice Phillips. New York: Macmillan, 1971. Experiments and suggestions for making marriage richer.

TWELVE
A
GROWTH
MODEL:
EQUALITARIAN
MONOGAMY

256

**A Growth Model:
Equalitarian Monogamy**

Power and Equality

Equalitarianism and Openness

The Growth Marriage

Commitment to What?

Trust and Fidelity
in the Growth Model

Defining Our Own Marriage

Summary

Questions for Study

Reading Suggestions

Power and Equality

Barbara and Donald

I don't know quite where we're at but I have the feeling that we're on more solid ground than we have ever been before. I went through a period of restlessness when I first started getting caught up in women's lib. I had a couple of rather meaningless relationships before I read Open Marriage. *When I read* Open Marriage *I really was turned on to the ideas of growth and intimate friendship—the trouble was that I knew darn well Don and I didn't have the strong relationship going for us that is so important to an open marriage.*

Well, I tried to manipulate Don—to get him to see what I saw—to get him to feel what I was feeling. But that never really works. He just wasn't where I was. Don wasn't against equality at all—it's just that he had learned all the ways a male is supposed to exercise power and authority, and he couldn't see what this did to me. I felt I had the right to be myself but that this better not conflict with his ideas of what I ought to do or be. By then it was no longer a question of openness in our marriage— hell, we were far from home base on that. Now it was a basic issue of whether or not I was to build my whole daily existence around him and his career.

I never had a career. I was a secretary before we were married and I had worked for about two years after we were married—until our daughter was born. What kind of a chance did I have for a career? What's all this self-fulfillment talk mean when you can't even get out of your own house or away from the daily routines of your children? I was getting desperate! I thought my life was ebbing away. Everybody wanting a part of me. The women's support group only made me more frustrated and angry. They could be sympathetic but I still had my responsibilities.

So one day I came to a decision. I told him I was not intending to manipulate him in any underhanded way but that I needed his help and his support if I was going to make it. I had some depression but I had full

*awareness of what I was doing. Poor Don! He really didn't know what
had been going on inside me. How could he? I never really talked openly
with him about my feelings. I always felt so guilty that I kept my real
feelings secret. That's when Don and I came to you. Don hated you for
a while. But I think something penetrated him that had never gotten
through to him before. It sounds so simple now—but it wasn't then. You
know what I think? I think for the first time in our marriage he was
scared of losing me. I think this helped open him up so that he started to
let me in.*

*There's really no fairy-tale ending to all of this. Since we last saw you we
have moved to Dover. Don likes his work and I am combining housekeeping with part-time school to get an associate degree. We have an amazing
equality. Don thinks he's crazy to mortgage his whole future to his job
and he says why should it be the man's burden to feel he has to compete
with every other male for top honors and achievement. He says now the
sooner I get out working the better because he's got a lot of hobbies and
interests that he has never really had the time to pursue.*

*As far as openness, well, if you mean are we involved in sexually in-
timate relationships with other people or couples, the answer is no. But
we have a much more open marriage now than I ever dreamed possible.
And you know what, it's an openness that grew out of a strong internal
rebuilding process between Don and I. I don't think open marriage can
cure anything. It's the other way around. As far as my previous escapades
go—I really don't desire anything like that right now, but if I ever should
Don would be the first to know what I'm feeling and I honestly believe
we could deal with it.*

Equalitarian monogamy is the term I have chosen to indicate the nature
of the power relationship between partners. The power translates directly
into privileges, duties, rights, and responsibilities. The naive may say this
is bad—marriage should not be concerned with power. Not so! If we fail
to deal with the issue of power we are faced with the age-old problem of

equalitarian monogamy in contrast to patriarchal monogamy, equalitarian monogamy indicates an equal balance of power and authority between husband and wife.

overt power by the male and covert power by the female. Only the terribly naive can close their eyes to the power issue. Direct confrontation of issues—including the issue of power—demands openness, honesty, leveling, acceptance of self, and positive self-feelings. Equalitarianism is the key to the growth model, because without it the two partners will not have equal opportunities for growth. And then the female finds herself in a one-down position. This is what happened to Barbara. She had experienced increasing depression directly related to her feeling of helplessness. She was without power, or she felt she was without power. The answer for her was in learning to assert herself and to confront Donald.

Rollo May has stated that there are five levels of power: (1) to be, (2) to affirm oneself, (3) to assert oneself, (4) to aggress, and (5) to violate or do violence. He points out that we are most likely to become violent when we feel most helpless. And we are bound to feel helpless when we fail to learn the prior levels of power—to affirm, to assert, and to aggress. May claims violence is the logical result of helplessness. If we fail to learn a sense of self-strength and its logical expression within human relationships we are, indeed, impotent.[1]

Equalitarian relationships are relationships between equals. This equality is both psychoemotional and socioethical. Obviously, no two people are at the exact same place of growth at the same time. Thus, an equalitarian relationship is one in which, over the long term, there is room for fluctuation and change. Figure 12–1 illustrates this:

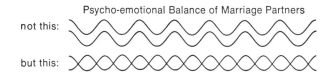

Psycho-emotional Balance of Marriage Partners

not this:

but this:

Figure 12–1
A Flexible Equality

The diagram illustrates that at times one partner may be less equal than the other but that at other times the situation is reversed. In the long run a balance is maintained; in the short run there is flexibility to accommodate changing needs and situations.

Equalitarianism and Openness

Equalitarian monogamy may or may not include openness. If we are faithful to the O'Neills' concept of open marriage, we must think in terms of degree of openness, rather than in terms of contrasting an open relationship with a closed one. Figure 12–2 illustrates how the degrees of openness can vary, even within an equalitarian growth model.

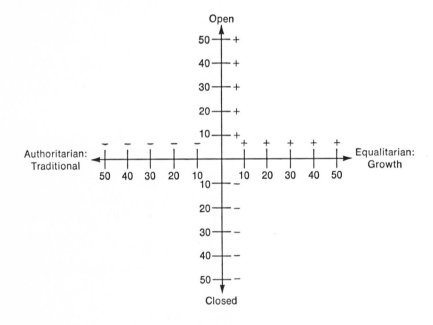

Figure 12–2
Degrees of Openness and Equality

Figure 12–3 illustrates an essentially closed marital relationship that is highly equalitarian. This arrangement is rare, but it is definitely a possibility. It could well be an illustration of one of the growth orientations described in Chapter 11.

One need not interpret either the O'Neill concept of open marriage or the concept of equalitarianism as either-or propositions. A relationship can be as open or as closed as the partners want, and as authoritarian or equalitarian as they want.

It is true, however, that openness is more likely in an equalitarian marriage than in an authoritarian marriage. It is also likely that as equalitarianism increases there will be at least some corresponding increase in

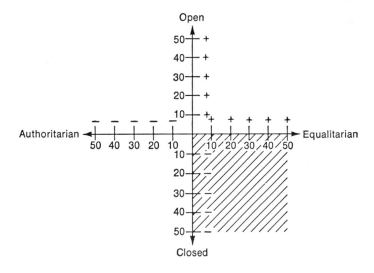

Figure 12-3
A Closed Equalitarian Relationship

openness, but not always and not necessarily. For example, many couples will commit themselves to total equalitarianism but to only a medium degree of openness. The dividing line in openness is usually the line between sexual exclusivity and sexual permissiveness.

I believe that the primary issue is power, not openness. Openness, vital as it is, is really a function of the distribution of power. Until the sexes feel that they are truly equal in terms of rights, privileges, and responsibilities (not just a lip-service belief or a nod to the god of equality), there can be no real movement toward a growth marriage. The inherent human

right to growth is the most basic of all the rights, privileges, and responsibilities. Speaking to the issue of power and equality, Seidenberg has
written:

*It is this writer's contention that behind the facade of love, devotion, and
compassion, the specter of power looms to take its toll in marriages. The
toll that is taken is really not measurable in terms of divorces and sep-
arations, for power can create inescapable traps in which all that are left*

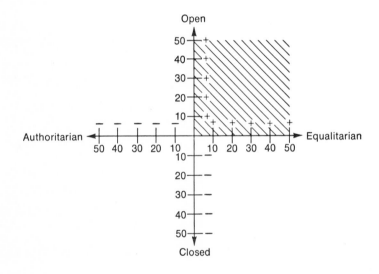

Figure 12-4
An Open Equalitarian Relationship

*are resignation and apathy. These, ironically enough, because there is
no movement or resistance in them, are often called happiness and contentment. Here there may operate a relentless spirit-destroying machine
that leaves the body intact but spineless without an apparent wound. . . .
The hope for our times and the future is a climate of understanding that
may allow young people to work out their destinies* with passion *but also
with autonomy which demands the elimination of power as an interpersonal demiurge, and with love which has an authentic concern for the
identity of the other and the self.*[2]

If the primary commitment in marriage is to equality, and if the primary concern is equality of power, and if the key issue of power is the growth of the mate, then we can assert with confidence that there will be increased realization of both equality and openness.

The Growth Marriage

We have considered open marriage and equalitarian marriage. What are the possibilities of an integration of these two basic phenomena? What is a true growth marriage? How would it look?

A growth model would be based on a **contract** that has been thoroughly discussed so that there is no ambivalence or misunderstanding. This contract may be a statement of intention and attitude as well as an item-by-item analysis of specific points. A well-written contract could easily be translated into a statement for use in the wedding ceremony (see Appendices A and B). I endorse a trial relationship as a helpful prerequisite for a growth model. A trial relationship allows the experience of living together to begin as a conditional experiment without constricting bonds. Although trial marriage is not for everyone, I endorse it as a natural, human, and logical plan that should be made legal.

Growth begins with one's attitude toward the dignity of life itself. The real enemy of marriage is not as much the institution as the personalities of the participants and their life-destroying notion of marriage as mutual possession of each other. Once we understand that, we can then see with greater clarity how to redeem, redefine, and even renovate marriage.

The growth model is being redefined and reinvented continually. This is not a conscious daily process, but rather an underlying realization that what seems right for today may not fit well tomorrow. This is why I am skeptical of contracts that spell out an exact length of time. We are all tempted to try to gain personal security by securing the future. This is

contract an agreement, mutually negotiated, that spells out the terms, definitions, and policies of a relationship; contracts may be open-ended in terms of time or for fixed periods of time.

the first step toward decay, because the idea of future control has a choking effect on the present.

Commitment to What?

Within the growth model, enslavement of any person and rigidity of contractual definition are impossible. This does not denigrate the idea of commitment. Indeed, I believe that commitment is too much lacking in marriage today. But we must ask: Commitment to what, to whom? If our commitment is to the words of the wedding ceremony, then this ceremony should be called a statement of intention rather than a commitment. And if the commitment is to a concept, even to a good concept, this automatically puts the partners in second place. The growth model emphasizes commitment to individuals, not to vows or concepts.

The primary commitment is to the self, the mate, and the relationship. This triple commitment recognizes that if we neglect the self, or obliterate the self in deference to the other, we bring decay and destruction to both the self and the other. If I do not believe in myself, I cannot believe in us. If commitment to the relationship takes priority over commitment to the self and to the other, the partners then defend the relationship at the expense of the well-being of the partners.

If we accept authentic self-love as a prerequisite for emotional health, it is not at all illogical to claim that self-love is a prerequisite for a healthy marriage. The triple commitment, then, is more important than any other single concept within the marriage contract, precisely because this commitment underlies the issues of trust and fidelity, role definition and division of labor.

It is a mistake to imagine that we can have as much freedom in the marriage relationship (legal or extralegal) as we have as unattached individuals. There simply is no way that a relationship can be nurtured if both partners covet total independence and autonomy. And so a satisfactory level of autonomy and identity must precede intimacy. Only the mature person can choose to limit some of his or her freedom for the sake of the other and the relationship.

Each individual has some reluctance about relinquishing freedom. And each individual desires the security of a mutual commitment. Jessie Bernard addresses this point when she writes:

For—and it can hardly be said too often—there is an intrinsic and unescapable conflict in marriage. Human beings want incompatible things. They want to eat their cake and have it too. They want excitement and adventure. They also want safety and security. These desiderata are difficult to combine in one relationship. Without a commitment, one has freedom but not security; with a commitment, one has security but little freedom. . . . My own observation of young people convinces me that in the future the emphasis among both men and women may well be on freedom rather than on security, at least to a far greater extent than today. Conceivably to a too great extent.[3]

How difficult is it to combine both freedom and security within a marriage? We shall consider this question in terms of trust and fidelity.

Trust and Fidelity
in the Growth Model

Within the growth model trust and fidelity are based on the commitment of both the self and the mate (1) to themselves, (2) to the other, and (3) to the relationship. The integrity of the partners is in their resolute intention to cultivate and nurture themselves and each other within the relationship.

Traditionally, trust and fidelity have been based on an implicit threat or dare. The partners, not trusting each other, draw their security from a pledge. This pledge gives the partners a sense of security—but it is a security based on proscription, on what both have agreed should be outlawed. It is not based on a faith that the partners will act in a responsible way to safeguard the vital growth-bond of the relationship.

When our faith is based on the goodwill and intention of the other, rather than on a pledge to observe ritualized restrictions, we stand on the brink of a new security based on *commitment to build and nurture the mutual growth bond.* It is a fidelity that transcends the narrow sexual taboo. It is based on integrity of spirit rather than the restrictive force of law.

Kris and Tony

All this might sound as though Kris and I were swingers or always on the make. This is not true. It is true that I had a cheating kind of relationship once and I felt lousy—the guilt, the deception, the unfaithfulness of daily cover-ups. Kris too had a brief relationship, and she was really turned off after a while. We decided, after much mutual hurt and distrust (I guess this was all mixed in with feelings of rejection and inadequacy) to attempt a new beginning in our marriage. We made a verbal contract that covered many things, but primarily we agreed that there would be no outside sexual relationships unless and until two things happened first: (1) We had successfully rebuilt our own marriage, and (2) we had talked openly about our feelings of attraction and interest in new persons. I knew this was quite a restriction because one never knows these things ahead of time. But we both were quite serious about protecting our newly developing relationship, and this way we could deal with our feelings and ask for reassurance. This was the way we could unlearn possessiveness and jealousy and learn a deeper trust—a trust that the other is not going to do anything that would be contrary to the best interests of both of us, a trust that lets us know that our security is not being threatened and that lets the partner having the outside friendship know where he stands regarding the risks and the responsibilities. This is a trust in the person, not in any law or code that says nice people should never acknowledge or act on an attraction.

Well, that was our intention and on the whole it's been great. I have been learning this new kind of trust—something so deeply rewarding that I would hate to think of going back to the old ways. Now I know Kris loves me and chooses me—it's a love coming out of freedom rather than out of coercion.

You know what we did first? We decided to have an affair with each other! Sounds silly, doesn't it? But we did. We met secretly for lunch, we had rendezvous at night, even at motels where we would meet and would register using aliases. For about two years we really committed ourselves to a total rebuilding of our marriage. When the first real attraction came I still felt uneasy and unready. Kris and I discussed it, and because the other person was involved in a very unstable marriage situation, we decided that this was not the right choice—all things considered.

Since then there have been two relationships for Kris and one for me. Now we are involved with a beautiful couple who seem to really know where they are. But the important thing is that I feel more security and trust than I ever have in my whole life. I won't say I never feel anxious or threatened, but I have a deeper faith in Kris than I ever dreamed possible. We love each other very much and there is simply no one with whom I'd rather spend my daily life. I have come to believe and trust that she feels this way about me too. It's the most wonderful feeling I've ever known. Of course we're not problem free, but we handle issues, not each other, and we are more direct and less afraid to own up to our feelings.

Are Kris and Tony unique? Yes, in many ways. They know where they are and they handle it. They are under no illusions about meeting all of each other's needs. They recognize that open marriage is no cure-all for an unsatisfactory primary relationship. They did not mention power or equality, but I would guess that they are learning, especially Tony, to be equalitarian.

Regarding trust and fidelity as these terms relate to consensual sexual relationships, let it be said that too many people use extramarital sex as a stop-gap measure to patch up an ailing marriage. They believe that outside relationships will make things right between the couple because their outside liaisons will make each of them feel better. This is a stop-gap approach, because it does not deal with the real problems of the marriage, even if for a brief time the couple feels better about the marriage. If, however, a couple has first relearned a more nearly total kind of trust and fidelity, there is a different basis for consensual sexual relationships.

Seidenberg says that few of us can stand complete sexual freedom for our mates.[4] We are simply not secure enough, and we may doubt that we will or should ever be that secure. But it is of vital importance to understand that Kris and Tony have learned a kind of trust which is essentially faith in the other. This is the very essence of trust and fidelity. It is the trust implicit in Buber's "I and Thou"—it is the trust of an "I" in a "Thou."

This kind of faith leaves one completely and totally vulnerable, completely open to the possibility of hurt, pain, and loss. It is an unlimited love because it does not withhold anything in the interest of self-protection. When we withhold love in order to protect ourselves, we (perhaps unknowingly) create defense mechanisms and engage in compensatory ploys. We resist the total investment of our egos in the partner and the relationship. We compensate by doing things, buying things, creating things (all of which may be innocent enough and justifiable in their own right) that serve as barriers against investing too much of ourselves in the other. We defend ourselves, often by telling ourselves that the other person really is not that important or precious to us. Sometimes there is a temptation to further protect ourselves by getting even—by finding a new love to use to hedge our bet. This puts the process of mutual marital destruction into motion—because we were afraid of being totally vulnerable. Yet it is this very vulnerability that underlies the growth process, including the learning of trust.

It is not easy to learn this most basic trust. The essence of trust is in the *willing and giving of freedom*. We have all heard a parent say to a teenager, "I trust you, dear, but you still can't go." Trust is a meaningless abstraction unless and until the one who trusts wills and gives the freedom that expresses trust. If I say I trust you and then deny you freedom, I have demonstrated my lack of trust.

Erich Fromm has said that love is always the child of freedom, never of domination.[5] I would paraphrase this by saying that trust is always the child of freedom, never of domination or of attempts to control, possess, or manipulate. In order to learn this kind of trust, we must take the risk of giving freedom, for only in the act of giving freedom can we finally unlearn the fear that prevents us from trusting. As Camus has said, "To know yourself you must act." This means, for our purposes, that the mind "willing" freedom is not enough if we are to truly learn to trust. We need further to act, to give freedom, for only in the process of giving freedom can genuine trust be learned and experienced.

I have talked of the triple commitment to the self, the other, and the relationship. And I have stressed that the essence of trust is in giving freedom. I conclude this discussion by adding another triple commitment—to ideas rather than to persons. This second set of commitments is secondary but obviously of great importance. These are commitments to (1) growth, (2) honesty and openness in self-disclosure, and (3) the ongoing process of **depth-leveling** in communication about both positive and negative feelings. Each of these has been talked about in earlier chapters.

Without the commitment to growth we may soon fall prey to disillusion and loss of vitality. I believe that our emotional-mental health, as living organisms, is directly affected by our openness for growth. We are alive as long as we are open to growth; we begin to die when we say no to the possibility. No human being can enter deeply and meaningfully into the life of another being without penetrating self-revelation. This is the very essence of a shared intimacy. Depth-leveling in communication is the process by which we keep in touch with the deepest parts of the other. This process enables us to be authentic human beings, refusing to repress our negative feelings and cultivating the excitement of sharing our positive feelings.

Defining Our Own Marriage

Every person is free to choose a married life style or an unmarried life style. This choice has never before been so openly available to any American generation as it is today. If you choose marriage, you have a new series of options. Do you want children, natural or adopted? Do you want a monogamous or multilateral marriage? Do you want monogamy with or without extramarital sexual relationships? Do you want an open or closed, authoritarian or equalitarian marriage? Do you want growth or stagnation? Do you choose an A-frame, H-frame, or M-frame relationship? Figure 12–5 illustrates some of the possibilities.

depth-leveling the process of revealing one's deepest and innermost thoughts and feelings; honest self-disclosure, nonsadistic in nature and intent, that enables intimates to be fully informed about each other's deepest and most powerful thoughts and feelings.

Regardless of which option you choose, there is no substitute for on-going redefinition, negotiation, and perhaps also reconsideration of expectations, assumptions, and boundaries. I hope I have persuaded you that we are the ones who destroy our own marriages. Society is partly at fault, and so is the cultural tradition. But the source of the problem, and of the solution, is within ourselves, our personalities, and our determination to nurture and cultivate our relationships.

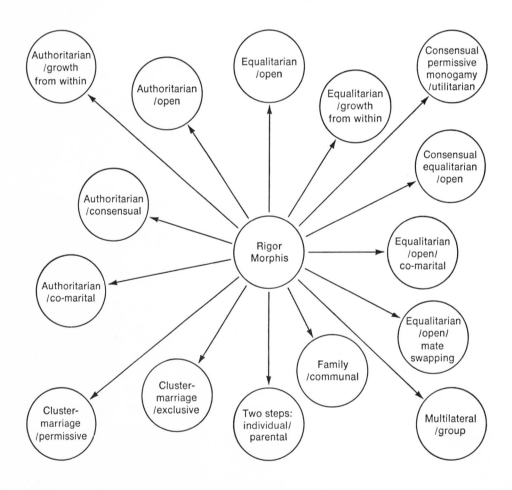

Figure 12–5
Alternatives to Marital Rigor Morphis

In all the options there may be growth. I believe that the growth model described in this chapter—with or without extramarital sexual relationships (but with positive openness up to that point) and with full equality, provides the greatest promise within a monogamous framework for realization of shared happiness, the joy of growth, and the growth of joy.

Summary

Power is the key factor in the concept of equalitarianism. Without meaningful and genuine equality of power there is no possibility for equality in other rights, duties, and privileges.

Equalitarian monogamy encourages openness in marriage, and increasing openness usually helps to develop greater equality. This is not always true, however. There can be equality without openness, and there can be openness without equality, although these are harder to imagine as truly open.

The growth marriage was strongly emphasized as the most promising model for a redefinition of monogamy. The growth model is continually in process. It never stops and says "here we are, let's always keep it just like this." The growth-oriented marriage is not committed to mere words, ideas, or vows of the wedding ceremony. It is committed to the marriage partners. The primary focus of commitment is to growth of the self, growth of the mate, and growth of the relationship. Within this ongoing commitment a married person cannot have as much personal behavioral freedom as a single person. Only the truly autonomous and mature person can voluntarily choose to relinquish some freedom.

Most people want freedom and security within marriage, but these two constructs are often difficult to reconcile. The more freedom we allow each other, the less security we have. The more security we demand, the less freedom we are likely to permit. The growth model attempts to combine freedom and security. The new freedom must be a "freedom to be" or a "freedom to become" and is based on the partners' commitment to build and nurture their mutual growth bond. In the growth marriage, trust and fidelity mean faith in the partner to act in a responsible way to safeguard the vital growth bond of the relationship. Trust and fidelity are not based on an implicit dare, threat or proscription.

Only when trust and fidelity are seen in a total sense, rather than in a narrow sexual sense, is it possible to speak of consensual sex as not being an act of infidelity. The essence of trust is in the willing and the giving of freedom. The giving of freedom always leaves the giver vulnerable. Yet it is this vulnerability that keeps open the ongoing possibility of growth and intimacy.

Marriages are no longer guided by simple rules about what is right and what is wrong. Today every person has the right and the responsibility to define and create his or her own marriage. We are the ones who effectively kill marriage. And we are the ones who can redeem it and revitalize it.

Questions for Study

1. Explain how Rollo May's concept of power relates to marriage.

2. The author suggests that a contract is a necessary part of the growth marriage. In your opinion what are the positive and negative aspects of using a marriage contract?

3. Jessie Bernard says, of future trends in marriage, that the emphasis "may well be on freedom, rather than security." Assess this statement, basing your conclusions on your own beliefs as well as those of others you know.

4. Explain the importance of the triple commitment (to the self, the mate, and the relationship) to the growth marriage.

5. Describe specifically the type(s) of marriage or relationships you would choose for your own future.

Reading Suggestions

Power and Innocence by Rollo May. New York: W. W. Norton, 1972. An analysis of the nature, function, and importance of power, with an emphasis on the kinds and levels of power. Illustrates the necessity for open acceptance and use of power in the functioning of the healthy personality.

Marriage Between Equals by Robert Seidenberg. Garden City, N.Y.: Anchor, 1973. An analysis of the struggle for power by unequal partners in marriage; illustrated by clinical case studies and excerpts from literature.

Open Marriage by George O'Neill and Nena O'Neill. New York: M. Evans and Company, 1972. A description of a new type of marriage in which each couple designs the relationship that is best for them.

The Future of Marriage by Jessie Bernard. New York: Bantam, 1972. An analysis of the past, present, and future of marriage; includes a discussion of the conflict between freedom and security.

Shifting Gears by Nena O'Neill and George O'Neill. New York: M. Evans and Company, 1974. A description of the internal dynamics involved in coping with the insecurity of change. A sine qua non for individuals committed to personal growth.

An Afterword

We have inherited our marriage tradition as a legacy from the past. The value and purpose of any tradition may be lost during the process of transmission. When this happens the recipients of the legacy may find themselves enslaved by the tradition and its failure to convey meaning and purpose. When confronted with a worn-out tradition, there are three options: (1) accept it lock, stock, and barrel; (2) reject it and rebel against it; or (3) reshape, re-create, and redefine it.

In the foregoing chapters I have attempted to carry out option three. The first two options are nonliberating. The person who feels constrained about marriage and consequently rejects the entire legacy is certainly not liberated. He is a prisoner of his own disgust and hostility. Option three requires individuals who are first committed to achieving autonomy. Only the autonomous individual knows himself or herself well enough to separate legitimate ego needs from illegitimate ego needs and to build a fulfilling marital relationship.

As I have worked with the material presented in this book, I have come to some conclusions.

1. Prophets of doom and prophets of utopian panaceas are both off base.[1] Both should be given a fair hearing. But critical judgment must be exercised as these positions are evaluated. A sense of historical perspective combined with a sober commitment to future generations leads me to conclude that the most fruitful progress in marriage depends on our ability to reject panaceas and prognostications of futility in favor of the slower and perhaps more painful redefinition and concentration on intrapsychic and interpsychic dynamics.

2. Variety in marital and familial structures is here to stay. The only critical issue is the establishment of the individual's right to decide whether any kind of marriage is desirable and, if so, what kind of marriage it should be. There will always be at least a small percentage who will opt for the group structures and for total permissiveness within monogamous unions. This development need not be feared; indeed, it should be encouraged and welcomed even by those who, in their own lives, do not choose those particular paths.

3. Sexual liberation is more than freedom from Victorian taboos and inhibitions. The truly liberated are those who, in the exercise of freedom, are not enslaved by their freedom. Sexual liberation implies not only a demythologized sexual stance but also a deidolization of sex. The commanding power of sex has been recognized by both the repression of the Victorians and the permissive hedonism of the sixties and early seventies. We can be enslaved not only by what we submit to but equally by what we reject. In growing out of Victorian practices and attitudes, we may still be sexually enslaved by the total celebration of the very thing we rejected. In both cases, sex is enshrined on a pedestal and the individual is in bondage.

4. If we are to be emancipated from restrictive dogmatic positions of the past, we must do more than reject authoritarian prescriptions. Here again we run the risk of becoming enslaved by what we reject. The tradition of humanistic ethics has much to recommend it to today's generation, especially to those who, having discovered that traditional codes no longer work for them, experience uncertainty in developing their personal ethical codes. Man's search for meaning and purpose is not a modern phenomenon, nor have dogmatic answers always prevailed. Authoritarian and humanistic traditions have existed both within and outside of Christendom. The specific danger to which I am here referring is the danger of rejecting humanistic traditions as proof of our "liberation."

5. Often in these pages I have called attention to the inadequacy of the English word *love*. As long as we insist on dealing with subjects such as marriage, mate selection, family, sex, sexuality, and romance in terms of this single four-letter word, we will be unable to adequately conceptualize the problems of each area of human fulfillment. I have employed the language of the Greeks and, following Rollo May, have attempted to give content to four types of love: libido, eros, philos, and agape. I do not know of any other satisfactory way to get at the dynamics of the interpersonal sexual, marital, and familial relationships. The romantic tradition has militated against such an analysis and synthesis of love. Rejection of *romanticism* need not imply a lack of emotion and tenderness in the relationship between the sexes—the excitement and passion of eros capture the root meaning of romance.

6. The emphasis on conflict facing and conflict resolution seems to me to be the most satisfying approach to successful marriage. Yet, within our society conflict is considered improper and even sinful. I have attempted to show the importance of dealing first with intrapsychic conflict in order to learn to face interpsychic conflict. There is conflict present in practically every human relationship; it is inevitable. We feed on illusion if we allow ourselves to naively believe that all conflicts can or ought to be resolved. And so we must recognize the importance of facing and handling conflict, even conflict that cannot be resolved. Indeed, to the extent that we embrace the concept of the individual's right to self-fulfillment, we may continue to live with conflict that, at heart, is not resolvable.

7. The interaction of women's liberation, human sexuality, and interpersonal oneness is far more subtle and dynamically volatile than our society is presently prepared to admit. When either sex is "up" or "down," both sexes are dehumanized and alienated from each other. Female dehumanization tends to be disguised by culturally patterned rituals which make the female either into an object of adoration (a sex object or sex symbol) or into an object in need of protection "for her own good." In either case, the female is relegated to an inferior status resembling a "china doll"—beautiful, but brainless and nonhuman. This perpetuates the process of mutual dehumanization, because an unrealistic valuation of a human being can lead to possessiveness and manipulation by both sexes. Things are possessed; people are loved. Love that attempts to possess is not love but bondage. Love is always the child of freedom. A total union or oneness between a man and a woman includes both psychic and sexual intimacy. This intimacy is not possible unless the two people are free to embrace the humanity of each other. If either partner has the attitude that the body is an object, alienation will result. In love and in marriage it is impossible for only one partner to be liberated or human. Both are enslaved, or both are free.

8. An emphasis on self-actualization is vital in the quest for meaning in human existence. However, if any limitation of personal freedom implies a frustration of self-actualization, then this concept can create pain and grief. Suffice it to say that two or more people cannot live together in any form of the married state without each voluntarily accepting partial limitation of his or her behavioral freedom (as opposed to psychic freedom, which need not be affected by marriage). Limitation of behavioral freedom may place constraints on self-fulfillment. Further, one's quest for self-fulfillment may lead to frustration if it is allowed to give rise to a set of expectations that are unrealistic. The expectation of highly charged intimacy as an ongoing, continuous phenomenon is clearly unrealistic. We must not allow ourselves to be frustrated by intimacy fulfillment expectations as we were by romantic expectations. If the agent of liberation (self-fulfillment and marital fulfillment) becomes, due to excessive and unrealistic expectation, an agent of excessive frustration, then the gain may prove to be merely illusory.

9. The socialization process is, in my opinion, the key to the future of human happiness, including marital and familial happiness. Social scientists, psychologists, psychiatrists, and educators are widely divided in their beliefs, attitudes, and prescriptions for human socialization. But we must continue to search, we must continue doing research, and we must seek to humanize every person, every relationship, and every institution.

Appendix A

Sample Marriage Contract

When filled out by only one partner, this sample contract reveals one set of expectations. When both partners compare and negotiate the differences in their expectations, the end result may be called a contract or working marital agreement.

Preliminary Statement of Marital Goals:

Provisions for Revision and Renewal of Contract:
Provisions for Dissolution of Contract:

Division of Household Labor:
Her Employment:
His Employment:
Financial Responsibility:
Allocation of Funds (His/Hers/Ours):

Methods and Responsibility for Birth Control:
Intended Number of Children:
Intended Spacing of Children:
Division of Labor for Child Care:
Discipline of Children:
Children's Religious Orientation and Instruction:
Children's Education:

Religious Beliefs and Practices:
Educational Goals:

Expectations for Primary-Pair Sexual Relations:

Extramarital Friendships (Psychic Intimacy):
Extramarital Friendships (Sexual Intimacy):
Boundaries of Openness:

Privacy Expectations:
Communication Expectations:
Enrichment Expectations:
Growth Expectations:
Handling of Conflict Expectations:

Vacations (Couple Only):
            (Including Children):
            (Separate):

Definition of Equality:
Definition of Open and Closed:
Definition of Commitment:
Definition of Trust:
Definition of Fidelity:

Appendix B

Sample Wedding Ceremony

The wording of the wedding ceremony should be based on the principles agreed upon in the contract, but with a wording less specific to the various items and more directly related to the intentions regarding commitment.

Opening Statement

Friends and family of _____ and _____, we are gathered together today for the purpose of sharing the joy that has led _____ and _____ to want to make a public statement regarding their relationship. _____ and _____ do not wish to be given away or to be taken in marriage, but they do desire your thoughts, prayers, and blessings. They have given a great deal of thought as to whether or not they have sufficient maturity and commitment to share their lives in marriage. What they do and say here in our presence reflects the honesty and integrity of their decision and the genuine love they bring to it.

(Here may be inserted music, a Scripture reading, poetry, or prayers. One, or at most two, items could be used here.)

Suggested Song

For All We Know[1]

Suggested Poem

"Let Us Walk Together"[2]
(See Appendix C)

Suggested Old Testament Reading

Ruth 1: 16–17

This passage should be read twice, once by a male, representing the groom, and once by a female, representing the bride; or it could be read by both the bride and the groom.

Suggested New Testament Reading

I Corinthians 13: 1–13

Suggested Prayer

Eternal God, Thou who art the source of creation, in whom we live and move and have our being, we express our feelings of joy and happiness on this occasion, giving thanks that _____ and _____ _____ have experienced a fulfillment in themselves through their shared love and commitment to each other.

We celebrate with them as they seek to honor themselves by creating a solid foundation for their life together, based on their trust in each other as friends, companions, and lovers.

May they be strengthened in their resolve to deal honestly with the issues that so frequently separate and divide; may they learn that pain and hurt are often the price of joy and love; may they learn that their vulnerability to each other is the secret to growth and the depths of intimacy; may they discover that to close themselves off from each other or to shield and protect themselves from each other is to destroy their spontaneity and openness to each other.

May they experience the shame and the joy of sharing their deepest feelings with each other, feelings of anger and hurt, rejection and resentment, knowing that this makes possible a depth of oneness and keeps open the pathway of forgiveness and reconciliation. May they learn to drink of the spirit of inner growth whereby they serve each other in love and devotion even as they continue to nourish their own life spirit.

May they grow together rather than apart. May they strengthen one another rather than weaken one another. May one be strong when the other is weak. May they learn that true peace is not the absence of conflict but its resolution. May they learn that giving in to the other is not the same as negotiation and compromise.

And even while we know and believe that their future joy and fulfillment rests squarely upon their own steadfast commitment, we ask this prayer in Thy Name (in the Name of Jesus), the source of life itself. Amen.

(At this point in the ceremony the bride and groom may either respond to questions or make first-person statements to each other. These statements constitute the primary vows.)

Exchange of Vows

Bride: *I commit myself to my own growth, to your growth, and to the growth of our love relationship. I commit myself to honesty in expression of my feelings and to true openness in communication.*

I commit myself to our relationship and I promise that I will nourish and cultivate the bond of love which I experience between us.

My intention is to strive for an enduring relationship and I promise to safeguard this intention of permanence by striving for fidelity to you in the goals and purposes which we have defined for ourselves.

Groom: (*May repeat the same words.*)

(The personal meaning of the ceremony is in the honest self-expression of the intentions, promises, and commitment of the bride and groom to each other. Therefore, the primary vows may be far more meaningful if they are original statements of the bride and groom. The primary vows above are only intended to be suggestive.)

A Question and Charge
to the Family and Friends

We, the witnesses of these pledges, also have a responsibility to _____ and _____. It is our task to support them in their resolve, to refrain from unsolicited advice and comment, to encourage and sustain them in times of trouble and pain, to rejoice with them in times of joy. If you concur with these thoughts will you please indicate your commitment to them by saying "I do."

Family and friends respond: "I do."

Exchange of Rings (optional)

To the Groom: "What token of this commitment do you choose to give?" The ring is presented and the groom places it on the bride's finger. As the ring is placed on the bride's finger the groom says: "This ring I give you in pledge of my commitment to you in our relationship." The procedure may then be reversed, Bride to Groom.

(Here may be included another poem, musical selection or reading. Alternatives not used earlier may be included here. Preferably the Scripture or prayer should be utilized in the earlier time slot.)

Concluding Statement:
A Charge to the Bride and Groom

The union of _____ and _____ is now publicly recognized. We, your friends and families, charge you both to keep faith in the commitment of intentions which you have professed in our presence. We charge you to the task of remaining faithful to your own goals and purposes. We charge you to weigh your expectations, that they may be realistic and honest, yet beautiful in their intent. We charge you to look deeply within yourselves before you seek to place responsibility on the other. We charge you to honor and cherish one another as you grow and learn together. May yours be the experience of true peace and fulfillment as you open yourselves to the responsibilities, the privileges, and the vibrant joys of life together.

Benediction

Go in peace: and may no person deter you from your mutual quest. Amen.

Or: May (the God of Abraham) (the God of Jesus who was called the Christ) bless you and keep you; may he cause his grace to be upon you; and as creators with the Creator may you find peace. Amen.

Or: May the God of Peace be with you. Amen.

Appendix C

Let Us Walk Together

Let us walk together
yet not as one
such that our shadows
are separate and distinct
such that our souls
are unbound and free.
Let us share our time
yet do not give all your time
nor take all of mine
for in order to develop to the fullest
to be free
we must have solitude
and individuality.
Let me wander in solitude
when I need to be alone
yet be near
when I need you.
Let us share our love.
Give freely of your love
but do not smother me
my soul must breathe of free air.
Take my love
but do not demand it
for love given of obligation
is stale and without life.
Let us share our lives.
Share my life
but do not try to shape it.
Let me share your life
but do not let it revolve around me.
Let us share ourselves.

Accept me as I am—
                    do not attempt to change me
to fit your dreams.
Respect me for what I am
                    not for what I was
or may one day be.
                    Share yourself with me
but do not allow me to limit your freedom
or bind your soul.
            Let us share our minds
thoughts
                    goals
                        values
                            and dreams.
Let us develop these in ourselves
without restriction or loss of freedom.
        Thus
                our two free souls
                        may wander together
as they develop in freedom.
            As we share our lives—
as we walk through life together
                        know my love is yours
but not my soul
                for it must be free!

Tom McFee, from *Love and Other Painful Joys*

Notes

Chapter 1

[1] Sigmund Freud, *The Future of an Illusion* (Garden City, N.Y.: Doubleday Anchor, 1964), p. 49.

[2] *The Random House Dictionary of the English Language, College Edition* (New York: Random House, 1969).

[3] "To Make Divorce Less Painful" (editorial), *Louisville Courier Journal*, June 28, 1971, Louisville, Kentucky, p. A-6. Reprinted by permission.

[4] Andreas Capellanus, *The Art of Courtly Love*, abridged and edited by Frederick W. Locke (New York: Columbia University Press, 1941). Reprinted by permission.

[5] Albert Ellis, *American Sexual Tragedy* (New York: Lyle Stuart, 1962), pp. 97–121. Reprinted by permission.

[6] Erik Erikson, *Childhood and Society* (New York: W. W. Norton, 1950).

[7] Erich Fromm, *Man for Himself* (New York: Holt, Rinehart and Winston, 1947), pp. 75–89.

[8] Talcott Parsons, "The Superego and the Theory of Social Systems," in *Working Papers in the Theory of Action*, ed. Talcott Parsons, Robert F. Bales, and Edward A. Shils (New York: Free Press, 1953), pp. 13–28. Reprinted by permission.

[9] Fromm, *Man for Himself*, Chapter 3.

[10] Karen Horney, *Our Inner Conflicts* (New York: W. W. Norton, 1945), especially Chapter 3, "Moving Toward People."

[11] Ibid., Chapter 4.

[12] Fromm, *Man for Himself*, p. 73 (paperback edition).

[13] Horney, *Our Inner Conflicts*, Chapter 5.

[14] Fromm, *Man for Himself* (paperback edition).

[15] Rollo May, *Man's Search for Himself* (New York: W. W. Norton, 1953), p. 52 (Signet paperback edition). Reprinted by permission.

Chapter 2

[1] W. T. Jones, *A History of Western Philosophy* (New York: Harcourt Brace Jovanovich, 1952), pp. 219, 233. Reprinted by permission.

[2] Abraham Maslow, *Toward a Psychology of Being*, 2nd ed. (Princeton, N.J.: Van Nostrand, 1962), p. 24 (italics mine). Reprinted by permission.

[3] Aron Krich, and Sam Blumb, "Marriage and the Mystique of Romance," *Redbook* (November 1970). Reprinted by permission.

[4] Erich Fromm, *The Art of Loving* (New York: Harper and Row, 1956), pp. 40–41 (Harper Colophon). Reprinted by permission.

[5] Erich Fromm has treated the subject in Chapter 2 of *The Art of Loving* and in Chapter 5 of *Escape from Freedom* (New York: Holt, Rinehart and Winston, 1941).

[6] From Karen Horney, *The Neurotic Personality of Our Time* (New York: W. W. Norton, 1937), Chapter 4. Reprinted by permission.

[7] Karen Horney has amplified her remarks throughout three chapters in *The Neurotic Personality of Our Time*. See Chapter 6, "The Neurotic Need for Affection," Chapter 7, "Further Characteristics of the Neurotic Need for Affection," and Chapter 9, "The Role of Sexuality in the Neurotic Need for Affection."

[8] See Abraham H. Maslow, "A Theory of Human Motivation," *Psychological Review*, 1943, 50, 370–396. Quotations from this article are reprinted by permission.

[9] See William Glasser, *Reality Therapy* (New York: Harper and Row, 1965).

[10] See Eric Berne, *Games People Play* (New York: Grove Press, 1964) and Thomas Harris, *I'm OK—You're OK* (New York: Harper and Row, 1967).

[11] See Stanley Coopersmith, *The Antecedents of Self-Esteem* (San Francisco: W. H. Freeman and Company, 1967), especially Chapters 2 and 13.

[12] See Chapter 2 on "Self-Love" in Fromm, *The Art of Loving*.

[13] The list includes Everett Shostrom, Rollo May, Eric Berne, Thomas Harris, Virginia Satir, Harry Stack Sullivan, Karen Horney, Abraham Maslow, William Glasser, Erik H. Erikson, and Andras Angyal.

[14] Fromm, *The Art of Loving*, p. 26.

[15] Ibid., p. 28.

[16] See Fromm, *The Art of Loving*, p. 23. Reprinted by permission. For similar thoughts see Allan Fromme, *The Ability to Love* (North Hollywood, Calif.: Wilshire, 1966).

Chapter 3

[1] Denis DeRougemont, *Love in the Western World* (New York: Harcourt, Brace, 1940), p. 25. Reprinted by permission of Pantheon Books.

[2] William H. Halcombe, *The Sexes Here and Hereafter* (Philadelphia: J. B. Lippincott, 1869), pp. 56, 58, 86–87.

[3] George Henry Napheys, *The Transmission of Life: Counsels on the Nature and Hygiene of the Masculine Functions* (Toronto, Canada: Rose Publishing Company, 1886), pp. 164–165.

[4] From Hugo Beigel, "Romantic Love," *American Sociological Review* 14 (1951): 326–334. Reprinted by permission.

[5] Ibid.

[6] Ibid.

[7] Ibid.

[8] See Donald Horton, "The Dialogue of Courtship in Popular Songs," *American Journal of Sociology* 62(1957): 569–578.

[9] Rollo May, *Love and Will* (New York: W. W. Norton, 1969), pp. 45–46. Reprinted by permission.

[10] From Albert Ellis, *American Sexual Tragedy* (New York: Lyle Stuart, 1962), pp. 97–121. Reprinted by permission.

[11] Ibid.

[12] Ibid.

[13] See Ira L. Reiss, *Premarital Sexual Standards in America* (New York: The Macmillan Company, 1960).

[14] For a theoretical treatment of some of these questions, see William J. Goode, "The Theoretical Importance of Love," *American Sociological Review* 24(1959):38–47

[15] May, *Love and Will*, p. 65.

[16] Ibid., pp. 73–74.

Chapter 4

[1] From Victor Frankl, *Man's Search for Meaning* (New York: Washington Square, 1963), p. 159. Reprinted by permission.

[2] Ibid., pp. 153–154, 164.

[3] See Karen Horney, *The Neurotic Personality of Our Time* (New York: W. W. Norton, 1937), Chapter 9. Reprinted by permission.

[4] See Erich Fromm, *Man for Himself* (New York: Holt, Rinehart and Winston, 1947), Chapter 4. Reprinted by permission.

[5] Ibid.

[6] Frankl, *Man's Search for Meaning*, p. 170.

[7] From Paul Tillich, *The Courage to Be* (New Haven, Conn.: Yale University Press, 1952), p. 50. Reprinted by permission.

[8] Ibid., p. 76.

[9] Rollo May, *Man's Search for Himself* (New York: W. W. Norton, 1953), Chapter 6.

[10] May, *Love and Will* (New York: W. W. Norton, 1969), p. 39.

Chapter 5

[1] *The Herald Telephone*, Bloomington, Indiana, April 1974.

[2] Gordon Drake, *Blackboard Power* (Tulsa, Okla.: Christian Crusade Publications, 1968).

[3] Robert Seidenberg, *Marriage Between Equals* (Garden City, N.Y.: Anchor Press, 1973), pp. 238–239. Reprinted by permission of Philosophical Library, Inc.

[4] J., *The Sensuous Woman* (New York: Lyle Stuart, 1969).

Chapter 6

[1] John Powell, S. J., *Why Am I Afraid to Tell You Who I Am?* (Niles, Ill.: Argus Communications, 1969).

[2] Karen Horney, *The Neurotic Personality of Our Time* (New York: W. W. Norton, 1937), Chapters 4 and 5.

[3] Jay Kuten, *Coming Together—Coming Apart: Anger and Separation in Sexual Loving* (New York: Macmillan, 1974), pp. 177–178.

[4] Rollo May, *Love and Will* (New York: W. W. Norton, 1969), p. 148. Reprinted by permission.

[5] From George R. Bach and Peter Wyden, *The Intimate Enemy* (New York: William Morrow, 1969), Chapter 1. Reprinted by permission.

[6] Personal communication to the author from one who experienced it.

[7] Sidney Jourard, *The Transparent Self* (New York: D. Van Nostrand, 1964), pp. 5, 24, 25, 26 (1964 Insight Book Edition).

[8] Jessie Bernard, *The Future of Marriage* (New York: Bantam, 1972).

Chapter 7

[1] George R. Bach and Peter Wyden, *The Intimate Enemy* (New York: William Morrow and Company, 1969).

[2] From Victor Frankl, *Man's Search for Meaning* (New York: Washington Square Press, 1959), p. 160 (paperback).

[3] Virginia Satir, "Marriage as a Human-Actualizing Contract," and Herbert A. Otto, "The New Marriage: Marriage as a Framework for Developing Personal Potential," in *The Family in Search of a Future*, ed. Herbert A. Otto (New York: Appleton-Century-Crofts, 1970).

[4] Eric Berne, *Games People Play* (New York: Grove Press, 1964).

[5] From Thomas A. Harris, *I'm OK—You're OK* (New York: Harper and Row, 1967), p. 18. Reprinted by permission.

[6] Ibid., pp. 18–19.

[7] Ibid., p. 20.

[8] Ibid., p. 25.

[9] Ibid., p. 26.

[10] Ibid., p. 29.

[11] Ibid., p. 32.

[12] Ibid., p. 52.

[13] See Karen Horney, *Our Inner Conflicts* (New York: W. W. Norton, 1945), Chapters 3, 4, and 5.

[14] Everett L. Shostrom, *Man the Manipulator* (Nashville, Tenn.: Abingdon Press, 1967), Chapter 3.

[15] Harris, *I'm OK—You're OK*, pp. 126–127.

Chapter 8

[1] Nena O'Neill and George O'Neill, *Open Marriage* (New York: M. Evans, 1972).

[2] Ibid., p. 248.

[3] Erich Fromm, *The Art of Loving* (New York: Harper and Row, 1956), Chapter 2, Section 3. See also *Man for Himself* (Holt, Rinehart, and Winston, 1947), Chapter 4, Part I, "Selfishness, Self-Love, and Self-Interest."

4 O'Neill and O'Neill, *Open Marriage*, p. 250.

5 Paul Tillich, *The Courage to Be* (New Haven, Conn.: Yale University Press, 1952), p. 181 (see also all of Chapter 6).

Chapter 9

1 See Margaret Mead, "Marriage in Two Steps," *Redbook*, July 1966. Quotations from this article are reprinted by permission.

2 Ibid.

3 Ibid.

4 Ibid.

5 Eleanor Macklin, "Going Very Steady," *Psychology Today*, November 1974, p. 55.

6 Janis Petty, Master's thesis, Indiana University, 1975.

7 Bronislaw Malinowski, "Parenthood—The Basis of Social Structure," in *The New Generation*, ed. V. F. Calverton and S. D. Schmalhausen (New York: Macaulay, 1930), p. 140.

Chapter 10

1 Robert Seidenberg, *Marriage Between Equals* (Garden City, N.Y.: Anchor Press, 1973), p. 110.

2 George P. Murdock, *Social Structure* (New York: The Macmillan Company, 1949), p. 264.

3 II Samuel 11:16; 12:9 (Revised Standard Version).

4 Genesis 16:1–6; Genesis 30:1–12 (Revised Standard Version).

5 From Edward C. Hobbs, "An Alternate Model from a Theological Perspective," in *The Family in Search of a Future*, ed. Herbert A. Otto (New York: Appleton-Century-Crofts, 1970), p. 37. Reprinted by permission.

6 John F. Cuber and Peggy B. Haroff, *The Significant Americans* (New York: Appleton-Century-Crofts, 1965).

7 For further elaboration on open marriage, see Nena and George O'Neill's book, *Open Marriage: A New Life Style for Couples* (New York: M. Evans, 1972).

8 Larry Constantine and Joan Constantine, "Where Is Marriage Going?" *The Futurist* (April 1970). Reprinted by permission.

9 From Gerald Leslie, *The Family in Social Context* (New York: Oxford University Press, 1968), p. 143. Reprinted by permission.

10 Ibid.

11 From Margaret Mead, "New Design for Family Living," *Redbook*, October 1970. Reprinted by permission.

12 From Frederick Stoller, "The Intimate Network of Families as a New Structure," in *The Family in Search of a Future*, ed. Herbert A. Otto, pp. 145–159.

13 Ibid., p. 158.

14 Albert Ellis, *Sex Without Guilt* (New York: Lyle Stuart, 1958), pp. 51–65.

15 Carl Rogers, *Becoming Partners* (New York: Dell, 1972), p. 213.

Chapter 11

[1] See Albert Ellis, "The Folklore of Marital Relations—The Great Coital Myth," in *American Sexual Tragedy* (New York: Lyle Stuart, 1962).

[2] Thomas Harris, *I'm OK—You're OK* (New York: Harper and Row, 1967), pp. xvi–xix, 170–177.

[3] See Sidney M. Jourard, "Reinventing Marriage: The Perspective of a Psychologist," in *The Family in Search of a Future*, ed. Herbert A. Otto (New York: Appleton-Century-Crofts, 1970).

[4] Herbert A. Otto, ed., *The Family In Search of A Future* (New York: Appleton-Century-Crofts, 1970), pp. 111–118.

[5] See Herbert A. Otto, "Has Monogamy Failed?" *Saturday Review*, April 25, 1970. The quotation from this article is reprinted by permission.

[6] Ibid., p. 23.

[7] See Virginia Satir, "Marriage as a Human-Actualizing Contract," in *The Family in Search of a Future*, ed. Herbert A. Otto, pp. 57–66.

[8] Ibid., pp. 201–204, for a list of such centers.

[9] See Richard Farson, "Why Good Marriages Fail," *McCall's*, October 1971, pp. 110ff. The quotation from this article is reprinted by permission.

[10] Ibid., p. 170.

Chapter 12

[1] Rollo May, *Power and Innocence* (New York: W. W. Norton, 1972), pp. 40–45.

[2] Robert Seidenberg, *Marriage Between Equals* (Garden City, N.Y.: Anchor Press, 1973), pp. 327 and 331.

[3] Jessie Bernard, *The Future of Marriage* (New York: Bantam, 1973), p. 89.

[4] Seidenberg, *Marriage Between Equals*, pp. 329–330.

[5] Erich Fromm, *The Art of Loving* (New York: Harper and Row, 1956), p. 28 (Harper Colophon).

An Afterword

[1] See, for example, David Cooper, *The Death of the Family* (New York: Random House, Vintage Press, 1970) and the utopians who advocate a complete swing to communal experiments and group marriage.

Appendix B

[1] Fred Karlin, Rob Wilson, and Arthur James, *For All We Know*, Tamco Music Inc. B.M.I.

[2] Tom McFee, "Let Us Walk Together" from *Love and Other Painful Joys* (Philadelphia: Dorrance, 1970).

Index

Books of Related Interest

The Individual, Marriage, and the Family, Third Edition

Available for use January 1977

Lloyd Saxton
College of San Mateo

Lloyd Saxton is an experienced marriage counselor and teacher of marriage and the family courses. His bestselling text on dating, marriage, and familial relations has been updated in this edition to include material on sex role interaction and prospects for marriage failure. (500 pages. 7⅜ x 9¼. Clothbound. Teacher's Manual and Student Study Guide available.)

Contents

Also of Interest

Human Sexuality:
A Psychosocial Perspective

Richard
F. Hettlinger
Kenyon College

Richard
Hettlinger was
educated at
Cambridge
University in
England and is
now a Profes-
sor at Kenyon
College, Gam-
bier, Ohio. Two
of his four chil-
dren are cur-
rently college
students. His
previous books
include *Living
With Sex, Grow-
ing Up With Sex,*
and *Sexual
Maturity.* He has
contributed ar-
ticles to *Sexual
Behavior,
Sexology,* and
*Medical As-
pects of Human
Sexuality* (of
which he is a
Consulting
Editor). (315
pages. 6½ x
9¼. Paper-
bound)

Contents

Foreword James Leslie McCary
Introduction
1 Sex and Society
Reading Should There Be Censorship of Pornog-
raphy? *Harry M. Clor and Richard Hettlinger*
2 Values on Campus
Reading Is It True What They Say about Harvard Boys?
Rebecca S. Vreeland • *Reading* The Right to Say
"No" *Richard V. Lee*
3 Sex before Marriage
Reading Rules and the Ethics of Sex *Joseph C.
Hough, Jr.*
4 Recreational Sex
Reading Sex and the Single Man *Albert Ellis* •
Reading The Civilized Rapist: Checkmate in Bed *"S"*
5 The New Sexuality
Reading Paradoxes of Sex and Love *Rollo May*
6 Love and Commitment
Reading Love *Ingrid Bengis*
7 Gay Can Be Good
Reading I Am a Homosexual Physician •
Reading Lesbian/Woman *Del Martin and Phyllis Lyon*
8 Sexual Liberation
Reading Psychology and the Sexual Body *Judith
Bardwick*
9 The Future of Marriage
Reading Group Marriage: A Conversation with Robert H.
Rimmer *Elizabeth Hall and Robert A. Poteete* •
Reading Sex and Love in a Commune *Kathleen
Kinkade*
Epilogue
**Appendix: Birth Control, Abortion, and Venereal
Disease**
Reading The Woman and the Fetus: One Flesh?
Rachel Conrad Wahlberg • *Reading* A Religious Pacifist
Looks at Abortion *Gordon C. Zahn*
References